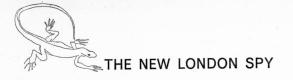

THE NEW LONDON SPY

THE NEW LONDON SPY

A DISCREET GUIDE TO THE CITY'S PLEASURES
EDITED BY HUNTER DAVIES

ANTHONY BLOND

First published in Great Britain 1966 by Anthony Blond Ltd.,
56 Doughty Street, London, W.C.1. © Copyright 1966 by
Anthony Blond Ltd. Printed in Great Britain by Tonbridge Printers
Ltd., Peach Hall Works, Tonbridge, Kent.

Contributors

Michael Bateman
Dominic Behan
David Benedictus
Chaim Bermant
John Betjeman
Anthony Blond
David Carritt
Nicholas Carroll
Quentin Crewe
Maureen Duffy
Roy East
Peta Fordham
Gillian Freeman
Martin Green
Ramsden Greig
Tim Heald
James Henry
Michael Horowitz
Philip Knightley
Anthony Lejeune
Andrew McCall
George Mikes
Philip O'Connor
Jonathan Routh
Andrew Salkey
Miles Tomalin
John Trevisick
Jane Wilson

drawings by Kaffe Fassett

Introduction

This is a guide book to London. Most guide books to London try to be comprehensive. All of them fail. This one doesn't even try.

This is a guide book to the *pleasures* of London. Nobody seems to have taken pleasure as a guide before, at least not for a couple of centuries. They've all been so busy piling on the facts about museum opening times or tube maps or how to recognise Buckingham Palace.

This guide book to the pleasures of London has been split up into different sections. Each one has been contributed by an expert. Not just someone expert in knowledge alone, but expert in describing events and experiences as vividly, amusingly and exactly as possible.

Pleasure is a personal thing, so the aspects of London dealt with here are dealt with personally. This means the opinions are as prejudiced and the comments as critical as the laws of libel will allow.

How this guide book to the pleasures of London decided which pleasures of London to guide people to is another matter. We could have gone on for ever.

One man's pleasure is another man's passion is another man's pain. So, the decisions again were personal. We've kept off some of the large-scale pleasures, like sport and music and opera, because expert information on them is always available. And not just information. Every newspaper every day also provides the latest opinions.

There are some large-scale pleasures we have included—like eating, drinking and staying at hotels. We haven't tried to cover the whole field. Enough books already try to do this. We have given just a brief, opinionated introduction. This is sufficient in itself, as the eating and drinking business is taken up with so much cant and nonsense.

We've gone more for the pleasures which haven't been charted before—from sex to sermons. And for those pleasures you might not immediately categorise as pleasure—such as a guide to Jewish London, or to Australian London. There are six foreign Londons, all chosen at random. To do any more would have meant a book in itself.

We've done our best to make sure every fact is correct and up to date. But there is always a gap between writing and publishing which bedevils any book which purports to guide. (Even museum times can change, tube stations close and Buckingham Palace lose its outside guards overnight.)

It is always best, therefore, to check if possible beforehand. The Savoy Hotel and the National Gallery and Westminster Abbey aren't likely to disappear without people noticing and commenting, but a little club, an old church, or a street market, however fascinating, can just move on or be knocked down without anyone ever bothering to announce it.

Anybody who hopes to do a book on London with every fact always correct has little chance. The London Telephone Directory, for all its 3,628 pages, is full of people whose telephone numbers have changed. Apart from being not correct, it's not even comprehensive. There are several thousand ex-directory numbers which are not listed. So, we apologise in advance for any mistakes.

The title of the book comes from *The London Spy*, first published in 1703. This was written by Ned Ward, landlord of the King's Head, a tavern next to Grays Inn. (Exactly the same area in which the publisher and the editor of this present volume both work, which proves something.)

Ned Ward went round London describing all the pleasures and diversions he came across. He got rather carried away with some of his pleasures, which explains why even today it is hard to find an unexpurgated version of his book.

He started and finished in a tavern. In between, he visited harlots and astrologers, parties and gaming houses, bated the lunatics at Bedlam with silly questions and watched a woman being whipped at Bridewell. But he also described some sedater pleasures, like Covent Garden and Westminster Abbey.

The topics in this, *The New London Spy*, are equally diverse and entertaining, equally scandalous and sedate.

But the intention is neither to condone nor corrupt. Homosexuality, for example, is reported because it exists. We are revealing what is there, but what few have ever bothered to reveal. Our Spy, uncovering layers of London life as he moves around, will be presenting an anatomy of London as much as a guide book.

But the overall intention is pleasure. It is a guide to certain London pleasures. But we hope that even those who will never come to London will still get a certain pleasure, just by reading it.

Contents

PUBLIC

PLEASURES

Almanack

January
Begins with New Year's day. In Scotland this is called Hogmanay ('People, being sick on the pavement in Glasgow'—E. Waugh) and is a Bank Holiday. No bank holiday in England but celebration road casualty statistics published. Also list of honours.

First half of bleak month lightened by fortnight of *Daily Express* Boat Show at Earls Court. Sir Max Aitken, Uffa Fox and goose-pimpled bikinis much in evidence. Soccer every Saturday and beginning of international rugger season. Wales *v.* England towards end of month. Rather tame if held at Twickenham—Welshmen in red berets plant leeks on top of goal posts. But worth a trip to Cardiff to hear massed miners singing 'Land of My Fathers'.

Christmas decorations down by twelfth night (5th). Frost, snow, rain. Londoners prefer abroad.

February
Begins with end of pheasant and partridge shooting. Aristocracy take off plus fours and return to London for Cruft's Dog Show at Olympia and Balls. Young Farming aristocracy have Ball at Cirencester. Curious minority groups have balls at London hotels (Rugger Ball, Ladybird Ball, George Washington Ball—exclusiveness based on price).

Anniversary of accession of Elizabeth II on the 6th. Birthday of Prince Andrew on 19th.

February 14. Valentine's day—traditional exchange of greetings cards between lovers. Possibility of Shrove Tuesday or Pancake Day arriving near end of month. Everyone eats pancakes. Villagers of Olney, Bucks. and natives of Soho, London have competition to see who can toss them best. Good month for snow. Londoners still complain about weather and go ski-ing in Switzerland.

March
Begins with St. David's day. Patriotic Welshmen wear daffodils in lapels. Prince Edward's birthday on 10th. St. Patrick's day on 17th —Irishmen wear shamrocks. Quite likely to get beginning of British Summertime (clocks forward one hour) and Easter (another Bank Holiday with a parade in Battersea park and a further dose of road fatalities). On Maundy Thursday the Queen distributes bags

of specially minted money in Westminster Abbey to specially selected old age pensioners who then sell them to antique dealers.

The *Daily Mail* organises an Ideal Home exhibition at Olympia. This consists largely of demonstrations of Instant Zabaglione Mix and revolving circular beds with built-in cocktail cabinets.

More Balls at London hotels. Different names. Same people.

Football season begins to come to an end, culminating perhaps in the Cup Final at Wembley (funny people in cloth caps and rosettes from the north shouting in Piccadilly) but football season gets longer every year and Cup Final more likely to be in May. Racing at Cheltenham in mid-month (Gold Cup, an in-event, tweeds and trilbies, nice setting), at Doncaster later (the Lincolnshire) and at Aintree (God and Mirabel Topham willing, the Grand National). Also the Oxford and Cambridge Boat Race (from Putney to Mortlake). Best watched on television—actually a great bore made interesting by custom.

Weather improves marginally. Londoners begin to plan summer holidays.

April

Begins with All Fools Day. Newspapers and radio occasionally produce bad joke, spoof interviews and stories. Ski-ing competitions in Cairngorms, Scotland. Season of Shakespeare plays open in Stratford. Season of plays opens in Pitlochry, Scotland. Hard-court tennis at Bournemouth. Spalding Tulip time in Spalding, Lincs. (about 20th, imitation Holland). Greyhound Grand National at White City. 23rd St. George's Day—flags on public buildings, sporadic outbursts of Morris Dancing and celebrations of Shakespeare's birthday. Very end of month 2,000 and 1,000 guineas flat horse races at Newmarket.

Polo season opens about 10th at Windsor Great Park, assorted Maharajahs, Prince Philip and Indian Army relics. 18th-19th approx. Berkeley Deb Dress Show: First glimpse of the season's debs. Badminton Horse trials—in Duke of Beaufort's Gloucestershire garden. Ultra tweedy with Queen in headscarf and expertly manoeuvred shooting sticks. (Other trials and point-to-points throughout April and March, see local papers for details.)

Queen's actual birthday on 21st (one day before beginning of Islamic new year). Celebrations confined to playing of National Anthem on Home Service. Real celebrations put off till official birthday.

May

Opens with choirboys singing from Magdalen Tower, Oxford. Undergraduates in punts in river below trying to drown each other. A glut of Morris Dancing. Royal Academy Summer Exhibition (grim trad. portraits and landscapes by home un-talent) opens in first week. Chelsea Flower Show at end of month—large numbers of women from Cheltenham in floral hats compete with the exhibits. Derby at Epsom—grey top hats for nobs, shirt-sleeves for others who watch from nearby Downs. Followed by the Oaks and Windsor Horse Show. Cricket season gets under way. Glyndebourne Opera (Sussex) opens at end of month for those who like to dress up for their entertainments—dark glasses, black tie and café society, very posh.

Festival gardens, Battersea open. Vintage Cars go to Brighton on the 1st. Padstow hold their hobby horse celebrations on the 2nd. On the 19th the Bounds are beaten at the Tower of London. On the 20th Morris Dancers dance for two days in Dunmow, Essex. Chichester Theatre Festival opens in last week (continues to September). Stanley Spencer Gallery in Cookham, Berks. opens. Possible culmination in Whitsun (Bank Holiday with usual sport and transport statistics), shortly preceded by Ascension Day (religious significance only).

More and more Balls. All of great social significance: Queen Charlotte's, Cygnet's in particular. Faces begin to grow over-familiar. Smart Londoners are now in London for nearly only time in year (provided socially O.K.). Weather erratic but country bright and beautiful.

June

Good leisured sporting month. Around 14th, Ascot—see *My Fair Lady*, rather passé apotheosis of English high society at play. Wimbledon tennis during last week (tea, blazers, more women in hats). Henley Regatta right at end and often into July (more blazers and boaters, champagne, strawberries and funny voices saying Good Show Chaps). Approx. 25th, the Greyhound Derby at the White City, election of the Mayor of Ock Streeta and yet more Morris Dancing in Abingdon, Berks. About 15th, 16th, the Lord's Test Match against whoever happens to be touring England. Ultra pleasant if good weather. Drink available throughout hours of play (10.30 a.m. to 7.00 p.m.).

11th—Queen's official birthday (10th is Prince Philip's real one) marked by Trooping of Colour. Great British Ceremonial Event—brigade of Guards marching about and fainting in hot weather on Horse Guards Parade, Whitehall. Impossible to get seats unless you're an Ambassador or have a friend in the Guards.

Mystery Plays in York, National Small Bore rifle meeting at Bisley. *Son et Lumière* at Hampton Court.

Oxford Commem Balls around 20th—pop groups, gay young things doing the Watusi and idiot dons doing the Black Bottom. Traditional good weather. Too good for London. Londoners start to leave for S. of France. Readers of Dickens' novels leave for Broadstairs, Kent, for their annual Dickens' festival.

July

Opens with the Hurlingham Ball at Hurlingham and the Eton and Harrow match at Lord's. Chaps in OE ties and Morning Dress, boxes draped in blue rags, attendance dwindling year by year. Festival of the City of London—relatively new idea with local cultural activities round Tower of London and Guildhall. The last day or two and first few of August are Cowes Regatta—another social event. Reappearance of Uffa Fox, last heard of at *Daily Express* Boat Show. Royal Windsor Rose Show during first week.

From about 13th the Royal Tournament at Earls Court—Musical Ride done by the King's Troop Royal Horse Artillery, the Naval Field Gun competition, and visiting colonials. Watch out for large parties of schoolchildren and lollies. 29th July Annual Feast of St. Wilfrid at Ripon, Yorks.

Swan Upping on River Thames (prob. 18th) and Doggett's Coat and Badge Race from London Bridge to Chelsea. Penultimate week: Royal International Horse Show, at White City; best seen on television. Invariably won by Irish or Italians.

Oxford and Cambridge play cricket at Lord's around the 10th. Society goes to Goodwood for racing around the 25th before Cowes. The Fleet Air Arm have a ball at the Hurlingham Club and the school summer holidays begin. Weather should be good. Usually not.

August

Begins with the Royal Yacht Squadron Ball at Cowes and the Royal national Eisteddfod of Wales. After which the Cowes lot go off to Dublin for the horse show where they spend their evenings spraying each other with soda siphons and their days recovering. The Druids start preparing for next year or go off to the English national sheepdog trials. Around the 13th to 20th the autumn illuminations are turned on in Southend, Morecambe and Skegness, there is a town crier's championship somewhere on the South Coast and a Test Match at the Kennington Oval.

Near the end of the month Edinburgh stages its International Festival which continues till early September. Famous military tattoo with bagpipers piping round Edinburgh castle but also the best serious international music festival in Britain. Battle of Flowers in Guernsey, Racing at York (round 16th).

V. important event of month on the 12th. Glorious Twelfth. Grouse shooting. Aristocracy back into plus-fours and up to grousemoors in Yorkshire and points north. First grouse arrive at ludicrous prices in the Savoy, Mirabelle, Caprice, etc., same evening. Don't be greedy. Wait.

Princess Anne's birthday is on the 15th and the county cricket championship virtually over by the end of the month. August is also famous for its bank holiday.

Also note—silly season. Departure of Loch Ness Monster-spotting teams for Loch Ness.

September

Partridge shooting begins. Entire Conservative Party, except E. Heath, now out on the moors. On 15th Jewish year begins and nation commemorates Battle of Britain. Remaining bits of R.A.F. fly past (embarrassing occasion) and a Spitfire and Hurricane are put on display in Whitehall. To placate working classes the Autumn illuminations are switched on in Blackpool—almost immediately after start of partridge shooting. There is an air show at Farn-borough, the St. Leger at Doncaster and the Royal Highland Gathering at Braemar, Aberdeenshire. There are Balls in Scotland. The football season starts again in England.

Sir Max Aitken and Uffa Fox come back for the International *Daily Express* sponsored offshore powerboat race from Cowes to Torquay. The final of the one day Cricket Cup is played at Lord's in the first week, there is motor cycling on the Isle of Man, the British Isles Bowls championships somewhere. On May 13th, Widecombe (Tom Pearce, Tom Pearce, lend me your grey mare) Fair is held at Widecombe, Devon. Leaves are turning gold. Weather cold.

October

Opens in a flurry of tweedy excitement with the beginning of pheasant shooting and the Cesarewitch at Newmarket. Shortly followed by the Horse of the Year Show at Wembley, a shark fishing and deep sea angling festival at Looe in Cornwall and the Goose Fair in Nottingham. There is a National Gaelic Mod in Scotland on about the 15th—the same day as the Cambridgeshire at Newmarket. On the 17th there are traditional pagan fairs at Sherborne, Dorset and Salisbury, Wilts. Near end of month, the International Motor Show opens at Earls Court, which is rivalled by the Dairy Show at Olympia. 21st is the anniversary of the B. of Trafalgar. (British summertime ends round 20th (clocks back one hour).

November

National Chrysanthemum Society have a show at beginning of month, Guy Fawkes and the Gunpowder plot commemorated on 5th, and inhabitants of Ottery St. Mary, Devon, roll tar barrels. On the 6th the R.A.C. organise their veteran car run from London to Brighton. The new Lord Mayor of London is elected and has a show and a parade (about 12th). Very cold girls with very little on ride mechanised floats. An international cycle and motor cycle show at Earls Court, not to mention the Red Cross Ball at the beginning of the month.

December

Almost as boring, but the London streets lights are always up by the first day of the month—Regent Street very smart, Oxford Street plebian. Everybody is busy preparing for Christmas. Oxford play Cambridge at rugger at Twickenham (note large numbers of bishops drinking in car park). Royal Smithfield Show at Earls Court—stock, live and mechanical. International Poultry Show at Olympia. Carol services, particularly in King's College, Cambridge. Christmas (super extraordinary road statistics as it's a bank holiday as well) followed by the Schoolboys' and Schoolgirls' exhibition at Olympia—a must to avoid. A few faintly nautical Balls at London hotels. Weather grim, but everyone praying for Christmas snow.

Like restaurants, there are guides galore. Unlike restaurants, there is none which can be honestly recommended. (None give real opinions, though something like the Automobile Association book is very good on the ratio of lavatories to bedrooms.)

So here are some selected opinions on selected hotels, based on a selection of reasons why you might want an hotel in the first place.

The reason for wanting an hotel might be general—such as a holiday. Or you might have a specific reason—from Sex to Suicide.

If you come to London from the provinces and dislike the way your friends live, or they refuse to have you, or you have none; if you are a visiting American, yet not staying with Fleur Cowles, the Ambassador or Mrs. Jack Heinz; if you were living with somebody and they have thrown you out; if you are a foreigner and have nowhere else to go—then you must put up at an hotel.

There are thousands in London to choose from. Most of them bad. All making a profit. But perhaps a score or so are worth the bill at the end. This guide is designed to help you choose the one best suited to your requirements or your pocket.

First of all, your requirements, however strange . . .

Sex
You might, in the pursuit of pleasure, want to spend the night with somebody in a London hotel bedroom. The simple rule is don't do it. Spend the night in her, or his, house, apartment, flat, pad or Dormobile; go out and stay up all night in a club, it is more fun; or take to the country, where there are places for illicit love. But not the bedroom of a decent London hotel. Whether you intend adultery or simple fornication, it will turn out a bleak and jumpy experience when you are cowering anxiously together between the sheets of some vast establishment, unable to make up your mind to say 'come in' or 'stay out' to a knowing knock at the door.

This pathetic state of mind has nothing to do with sexual guilt, shame, or our Puritan tradition. It is simple human misery and stems from the certain knowledge that the entire hotel staff, say 1,000 members of the Catering Union, know exactly what you are up to and despise you for not being able to arrange your sex life properly.

There is also the fact that the better London hotels object fairly strongly to being used as brothels and they will not trouble to hide the fact when you book in, if they let you in at all.

They will not mind so much if you take two rooms. But it is not very relaxing to have to hide in your chosen one's bathroom whenever one of the staff enters the room; to remember to rumple your bed before you leave your room for the night; to dash back for your toothpaste or ditty box; to stagger off at dawn to a cold bed before the papers and tea arrive.

There is, of course, a way out—if you can afford anything from twenty guineas to fifty guineas per day. This is the income bracket of cabaret stars, prime ministers of one-party states, and successful gamblers. If you have this kind of money you can have as many masters or mistresses as you please for as long as you wish, provided you take a suite of rooms. A sitting-room and a dining-room somehow put the bedroom in perspective. If you go to an hotel with a pretty partner and take a room and bath, everybody knows what you have in mind (unless you are married) and everybody, consequently, disapproves. But in a suite, you can entertain the biggest rake in London, or the gayest divorcee, until the small hours, and there will always be the possibility that you are just dining in the dining-room, or sitting in the sitting-room. And nobody minds at all.

Divorce

Hotels figure in the process of divorce as much as they do in the celebration of marriage. You go to them from the church and later, if you are unlucky, from them to the law courts. They are a half-way house between the rituals of the altar and the witness box. They provide the beds where, in relative privacy, the bonds of matrimony are implemented, and almost as often, dissolved. You should not use the same hotel for both purposes.

Any private detective worth his fee will give you a list of reliable divorce hotels. That is part of his job. He will not supply a reliable man or woman for you to clamber into bed with under the eye of the chambermaid or valet. That used to be part of his job. But since the scandal, trial and death of Stephen Ward, no private detective is willing to run the risk. The reason is that even though you probably would not—and one should not—have sexual intercourse with the hired evidence of your adultery, you must, to get a divorce, swear that you have had intercourse. This puts the agency in the position of having procured a man or woman for immoral purposes. And since the Ward case the police have been very tough on that particular offence.

So if you want to present your wife or husband with a tidily arranged divorce, you must shift for yourself in the sad hunt for a stooge (fee £75 to £100) who will neither blackmail you nor use you in their own divorce case. This may not be easy. You will not find an honest candidate in any of London's nightclubs, though this is the advice most often given. Aspiring female novelists in search of experience, or the less gifted students at art or drama schools may be glad of the fee and a good night's rest.

Once you have found your partner (their names need not be mentioned in court) the battle is more than half won and you can book in with a light heart at your divorce hotel. For some strange reason they are usually near railway termini—Victoria, Euston, Paddington. In atmosphere they are middle-class and respectable. The bedroom staff have photographic memories, and will not confuse your wife's passport photo with that of the girl you slept with for one night. The rooms are clean but gloomy, and the food is banal, but you should tip well. It is a small price to pay for reliable witnesses.

Animals

If you want to take your dog, cat, parrot or crocodile out to lunch you should go to the Ritz. There you should ask for the ladies' loo and present your pet to the attendant, whereupon she will offer you a selection of dainty collars. Most pets have necks small enough to be wrung by the average-weak pair of hands, but experience has shown that a number of poodle collars buckled together will fit the neck of the biggest Great Dane or Bull Mastiff. The beast will then be chained to the radiator and you can go to lunch in peace. What happens if dogs, cats and birds are chained together to the same radiator at the same time is open to question. You must ask the attendant.

Should you wish to move in for a longish stay with your pet you must go to the Kensington Palace Hotel. There a really thoughtful management have provided a dog, cat and bird baby-sitting service, and pages who will exercise your pets for you in the

Park across the road. The chef will prepare any dish your little friend may fancy from the carte, and the inevitable outcome can be disposed of in special 'dirt boxes' specially provided in your bathroom. The staff have strict instructions 'to speak nicely to the pets to make them feel at home' and, needless to say, the hotel is very busy during Cruft's, the Cat Show and the Bird Show. So book early. The charge for a pet is 7s. 6d. a night.

Honeymoons

Any London hotel will fall over itself to arrange your wedding reception. But there is one thing you cannot do, and that is to stay in the same hotel for your honeymoon. There is something just too brutally frank about seizing your bride by the hand and heading away upstairs the moment the speeches are done. And it would be boorish to expect your friends to stand in the stairwell chucking confetti over themselves as you make for the bridal suite, or to cluster mutely round the lift gates in the foyer, for it will be a very silent occasion; they can hardly cry 'Good luck!' or 'Have a lovely . . .' well, *journey* would be too much of a euphemism, in the circumstances.

So where you stay for your honeymoon depends on who you are. Anglo-American alliances should be consummated at the Connaught. Crumbs from the upper crust of English society seem to unite at Claridges. The Savoy, apt to treat young lovers with a certain grim reserve, if not actual suspicion, can be very kind if you really are just married and will keep the press, your creditors, even the police, for a time, from your door. Good for heiresses, ageing playboys and theatre people. If you have left the stage and married into films, you will sleep easier at the Dorchester, in the same beds Liz and Richard (Burton) used, if you take the Harlequin Suite. At the Ritz the feeling is so cosmopolitan, so chic, so utterly urbane that you might have to pinch yourself in bed to realise that it is your wedding night.

Work

If you come to London to do business you will want a hotel that takes telephone messages accurately, delivers telegrams promptly, and does not lose your letters or give them to someone else. You will need a good big writing desk, with a light or a window on the left, comfortable chairs for you and your secretary, a direct dial telephone for local calls and an efficient switchboard operator for long distance. You will want swift, courteous room service to impress your colleagues, and a floor staff that will clean and tidy your room while you are having breakfast, so that you may start work as soon as you have finished your coffee and morning papers.

Such places are hard to find. Here is the way to set about it. Book, in advance, at three or four hotels in that part of London where you wish to stay. Post yourself a couple of letters to each hotel. When you arrive at the airport or railway station, fill in the time waiting for the customs or a taxi by telephoning the hotels you have chosen and leaving long, complicated messages for yourself. Then go to the first hotel on your list and keep your taxi waiting. Ask for your mail and any messages. Inspect your rooms. Interview the chambermaid. Order a drink. Go downstairs to the public call box, ring yourself up and have yourself paged. Leave the receiver off the hook and follow the page boy on his route—check if he is thorough. If all these services meet with your approval pay off the cab and stay. If not, go on until you find the right hotel. Once there, check the switchboard operator's tact by telling her to call the other hotels on your list and cancel your booking. Charge your taxi to expenses and write a letter to *The Times* about your findings. If you are a businessman in Britain today, you are the most important person in the world and your demands can be correspondingly high.

Suicide

An hotel is quite the best place. Choose one that is fairly central and has a good reputation—however unjustified—to live up to.

Whether you favour the pill or the blade, take a room with bath and telephone near a hospital—you might change your mind half-way. Any hotel in Oxford Street, Knightsbridge, or the north side of the Strand will do.

Take care to commit suicide *in* the hotel, not from the hotel, however tall the building—jumping is the wrong way out, if you want tidiness and privacy. Hotel managements hate suicides, but it will save your family and friends from having to clean up the mess, and your remains will be disposed of discreetly and with a minimum of publicity. Your estate will have to foot the bill if you are successful, so to avoid more trouble than is necessary, pay in advance.

As a last gesture to society you might leave your body to the hospital that would have saved your life if you had telephoned in time; they never have enough.

And remember, for good service stick to the big hotels. The smaller ones in Earls Court, Bayswater or Notting Hill, accustomed though they are to finding guests stone dead in the TV lounge or crumpled under the geyser in the communal bathroom, will be scared by suicide and do a rush job.

So pick one of the best hotels for suicide. After all, you're not paying.

Pleasure

General pleasure—such as a holiday—rather than any of the specific pleasures already mentioned. In this case, your pocket is the first consideration.

Travel agencies will as a rule advise you to stay at the hotel which gives them the biggest cut of your bill. It is therefore wise to book your holiday hotel yourself; one that will suit your temperament, social milieu, taste and style—if you have any. But how to choose?

It is essential, if coming to London, to grasp the fact that British hotels exist primarily for the convenience of those employed in them and secondly for the profit of the owners. The public merely pays.

The vast majority of hotels charge you handsomely for the privilege of staying in them and doggedly refuse to give you any service worth the name. These hotels are staffed by Portuguese communists, Spaniards failing to learn English, Cypriot terrorists and petrol pump attendants who have come in from the cold.

A minority of hotels in Britain have realised that there is more money to be made in the long run by giving good service. They employ trained managers, tactful doormen, competent chefs, and the dwindling number of skilled barmen, good waiters and honest chambermaids left in Britain.

They tend to charge rather more than the others, but they are the ones to stay at—it is worth the money. They come in two sorts—Hotels of Character and International Jet Set.

The following list of Best Hotels should make it easier for you to choose the one that will give you most pleasure.

Hotels of Character

Quiet and dignified with a natural air of calm superiority, although here and there, the décor and the guests are beginning to fade.

CONNAUGHT. CARLOS PLACE, W.I. 100 ROOMS

Atmosphere of pleasant country house, lately done up by people with more money than breeding. Excellent American/English food, good wine list, freezing cocktails. Obliging hall porter, discreet and cheerful bedroom staff. Comfy, quiet, high-ceilinged rooms. Top place for chic sex. Likely fellow guests: Prince Rainier, David Niven, Ingrid Bergman, Walt Disney, Aaron Copland.

CLARIDGES. BROOK STREET, W.I. 250 ROOMS (ALL SUITES)
Opulent passé décor, obsequious service. Food rich and uninspired. Suites lavish but lack style. Used to be home from home for landed aristos who came to London for sex, or to attend political or religious rituals, and were assured of comfort without having to bring their own servants. If you can afford it, you will be treated like a gentleman, regardless. Likely fellow guests: Queen Victoria Eugenie, Yul Brynner, King Constantine, Jack Benny, Dr. Banda, Queen Anne-Marie, M. Dietrich.

RITZ. PICCADILLY, W.I. 132 ROOMS
Unique air of indefinable excitement. Haphazard décor of palms, brocade and marble. Best public gossip in London in Rivoli Bar. Tea time (Indian or China) a good moment to find out who is having a walk out with whom in London. Food undemanding, wines agreeable, service pleasant. Does not reveal guest list. May be empty and turn you away, or full and find you a room— depending on who you are. Duke of Windsor usually stays there. Has reputation of being the best hotel in London, nobody quite knows why. It probably is.

BROWNS. DOVER STREET, W.I. 136 ROOMS
A Trust House Hotel. Discourages tipping, adds 12% surcharge for service. If you feel you have had no service, you may dispute the surcharge. Comfy, chintzy, family hotel. Great character, but no excitement. Kurt Hahn, the Gordonstoun man, stays there.

BERKELEY HOTEL. BERKELEY STREET, W.I. 100 SUITES
Once the spiritual home of many a gallant officer. Atmosphere vanished owing to renovations. Somehow a lightweight hotel today. Popular with debs and their delights. Good lunches, and late grill. Food sound, some good wines. Likely fellow guests: Ava Gardner, Shirley Temple.

International Jet Set
Old and new, all trying hard to set and keep the pace.

SAVOY. STRAND, W.C.2. 500 SUITES
Atmosphere as well as pace. Good food, good wine, good cigars,

good service, high prices. London's top no-nonsense de luxe hotel. Ideal for rich busy people who know what they want and expect to get it. More celebrities to the square inch of red carpet than else-where. Atmosphere of purposeful expense. If you are poor, idle or obscure, you will feel guilty here. Likely fellow guests: Callas, Noel Coward, C. Chaplin, Jane Fonda, C. Ponti, R. Vadim.

DORCHESTER. PARK LANE, W.I. 280 ROOMS

Like the Savoy, it has character as well as excitement. Décor, atmosphere, irretrievably 1930s, like the façade. Caters know-ledgeably for lovers of international repute, working millionaires, tasteless eccentrics. Determined to provide whatever you may need. A whole roast sheep was once served to a sheik and his followers sitting on the floor. Likely fellow guests: King Hussein, Danny Kaye, Liz Taylor/Richard Burton, Gregory Peck, A. Hitchcock—Kirk Douglas, Mary Pickford. (Speciality—ladies' turkish baths.)

GROSVENOR HOUSE. PARK LANE, W.I. 550 ROOMS

Biggest ballroom (Queen Charlotte's ball held here), biggest hall, biggest . . . but not necessarily the best. A mausoleum of our time. Likely fellow guests: The Dockers, Sam Spiegel.

MAYFAIR. BERKELEY STREET. 450 ROOMS

Atmosphere of glittering sin. Plate glass, cushioned bars, black mirrors. Catering for every expensive taste, its character is chameleon-like. Has a cinema, theatre, night-club, coffee shop, Polynesian restaurant (with tropical thunderstorm every half hour) and casino, as well as rooms. A supermarket in raffish pleasures. Likely fellow guests: Dionne Warwick, Henry Mancini, Sammy Davis jnr.

LONDON HILTON. PARK LANE, W.I. 495 ROOMS

Owned by C. Clore, leased to C. Hilton, cost £8 million. Central heating, air-conditioning throughout. Speedy lifts (800 ft. per minute) to 28 floors. Five restaurants, four bars, car park, shops. Iced water on tap. The service is hectic and undistinguished, the food is pretentious, the wine list alarming. Best that can be said of this attempt to Americanize the London hotel scene is that it overlooks the gardens of Buckingham Palace (which should, one day, be the best hotel in London). Likely fellow guests: P. Ustinov, Francoise Hardy, R. Marciano, M. Luther King, S. MacLaine.

WESTBURY. CONDUIT STREET. 285 ROOMS

No service charge, good expensive drinks, excellent central location (the doorman will find you a parking place, in an otherwise unparkable area). Service efficient, pleasantly impersonal. Caters exactly for middle-class Jet Set. Likely fellow guests: Premiers of Sweden, Tobago, Trinidad, Gracie Fields, Petula Clark and visiting Americans.

CARLTON TOWER. CADOGAN PLACE. S.W.I. 318 ROOMS

Unpretentious jet age décor, good friendly service, modern, sensible rooms. Personalised bookmatches free to celebrities (others pay). Good restaurant—the Rib Room—specialises to some purpose in beef. Manager a music lover, will put ballroom piano at disposal of practising musicians for rehearsals. Likely fellow guests: A. Markova, Hans Hotter, Rudolfe Kempe, Willy Brandt, Elke Somner, Mel Ferrer, James Mason.

ROYAL GARDENS HOTEL. KENSINGTON HIGH STREET, W.8. 527 ROOMS

Like some other recent British enterprises on the grand scale, this one limps a little. It is big, it has pretentions, it is all-British, it is practically in the suburbs, and it may shake down sooner or later. Peter Sellers (always a good sign) has been occupying the penthouse lately. Other guests include Joe Louis and the Bolshoi Ballet.

There is a man in Kentish Town who burns pianos on the pavement. People, and firms, come from far and wide bringing him their pianos to burn. Go to Kentish Town High Road and ask, or smell.

Eating Out in London

Books galore have been written on London restaurants, so we don't presume to be even faintly comprehensive.

But here are some hard-won words of advice which all eaters in London should know. Plus a quick guide to a couple of dozen restaurants, depending on how much you want to spend, and a list of the best English restaurants. English food has to be tried. You're not likely to find it anywhere else.

The English have a determined sense of inferiority about their own cuisine, so most London restaurants ape that of other countries.

In London you can eat in an Anglo-French/Italian/Greek/Indian/Turkish/Indonesian/Chinese restaurant and get their national dishes tutored to the British palate more easily than you can get steak-and-kidney pudding, roast beef or roly-poly. (In approximately 3,600 meals eaten out in the last ten years, one well known gourmet says he has never seen roly-poly on the menu.)

Apart from jellied eel stalls, fish and chip shops and City Chop Houses, English food is only available at Simpson's in the Strand, Stone's, Grumbles, and the Hungry Horse. See Quick Guide pages 31–2.

Foreigners, especially Frenchmen, often pursue English sea-food and particularly the unique potted shrimp and the Scotch smoked salmon. These can be found at the Wheeler chains, where Chinese cooks are almost exclusively employed, at Overton's—try the Victoria branch—at Sweeting's in the City, and at Bentley's just off Piccadilly in Swallow Street. That favourite haunt of Frenchmen, Scott's in Coventry Street, is not recommended.

As a broad rule, French restaurants in London are run by Italians, Italian by Greeks, and Greek by Cypriots. The recent invasion of the trattoria has lifted the decor, quality and, it must be admitted, the price of Italian food to an excited pitch.

Soho is the traditional restaurant centre in London and is almost the only quarter with any street life. Traditional restaurants, which were strong before the War and still serve decent meals with professional waiters, clean tablecloths and cutlery, are no longer fashionable but still provide the most consistent value for money. These are, in no particular order of merit: Casa Pepe, Gennaro's, Leoni's, Kettner's, L'Etoile, L'Escargot Bienvenu, and indeed any restaurant where a chasseur can be seen in a brightly coloured soup-stained uniform looking around helplessly for taxis.

However, the younger set prefer the more expensive trattoria where the proprietor wears a light cashmere pullover and the décor is in the Milan Industrial Fair idiom.

It is not necessary to book tables for a traditional restaurant but better to do so for any in the second category.

Don't eat in your hotel. Very few London hotels operate the Continental en pension system and there is very little connection between the hotel restaurant and the hotel guests. The food is Babylon international and very expensive.

A service charge in London restaurants is very rarely added to the bill, but you should tip at the rate of 2s. if mean or 2s. 6d. if generous, in the pound.

The menu in London restaurants you will find tends to be of a pattern. The better ones have a choice of one or two plats du jour but far too many have far too many dishes. The best tactic is to ask to meet the head waiter and explain that you are an ignorant foreigner and place yourself in his hands.

The Englishman has the absurd notion that it is not manly to eat puddings, or sweets as they are called slightly lower down the social scale. The businessman's meal usually consists of one or two aperitifs, a plate of smoked salmon, a fillet steak, and coffee.

In very few places is there a menu à prix fixe and each item, including vegetables, is carefully itemized down to the last sixpence. The bill is usually correctly added up.

The English don't have long Continental lunch-hours (one hour off is standard) and therefore don't consume elaborate lunches, so the waiter will expect you to be impatient and will be himself.

England is the biggest European wine importer, and restaurants have staggeringly long and varied wine lists. Many Italian restaurants have family connections with vineyards in Italy but mostly the vin en carafe is not an open wine but tipped from a bottle into a carafe and you are charged less for it.

It is nearly always sound practice to have the cheapest wine on the menu but never the second cheapest as this is reserved for the genteel host who does not wish to be blatant.

Apart from Soho, restaurants are fairly dense in Chelsea and Kensington, and scattered round the Hampstead and St. John's Wood area. It is worth going to the East End to eat at the New Friends Chinese restaurant in Salmon Lane and certainly worth buying a copy of the *Good Food Guide* if you are staying in London for more than a few weeks.

Unlike Parisians or New Yorkers, Londoners don't have a favourite neighbourhood restaurant but will go miles to dine after lengthy hesitations. They are as fickle in their patronage as the restaurants are inconsistent with their food. Considerable social prestige is attached to frequenting the right place.

There are sadly no boulevard cafes in London and the existing coffeehouses are mostly patronised by the young and noisy and are ill-suited to a business conversation. The more serious kind of Englishman will prefer to converse in a pub and these of course are only open during licensing hours—generally 11.30 a.m. to 3 p.m. and 5 p.m. to 10.30 p.m., though there may be half hour variations either way.

There is absolutely nowhere for the visitor to go for a serious conversation at 10.30 in the morning. All he can do is to wait until half past eleven. Londoners lunch from one and dine from eight o'clock on. (Most of the restaurants listed in the Quick Guide are open until eleven.)

Almost all London pubs offer sandwiches and many have restaurants attached where a traditional three course English meal can be had for under £1. The service is more friendly than polite and they are usually crowded, but the value for money is incontestable.

Around Leicester Square and in crowded shopping streets, there are chain eating houses where chicken and mock hamburgers can be consumed under orange lights. The best dish they offer is a glass of cold English milk which is probably the most tasty in the world but otherwise they should be avoided by the gastronomically or aesthetically sensitive visitor to these shores. A possible exception are the Kenya Coffee Houses.

The Pan-Am lounge in Piccadilly is a far warmer and more comfortable place to meet friends than on the pavement outside Swan and Edgars.

Don't forget that the better hotels have headed notepaper and writing tables.

Best bird-watching pitches: the pavement outside Vogue in Hanover Square (weekdays 10–5), Kings Road (Saturday a.m.), Portobello Road (Saturday p.m.).

Quick Guide to London Restaurants

RESTAURANTS SPECIALISING IN ENGLISH FOOD

The Hungry Horse, 196 Fulham Road, S.W.10, FLA 7757, *or* 8081
Jasper's Eating House, 4 Bourne Street, S.W.1, SLO 6445
Peter Evans, 60 Fleet Street, E.C.4, FLE 4996
Rules, 35 Maiden Lane, W.C.2, TEM 5314
Simpsons in the Strand, 100 Strand, W.C.2, TEM 7131
Sweetings, 39 Queen Victoria Street, E.C.4, CIT 3062
Wheelers, 19 Old Compton Street, W.1, GER 7661
Wilton's, 17 Bury Street, S.W.1, WHI 8391

OTHER RESTAURANTS

In three categories, according to price:
*** You will have a good meal, expensively served and pay £4 a head including wine and tip.
** £2 should cover you.
* You can eat well for £1 or under.
There is no relationship between the price and the quality of the food. These stars only indicate the degree of attention and comfort the visitor may expect.

***

Caprice, Arlington Street, St. James's Street, S.W.1, HYD 3183
Coq d'Or, Stratton House, Stratton Street, W.1, MAY 7807
Etoile, 30 Charlotte Street, W.1, MUS 7189
Mirabelle, 56 Curzon Street, W.1, GRO 1940
Parkes, 4 Beauchamp Place, S.W.3, KEN 1390
Pruniers, 72 St. James's Street, S.W.1, HYD 1373

**

Chez Victor, 45 Wardour Street, W.1, GER 6523
Jacaranda, Walton House, Walton Street, S.W.3, KEN 2062
Lantern House (Chinese), 631 Watford Way, N.W.7, MUS 4470
Marynka, 232 Brompton Road, S.W.3, KEN 6753
Nick's Diner, 88 Ifield Road, S.W.10, FLA 0930
Silver Spur, 38 Thurloe Place, S.W.7, KEN 7717
Trattoria Parioli, 129 Crawford Street, W.1, WEL 9601
Trattoria Santa Lucia, 20 Rupert Street, W.1, GER 3818
Trattoria Terrazza, 19 Romilly Street, W.1, GER 8991

*

The Ark, 122 Palace Gardens Terrace, W.8, BAY 4024
Claridge's Causerie, Brook Street, W.1, MAY 8860

31

Cordon Bleu (lunch only), 31 Marylebone Lane, W.1, WEL 2931
De Hems, 11 Macclesfield Street, W.1, GER 2494
Gay Hussar, 2 Greek Street, W.1, GER 0973
Manzi's, 1 Leicester Street, W.1, GER 5131
Monplaisir, 21 Monmouth Street, W.C.2, TEM 7243

Press receptions given by firms launching new products, film companies launching new stars, and groups holding reunions are taking place all the time in London hotels. Some, like the Hilton and the Europa, make it easy for you by displaying a board in the foyer announcing the rooms in which these drink and canape affairs are taking place. You can always say, if challenged, that you got the rooms confused. Or that you're representing the East Nigerian Press Association.

Still better parties are held each night at the better embassies. Three out of every ten embassies you phone on any morning of the year to ask 'What time is the party tonight?' will tell you it starts at six. Either leave your name and a message that you may be up to half an hour late; or get on the mailing list as the Defence Correspondent of the East Nigerian Press Association. Reciprocal entertaining of Military and Air Attaches will also stand you in good stead.

London Pubs

Pubs are what other countries don't have. In England, country pubs are perhaps nicest of all. After that come the London ones.

Pubs change character as you tipple down from the top of Britain. In the dry areas of Skye you have none at all. In Glasgow they are just drinking shops. In Carlisle they are cheerless and state controlled.

But in London, there are pubs for all men and for all seasons.

Pubs, like people, have two faces. The one that the casual visitor observes, and the other which is only seen by the intimate regular.

It is really for the visitor that pubs have been put in the following categories: Rough Pubs; Posh Pubs; Arty Pubs; Pubs for Unaccompanied Men; Pubs for Unaccompanied Women, and for those with slightly more eccentric tastes, Pubs Associated with Crime. But the regulars will also gain by it. They tend to know no other pub but their own. And they know their own so well that they have lost sight of the features.

There are numerous other types of pub in London, and many individual pubs, that are worthy of attention. But it is hoped that the following pages will cater for the broader, or baser, social instincts.

Voyeurs can visit the rough pubs mentioned. Snobs can go to the posh pubs. Those who wish to be thought 'with-it' have the arty pubs. Men who like to drink in masculine company can go to the sporting pubs. Women who like to drink alone without being molested, but who enjoy male company, can find the pubs mentioned. And those with a taste for the macabre can drink from the bar that Christie drank from, or visit other famous crime pubs.

If you took the pub away from London, social life in public would almost cease to exist.

ROUGH PUBS

People talk about pubs being rough in Glasgow or Liverpool, but London has its quota for the enquiring drinker who likes a barney, or the proximity of physical violence and available women. The most obvious in this category are those around the docks where seamen drink. One of the nicest pubs, though not the kind of place you'd take a maiden aunt, is the Custom House Hotel, known as 'the Steps', Victoria Dock Road. This is a vast, sprawling pub, with a raised bar at the back. It provides live music, as well as throwing in a couple of juke-boxes. There are other lively pubs near by, including the Freemasons Tavern and the Railway Tavern, but the Steps takes pride of place. You could be in a waterfront bar anywhere in the world, and the atmosphere would be much the same. It is not unusual to see somebody almost kicked to death outside, so unless you are on the look-out for a rough-house or know how to take care of yourself in a fight, avoid getting into an argument.

A better known, and almost as rough, pub is Charlie Brown's (actually called the Railway Tavern, but known generally by its nick-name), West India Dock Road, which boasts a splendid museum of curiosa from all over the world, collected by one of the landlords. Another guv'nor was stabbed through the glass door, trying to get rid of an argumentative customer. It is also very handy for one of the best Chinese restaurants in London, the Old Friends, almost next door.

Nearer central London is the Admiral Blakeney's Head, just beyond the Tower, in the now rapidly disappearing Cable Street. Cable Street still manages to hit the headlines with the odd murder and the Blakeney's Head is as virile as ever. Juke-boxes, spades, seamen, tarts, mingle in a remarkably friendly atmosphere, and there are cafés nearby catering for all nationalities. The police still patrol Cable Street in twos.

For those who like their squalor without the atmosphere of violence, there is Dirty Dick's, opposite Liverpool Street Station. This has dead cats, cobwebs and sawdust by way of décor. But is in fact a genuine old pub keeping up the tradition of its founder, who amassed a fortune and refused to spend money on clothes. There is a curious collection of postage stamps on which couples have written their names.

In the West End, there are a couple of well-established rough and ready pubs. Much the most famous is the Duke of York's, Rathbone Street, the best meeting place in London. This marvellous pub, superbly managed in the face of terrible odds, has a fine and baudy museum, with a portrait of the late (and lamented) guv'nor, Major Alf Klien, framed by a lavatory seat. Every available inch of the walls and ceiling is taken up with paintings, seaside postcards, ties, sailors' hat bands and other totally obscure objects. Nearby, in Goodge Street, is the One Tun, known simply as Finch's, which caters for the overspill from the Duke of York.

POSH PUBS

There are any number of dreary 'posh' pubs in the West End of London, or around Chelsea and Belgravia. But very few actually manage to become 'smart' pubs, i.e., those that get used by a certain set—guardees, debs, advertising men, actors and the like.

One of the most obvious in this category, and yet not ruined for the casual, unpretentious drinker, is the Grenadier, Wilton Row. This serves very decent food, far better than the average pub meal (though naturally priced accordingly). It does have a great deal of physical charm, in a particularly nice setting. Its connection is really more with the Duke of Wellington than with the Grenadier Guards (though a Colour Sergeant is detailed to pose for the inn sign whenever it needs repainting, and the barmen wear mess jackets). It used, in fact, to be a mess for the Duke's officers, and the Duke himself is alleged to have played cards there.

Another smart pub, though one with a slightly sinister atmosphere, is the Star Tavern, Belgrave Mews West. This belongs to no clique that can actually be pigeon-holed, but you get the impression that if the master-minds behind the Great Train Robbery ever used a pub, it would be one remarkably like the Star. There is the atmosphere of discreet opulence about the place, and inevitably a Jaguar or two outside. Again, however, the casual visitor doesn't feel an outsider and playing darts is not discouraged.

Another smart pub is the Windsor Castle, Campden Hill Road. It is almost, but not quite, made totally impossible by the clientele who like to be seen there. But is after all a very handsome pub with a garden. There is also the Denmark, Brompton Road; the Elephant and Castle, Holland Street; the Australian, Milner Place, and the Markham Arms where, allegedly, the brightest conversation in London can be found. (Though don't turn up straight from footballing in Hyde Park—you will be called a Nuclear Disarmer). Finally, there is the Antelope Tavern, in Eaton Terrace, which is smart enough for those who like that kind of thing and serves very good food (though you cannot book a table).

ARTY PUBS

One of the most famous 'arty' pubs in Chelsea is the Queen's Elm, where the importance of the customer can be gathered by the way he is greeted by the landlord, who will rush forward if he is a famous novelist or actor, but who will also—let it be said—cash a cheque for the odd poet (Patrick Kavanagh, the Irish poet, uses the pub when in London).

Equally famous is Finch's (actually called the King's Arms) further down the Fulham Road. Finch's is slightly less pretentious than the Queen's Elm, and is excellently staffed (though it gets impossibly packed towards the end of the evening and at week-ends). It is patronised by actual painters and sculptors, Frank Bowling and Elizabeth Frink, for instance. There is also a hard core of regular locals, being the kind of place you could return to after ten years in Tangier and be sure of running into the people you used to know in Finch's in the old days. In Bayswater there is Henekey's, at the top of Portobello Road, which is a great meeting place on a Saturday lunchtime.

The most arty pub in the West End is, without doubt, the York Minster, in Dean Street, equally well known as the French Pub. This is the most enduring arty pub in London, having kept a faithful clientele of actors, journalists, writers, and painters over the past twenty or thirty years. It used to serve an excellent, unpretentious French lunch upstairs, but the restaurant is temporarily closed. This again, is the kind of pub you could return to after years abroad and meet your old friends who would greet you as if they'd seen you only last week.

The amazing thing about the popularity of the French, is its badness as a pub *qua* pub. There are no pint glasses, for instance, and your unsuspecting customer asking for a pint is simply served with a half, without explanation, and you can only get Watney's Red Barrel in the way of beer. On the other hand, the guv'nor serves an incredible range of aperitifs, and he does buy his own wine.

The great actors' pub is the splendidly victorian Salisbury, in St. Martin's Lane. This has been faithfully restored, the brewers intelligently resisting the temptation to modernise. The Salisbury also serves good food, and is large enough to accommodate its numerous clientele. The camp atmosphere of fifty or sixty actors of varying degrees of success is a bit overpowering, unless you like that kind of thing, but it is also a decent, well-run pub, with a good range of beers. Nearby, and also a popular meeting place for actors, though much more intimate, if not incestuous, is the Round Table, St. Martin's Court. The clientele here tends to be rather cliquey.

PUBS FOR UNACCOMPANIED MEN (NOT QUEERS—BUT HEARTIES)

The complaint most often made about pubs by women is that they are an exclusively male preserve. However, this is changing fast, and now men complain that there are no pubs where they 'get away from women'. Even sporting pubs, where a man could be sure of conversation on resolutely male topics, are no longer safe. But confirmed bachelors and grass widowers may still find kindred spirits in one or more of the following.

There are many football pubs in London. These are usually close to soccer grounds and are often the headquarters of supporters' clubs, such as the Highbury Barn Tavern, Highbury Park, for Arsenal, and the Boleyn, Barking Road, for West Ham. This is where it all happens after successful cup matches.

For those who prefer talk about rugby football, there is a cluster of 'rugger houses' in Twickenham: the Rugby Tavern is the sort of place where ex-second row forwards swill beer and reminisce; the Cabbage Patch, named after the famous ground, is far more democratic. A lot of drinking before internationals at 'Twickers' is also done at the City Barge, Strand-on-the-Green, Chiswick.

Cricket pubs also tend to be situated near grounds. The Lords Tavern, shortly to be rebuilt, needs no introduction, though its 'hearties' are now subject to fierce competition from show-biz personalities. The lunch interval there is like the foyer of a Shaftesbury Avenue theatre on a first night. For those who prefer quiet discussion of cricket, there is either the Crown, Aberdeen Place, or the Abbey Tavern, Violet Hill. South of the river, Lord's sister-ground, the Oval, has its adjoining Surrey Tavern and the nearby Hanover Arms in Kennington Park Road. In the West End, the Yorker, Piccadilly, is almost a cricketing shrine.

But far and away the most popular pub sport is boxing. Many pubs are run by ex-boxers (one of the most famous is still called after its guv'nor, the Tom Cribb, in Panton Street). Most famous is the Thomas à Beckett in the Old Kent Road, with its large collection of trophies. For a quiet chat, pick Len Harvey's Star and Garter in Islington. Or, early in the evening, Alf Mancini's Rifle, down the Fulham Palace Road.

PUBS FOR UNACCOMPANIED WOMEN

In Scotland and in the North of England it is still not done for women to go into any pubs. Although they are invading London pubs, women may not safely go into all pubs on their own. Until they can, so some people say, true social equality does not exist.

In some, even today, they will even be shown the door, no matter how respectable they look. In most others, they will be the victims of male predators.

But there are a handful of London pubs, growing in number,

where a lone woman is perfectly safe. One you can go to is the Queen's Arms, in Tyron Street, Chelsea, where both setting and clientele are almost exaggeratedly decorous. For women who like something a little livelier, there is the Bolton Hotel and its neighbour the Coleherne, in Old Brompton Road, though not the latter on Sunday mornings.

A pub where you can enjoy homely entertainment, varying in quality, is upstairs at the Chepstow, Chepstow Place, Bayswater, in 'Terry's Bar'.

If you want something slightly more louche, there's the Golden Lion, the York Minster's neighbour in Dean Street, Soho. If you're really in search of cheap but harmless thrills, you should take a trip down East, to dockland, where there's a huge, noisy pub with coloured lights and a couple of juke-boxes, in Victoria Road, called the Kent Arms.

PUBS ASSOCIATED WITH CRIME

For pub-goers of both sexes with a taste for the morbid, there is a large number of London pubs with criminal associations. This is a tradition that began with highwayman's inns, and it has died hard.

Many pubs still boast of their connections with Dick Turpin. There's a knot of them in the Hampstead-Highgate area, such as The Flask, Highgate West Hill, and the nearby Wrestler's, North Road, which claims a tunnel that Turpin used leading to Jack Straw's Castle, Whitestone Pond, two miles away in Hampstead. A few hundred yards away from that is the best-known Turpin pub in North London, the Spaniards Inn. It is said to be his last stopping place before riding north to York and execution.

Other pubs with Turpin legends are the Spotted Dog, Upton Lane, West Ham, and the George and Dragon, Acton High Street, said to be the H.Q. for his Hounslow Heath forays. One famous highwayman, Jack Law, was himself a publican, and the pub he owned, the Brockley Jack, Brockley Rise, was later named after him.

Several pubs gained notoriety as stopping places for condemned men and women on their way to execution: Ye Olde White Hart, Drury Lane; the Crown, Clerkenwell Close; the Mother Redcap, Camden Town; and the Three Tuns, South Portman Street, last port of call before Tyburn.

The Hog-in-the-Pound, a brand new house in Bond Street, carefully avoids any mention of its former landlady, Catherine

Hayes, who was actually burned alive at Tyburn for 'an atrocious murder' committed in her own pub.

In more recent times, pubs have been linked with Charlie Peace, Jack the Ripper, Dr. Crippen and others. Nearer to our own age, the K.P.H., Ladbroke Grove, was once the haunt of Christie, the sex murderer. Close by, the Ladbroke Hotel was the scene of a committee meeting held in 1965 to restore the name of his unfortunate lodger, Timothy Evans.

Finally, no survey of 'crime pubs' would be complete without a reference to the notorious Camley Arms, Camley Road, King's Cross. This canal pub, originally built to supply porter to navvies building the Regent's Canal, was the headquarters of a notorious group of criminals in the 1890s called the 'Regent's Men', who were surprised in the pub by the police. It is sad to have to report that the Camley Arms is in imminent danger of destruction.

London's Art Galleries

Each gallery gives a guide to its own collection, but which gallery is going to tell you what to look at and what not *to look at?*
Come to that, which galleries are worth looking at anyway?
This is an opinionated guide by an expert. Lesser experts might disagree.
All non-experts will be saved years of study.

An Art Fancier's Guide to London

Despite recent claims to the contrary, London is not an indisputable art centre of the world. Lack of funds makes our national collections less active than many across the Atlantic. And it is still too early to judge whether British artists now working and exhibiting in London are really as gifted and original as their opposite numbers elsewhere.

Nevertheless, London's permanent collections probably contain the largest and most varied assortment of masterpieces in the world, and her sale-rooms and art dealers unquestionably offer the most remarkable range of art-objects of any modern capital. But a brief guide through the tangled London art-thicket is needed to really see what's there.

THE NATIONAL GALLERY, TRAFALGAR SQUARE

Founded in 1824. The official policy of the directors and trustees has been to build up a representative collection of European painting, but as any alert visitor will discover, they have been just as much the victims of their own, or their time's, taste as anyone else; Giotto and Simone Martini are absent; apart from Cranach and Holbein, the German school is feebly represented; there is no major work by El Greco, Goya, Tiepolo, Watteau or Fragonard, and nothing by Georges de la Tour or Jacques-Louis David.

The Impressionists and Post-Impressionists (comparative newcomers, many appropriated from the Tate Gallery) seem to have been selected by a fruit-machine. One aim of post-war policy seems to have been to demonstrate what a bad artist Renoir could be. But, all in all, the National Gallery offers a greater variety of tip-top Old Masters than any other gallery in the world.

As individual pictures are frequently moved around, it is impossible to propose a permanently accurate itinerary. The following is the best advice for the time being.

Pause for a moment on the staircase landing and gaze at the floor.

There, in a huge mosaic allegory by Boris Anrep, you will find the likeness of such prominent contemporary figures as Greta Garbo and Bertrand Russell.

After that, take your choice. Rooms I, II, III, IV (to your left) contain what used to be called 'Italian Primitives' plus the Wilton Diptych, which is late fourteenth-century French, and depicts Richard II presented to the Virgin and Child by his patron saints— an adorably attractive picture as well as historically the most significant for mediaeval English history. Fine works by Duccio, Sassetta, Masaccio, Botticelli, the Pollaiuolo Brothers, and (in Room III) the best group of pictures by Piero della Francesca outside Italy: The Baptism, the Nativity, and Saint Michael.

Room V is a sort of aquarium displaying Leonardo's Virgin and Child with Saint Anne, acquired from the Royal Academy in 1962.

Rooms VI and VII, the High Renaissance in Italy: two Michelangelos, plenty of Raphaels, Bronzino's kinky Allegory with Venus, Cupid and Time; several Correggios; a dazzle of Titians, Veroneses and Tintorettos, mostly outsize.

Room VIII. Flemish pictures, good but not the best.

Back to the 'Italian Primitives'. Room VIIIa: a dazzling display of Mantegna, Tuna and Cossa, as well as three major works by Antonello da Messina: St. Jerome in his cell, the Crucifixion and a portrait.

Room VIIIb: Mostly Giovanni Bellini, ranging from the very early Agony in the Garden to the sublime late portrait of Doge Leonardo Loredan; also Pisandro's Vision of Saint Eustace. Room VIIIc: Botticelli's Venus and Mars and Adoration of the Magi, and, less spectacular but no less magical, Pollaiuolo's Apollo and Daphne and Baldovinetti's Portrait of a Lady.

Room VIIId: 'Flemish Primitives': Jan van Eyck's interior with Jan Arnolfini and his Wife takes pride of place, but the quality throughout is staggering: two van Eyck portraits, the so-called Donne Triptych of Memlinc (English donors), works by Roger van der Weyden, Campin, and Breughel's large Adoration of the Magi.

Room IX: German, more-or-less early: Holbein's Ambassadors and Christina of Denmark, beside which nice Cranachs and a tiny Altdorfer look pretty slight.

Dutch, seventeenth century. Room X: Finest possible 'cabinet pictures' by de Hooch, Steen, van Goyen, etc. Also some marvellous Hals, including a big family group, and (for the children) a peepshow by Hoogstraten. Room XI, Rembrandt: everything you could want except a landscape, a still life and a late figure-composition. Outstanding: the early Vistavision Belshazzar's Feast, and a unique large equestrian portrait. Room XII, mostly landscapes (among them Hobbema's Avenue at Middelharnis) but also two Vermeer interiors.

Room XIII: Venetian eighteenth century: Canaletto splendidly represented, Guardi charmingly, Tiepolo capriciously. Outside, in the vestibule, some very aristocratic-looking portraits by Baltoni.

Room XIII*a*: Milanese Renaissance. Apart from Bramantino's Adoration of the Magi, strictly for scholars.

Room XIII*b*: Venetian sixteenth century: three superb portraits and a Lucretia by Lorenzo Lotto.

Room XIII*c*: Nothing by Carlo Crivelli! For connoisseurs of fantasy and faultless drawing.

Room XIV: Flemish Baroque. Rubens, Van Dyck and Jordaens at their best. Easiest to enjoy are perhaps Rubens' view of his home, the Chateau de Steen, and his Chapeau de Paille (a plump girl in a big straw hat). But everything here is exciting.

English School. Room XV: Constable and Turner, mostly too often reproduced to be easily appreciated. Best to concentrate on the least known, such as Constable's Harwich, Sea and Lighthouse and Turner's Lake from Petworth House. Room XVI: Reynold's best hung with with Gainsboroughs and Hogarths, vastly to his disadvantage. Gainsborough's Mr. and Mrs. Andrews in a Landscape is, for me, the best of all English pictures; Hogarth's Shrimp Girl runs it close. Lawrence, Stubbs and Wilson, also far outpacing poor Reynolds.

Room XVII: Big Italian altarpieces.

Room XVII*a*: Baroque art in Italy, not all of it Italian. Only one Caravaggio, the Supper at Emmaus; beautiful Elsheimers.

Room XVII*b*: Seventeenth-century landscapes painted in Italy under Italian influence. Superb Claudes and Poussins.

Room XVII*c*: Italian Baroque for scholars.

Room XVII*d*: Less famous Italian sixteenth century, but don't miss Moroni's Portrait of a Tailor, ancestor of all bourgeois portraits, Velasquez, Manet, the lot.

Room XVIII: Spanish seventeenth century. Velasquez Rokeby Venus (note suffragette's slash-scars on behind), portraits of Philips IV and V, and two religious pieces; Greco's small Adoration of the name of Venus; Goya's sultry Dõna Isabel Cobos de Porcel.

Room XIX: French eighteenth century. Look at the Chardins, but only because there are none in the Wallace Collection; everyone else better shown there.

Room xx: French seventeenth century. Hard to find better Claudes and Poussins.

Room xxi: Nineteenth-century French pictures, thanks almost entirely to the late Samuel Courtauld: Seurat's Baignade, Manet's Servante de Bocks, Renoir's Première Sortie. Courtauld had *nothing* to do with Renoir's La Source.

Room xxii: Rush past Renoir's two Tadema-type Danseuses and his portrait of Madame Sert, and admire few but first-class works by Degas, Van Gogh, Cézanne. (Recent Cézanne purchases have been good, but haven't yet run to a still life.) Huge late Monet water-lilies.

Room xxiii: Nineteenth-century French, not Impressionist. Good Géricault, Boudin, Ingres, Couer, Delacroix, but no absolute masterpiece.

Stagger out past Zoffany's Portrait of Mrs. Oswald, and if you still have the strength, ask to be directed to the basement reserves. There, hanging floor-to-ceiling and frame-to-frame, are the several thousand pictures the authorities deem inferior to everything upstairs. Most disturbing.

THE NATIONAL PORTRAIT GALLERY

round the corner, is insufficiently visited. Goya's Wellington hung there for years on loan, and no one seems to have noticed it. Many of the exhibits are major works of art (e.g. Holbein's cartoon for his lost Whitehall portrait of Henry VIII, Hogarth's self-portrait, Lawrence's Canning), but almost equal pleasure can be derived from such curiosities as Blake's death-mask (source of inspiration to Francis Bacon) and a portrait of Peg Woffington in bed. If you prefer British history to European art, skip the National Gallery and spend your time here instead.

THE TATE GALLERY

so-called after the sugar-king who founded it with £100,000 and his own collection of English paintings, most of them hideous, is so schizophrenic in intention that no single director could ever hope to understand all its needs. English painting in all its phases, nineteenth-century art in all its aspects, and the Contemporary Scene from Tokyo westwards to Venice, California: no wonder it's a mass of gaps and curios.

The English School, sixteenth century to Sargent (American, but never mind) occupies Galleries i to xvi. Gallery i, Eworth to Kneller (both foreigners) contains much that is charming or odd. Gallery ii is devoted to Blake, includes his Illuminations to Dante and the Spiritual Form of Nelson guiding Leviathan. Galleries III to IV, eighteenth century, splendid Hogarths, among them the Graham Children and Calais Gate, Wilson's Cader Idris; Reynolds' Keppel (good) and Heads of Angels (silly); Stubbs' Mare and Foals, a good example of our purest classical painter; Wright of Derby's Experiment with an Air-pump; and—how on earth?—a Two Piece Reclining Figure by Henry Moore.

Gallery V: John Constable—superb, but must be supplemented by a study of his drawings and sketches in the Victoria and Albert Museum.

Galleries VI-X: Nothing but Turner, all from the artist's immense bequest to the nation. Might convert even Dali from his opinion that Turner was the worst artist who ever lived. Should be visited in winter when a number of Turner's iridescent water-colours are exhibited in Gallery X; in summer they are taken downstairs, presumably in case the roof leaks.

Gallery XI: The Pre-Raphaelites, and three wonderful Samuel Palmers. However well-disposed one may feel towards the Brethren, most of the pictures here display them at their most ambitious and consequently least winning. Brett's microscopic landscapes fare best.

Gallery XII: Victorian bourgeois painting, e.g. Frith's Derby Day, Martineau's Last Day in the Old Home, Augustus Egg's Past and Present. Irresistible. Also some proto-surrealism by the victorian patricide, Richard Jadd.

Gallery XIII: 'British Impressionism', charming but tres backwater. Utterly out-of-place but mesmeric is Aubrey Beardsley's only known oil-painting, Caprice.

Gallery XIV: Alfred Stevens, Watts, Whistler, Sargent. Strange bedfellows whom one hopes some future director will separate. All accentuate each other's faults: Sargent looks flashy, Whistler flimsy, Watts stodgy, and Stevens (except in his Mother and Child) duly academic. And yet all, in varying degree, are good.

Gallery XV and Annex A are devoted to 'English painting of the earlier twentieth century', including Kokoschka and Gaudier Brzeska, who I feel turn out to have been its leading lights. Otherwise the highest possible level of mediocrity is observable throughout.

Gallery XVII: late eighteenth- and early nineteenth-century English painting, mostly huge. Nothing here can be overlooked, however good or bad.

Galleries XXII-XXV: A first-class choice of modern (i.e. post-Euston Road) British painting. E. Corridor. Lots of Henry Moore.

(Gallery XXIII now also has Picasso's 'Three Dancers'.)

Gallery XVI: Sculpture from Degas to Noguchi, plus Matisse's huge late papier-cotté L'Escargot, two Resurrections by Stanley Spencer and abstracts by Rothko and Kline.

Galleries XXVII-XXX, XXXIV and XXXV are dedicated more or less to French painting from Manet to Picasso. Many of the best pictures which once hung here have recently been either sent back to Dublin, to accord with the wish of their donor, the late Sir Hugh Lane, or whipped off to the National Gallery. Even so, those remaining make a brave show, almost up to the standard of an American provincial museum.

Gallery XXXIV: Contains fine drawings by Cézanne, Klee and others.

The rest of the Tate Gallery (galleries and some corridor space) houses an often changing assortment of modern and recent all by non-British artists.

Visitors who like pretty things should visit the basement restaurant, painted with scenes illustrating the Pursuit of Rare Meats by the late Rex Whistler.

THE VICTORIA AND ALBERT MUSEUM

defies description. It was founded in 1852 with the very necessary aim of improving design in British manufacturers, but over the years it has expanded to embrace almost every artefact from every place and period, including some which can be more fully studied elsewhere (Chinese Art, for example). A free booklet entitled *Four Masterpieces to See in Fifteen Minutes* is slightly misleading since it includes the Great Bed of Ware, which is a masterpiece of nothing except capacity and, probably, discomfort. As the museum is constantly being re-arranged (always for the better) it is hard to propose a gallery-by-gallery tour. I would, however, suggest that the following marvels should be sought out by non-specialist art-lovers.

The galleries of Italian Renaissance and Baroque sculpture. These are so well arranged that the visitor is impelled towards the highlights. Enough to say they house superb works by Donatello, Michelangelo, Giovanni da Bologna and Bernini.

The West Hall, hung with seven of Raphael's cartoons for a series of tapestries commissioned by Pope Leo X (on loan from Her Majesty the Queen). Nothing else, outside Italy, gives such a complete idea of a major pictorial scheme conceived by a great Renaissance painter.

The Jones Bequest. A Victorian tailor's hoard of dix-huitième furniture, objects and pictures. Taste if anything more refined than that Victorian nobleman, Lord Hertford's.

The Constable rooms—hundreds of his best drawings and sketches.

The Ionides Collection, a mixed bag including a Botticelli portrait 'restored' by Rossetti (she emerges a Blessed Damozel), a Degas, and Le Nain's Peasants, of which Picasso believes he owns the original.

Early Mediaeval and Gothic, Islamic, Indian and Far Eastern art are superbly represented. So are European ceramics, glass, textiles, silver, furniture, tapestries and metalwork.

Please don't miss Nicholas Hilliard's Young Man leaning against a tree among roses. It is the most poetic of all English miniatures.

THE BRITISH MUSEUM

Unless you've some idea of what you want to see, stay away. It will only make your inferiority complex worse.

But if you do know, find out first when your particular gallery is open. Recent economies at the Treasury have necessitated a reduction of staff, so that certain galleries are often closed to the public. We must comfort ourselves with the reflection that the money saved may have gone towards something absolutely necessary, like that waterlogged underground tunnel at Hyde Park Corner.

As a picture-man, I cannot presume to comment on more than a fraction of the British Museum's treasures, except to say that I myself derive a purely aesthetic uninformed pleasure from almost everything later than the odds-and-ends from the Mesolithic settlement at Star Can and earlier than the Fitzgerald Air-Mail Collection.

Perhaps your best plan is to enter at the South Entrance and make your way to the Elgin Marbles, carved between 447 and 432 for the Parthenon, acquired between 1801 and 1803 by the 7th Earl of Elgin and sold by him in 1816 to the British Government. Had they remained *in situ* they would certainly have perished: our best, and only, argument for withholding them from the Greeks today.

You can view them with a 2s. 6d. 'sound guide' ('walkie-talkie').

Then set off on a seemingly endless walk to the North side, pausing to admire whatever you fancy *en masse*—Anglican, Egyptian, Magna Carta, the manuscript of *Alice in Wonderland*. At last you reach the King Edward VII Gallery, which contains a very varied assortment of masterpieces from Shang Dynasty ritual bronze vessels to Sèvres porcelain.

Upstairs is the Department of Prints and Drawings. The Print Room itself is impenetrable except with a letter of recommendation from someone known to the staff, but the galleries preceding it are usually devoted to some special exhibition drawn from its incredible riches—Raphael and his Circle, for example. If any one of these exhibitions were shown in the United States, it would attract a mile-long queue and a page in *Time Magazine*. Here they are poorly attended.

THE WALLACE COLLECTION

in Hertford (pronounced Harford) House, Manchester Square, was founded mainly by the 4th Marquess of Hertford, a nobleman with quarter-of-a-million pounds a year and an insatiable passion for the unspiritual in art. Fortunately so, since most of his English contemporaries abhorred rococo paintings (they associated it with French tarts), and without him London would not possess a single major work of Boucher or Fragonard, and only three Watteaus (one in the National Gallery, the others at Dulwich and in the Soane Museum).

Hertford lived chiefly in Paris and his taste was far more French than English. One might call his collection an anti-Ruskin collection. It contains almost nothing which would not have provoked the great moralist's wrath. The earliest masterpieces in the collection are Titian's Perseus and Andromeda, the latest Delacroix, Beheading of Marino Faliero. The line between the two is clearly illustrated; Rubens is chief intermediary.

The Wallace Collection is not so large that one is forced to plan one's visit beforehand. But the diet it affords is somewhat over-luscious, so to those with a tendency to artistic indigestion I would suggest that they confine their visit to rooms XVI and XVIII. The first contains the best of the larger pictures; Rubens' Rainbow Landscape; Velasquez' Lady with a Fan; the Laughing Cavalier; and a series of exquisite Rubens sketches. The second contains the pick of the smaller pictures, including half-a-dozen Watteaus and Fragonard's Swing—also some of the finest furniture and snuff-boxes in the world.

If, after all this, you feel a craving for something Ruskinian, go downstairs and take a long look at Cima da Conegliano's Saint Catherine of Alexandria or the little Saint Michael attributed to Memlinc. They belong in another world.

THE IVEAGH COLLECTION, KENWOOD

on Hampstead Heath, is a characteristic millionaire's collection of the first quarter of this century, the only one in London which in any way resembles those built up by such men as Huntingdon, Bache and Melton in American in the same era. It was founded by the 1st Earl of Iveagh, the Guinness magnate, and bequeathed to the nation in 1927, together with the unpleasant-coloured Adam mansion which houses it and a 200-acre park.

Like all such collections, it contains too many insipid English portraits (don't miss Reynolds' Miss Brummell, the ugliest girl on record), but also, as if by accident, Vermeer's Guitar-Player and what many would claim to be Rembrandt's finest self-portrait, a late half-length showing him standing before a canvas painted with one single sphere.

In the garden, a pop-art caravan of circa 1900.

DULWICH COLLEGE PICTURE GALLERY

Appropriately for the ultimate benefaction of a boys' school, the best pictures in the Dulwich College Picture Gallery were collected by a Frenchman called Desenfans. He brought them together to form the nucleus of a royal collection for King Stanislaus Lecszynski, but failed to deliver them before Stanislaus's abdication. Eventually Desenfans bequeathed them to an English painter, Sir Francis Bourgeois, and he in turn bequeathed them to Dulwich College. Hence one of the best small galleries in Europe.

Basically, this is a perfect reflection of the best eighteenth century taste: seven Nicholas Poussins, four Murillos, three Rembrandts, eleven Rubens, two big Guido Renis, two tiny Raphaels, and a host of nice little 'cabinet pictures' (one very rude Teniers). Later benefactors have added English pictures, including some of Gainsborough's best. The building, by Sir John Soane, is all that a small gallery should be.

THE COURTAULD INSTITUTE GALLERIES

are housed, ironically enough, in a hideous nondescript new building which belies everything Samuel Courtauld stood for. The first, and probably the last, major English collector of Impressionist and Post-Impressionist painting, his ambition was to open British eyes to the lyrical, orderly beauty of masters like Degas, Cézanne and Seurat. Now, to make a home for his collection, London University have ruined a corner of Woburn Square. I understand they now intend demolishing what remains of it.

You reach Courtauld's pictures through another collection, Lord Lee of Fareham's—lots of big names, but the best pictures bear small ones, such as Lely's, or none, like two superlative Florentine marriage coffers. The exception here is Rubens' modello for his Descent from the Cross.

The Courtauld pictures shine out even more splendidly after these dim Old Masters. Most of them are so famous, one is surprised to find them here. And indeed, until six years ago, many of them hung in the Tate Gallery or the National Gallery—Manet's Bar aux Folies-Bergère, Cézanne's L'Amour en Platre. In spite of efforts by the National Gallery and the Tate, this is the one place in London where the nineteenth-century French miracle can be properly understood.

At the end of the galleries is a room full of pictures and furniture collected by the Bloomsbury critic Roger Fry. Apart from one small Seurat, they succeed in looking both dowdy and tatty, which is disappointing since Fry's gospel was very close in spirit to Courtaulds.

SIR JOHN SOANE'S MUSEUM

at 13 Lincoln's Inn Fields takes its name from its founder, the architect Sir John Soane (1753-1837). Since he stipulated that it should never be added to or re-arranged it retains its original character throughout—the only private home thus preserved in London.

Soane's style may have been severe and monumental, but his house is anything but. Objects of innumerable periods and civilizations are crammed together less with the idea of displaying them to their best advantage than of creating a romantic and sometimes claustrophobic mise-en-scene. The building is not large, but Soane employed every conceivable device to make it seem, or act, larger: mirrors, glass panels, walls which swing out to reveal further walls behind. The general effect is fantastic and a little spooky.

Best things here are Hogarth's The Rake's Progress and the Election, a series of large Piranesi drawings, a Canaletto View of the Grand Canal and a Watteau Fête Champetre. The sarcophagus of Seti I in the Sepulchral Chamber is apparently an object of the highest importance.

Not to be missed by connoisseurs of the off-beat.

ROYAL COLLEGE OF SURGEONS

Almost facing the Soane Museum. Containing the greatest medical

Sir John Soane's Museum

museum in the world and also a number of astonishing portraits
of rare animals by George Stubbs. These include Warren Hastings'
Yak, which died of the heat in Gloucestershire, and a rose-pink
rhinoceros.

THE ROYAL ACADEMY
in Burlington House, Piccadilly, is more famous for its huge
exhibitions, but permanently on view in the Diploma Gallery are
some first-rate English pictures, including the Leaping Horse by
John Constable. Elsewhere, 'freely accessible' but seldom seen, is a
marble tondo by Michelangelo, surely the most important piece of
sculpture in England.

51

HAMPTON COURT PALACE

Huge but not especially palatial, contains a large number of paintings from the Royal Collection, many from the collection of Charles I, and few painted later than 1700. The collection is not entirely static, but a nucleus of superb Venetian pictures (Tintoretto, Titian, Lotto, Giogione) never changes, except when one or two are removed for display in the Queen's Gallery at Buckingham Palace.

Although the general standard is amazingly high, not everything here demands a purely artistic response. There is a portrait of Sir Geoffrey Hudson, Queen Henrietta Maria's dwarf, immortalised by Sir Walter Scott in *Peveril of the Peak*, and a whole gallery of voluptuous ladies by Sir Peter Lely, including the Duchess of Richmond who was the model for Britannia in our coinage.

No gallery in England possesses greater charm. With its high narrow windows and sombre panelling, Hampton Court can only be compared to the Mauritshuis in the Hague.

THE QUEEN'S GALLERY

in the South Wing of Buckingham Palace, is the newest and best-designed art gallery in Central London. Temporary exhibitions there are drawn from the apparently inexhaustible treasures of the Royal Collection. Their character ranges from the profoundly serious (whole walls of drawings by Leonardo da Vinci) to the historically intriguing (letters from infant princes, Fabergé Easter-eggs). Many visitors will feel themselves sufficiently rewarded by having their entrance-fee accepted by a super-footman in royal livery and gold-braided top hat.

THE FOUNDLING HOSPITAL

at 40 Brunswick Square contains an odd little museum which ranges from Hogarth's superlative portrait of the founder, Captain Thomas Coram, to a number of 'tokens' left with abandoned infants. There are other good pictures (Hogarth's March to Finchley, two small views of the original Foundling Hospital by Gains-borough) and a quantity of Handeliana, including the original score of the Messiah.

NATIONAL MARITIME MUSEUM AT GREENWICH

There are two good reasons why even the unnautically-minded should visit this museum.

It is housed in the Queen's House, designed by Inigo Jones for Anne of Denmark, and the first purely classical example of domestic architecture in England (begun 1618, finished 1635); and, besides a magnificent array of chronometers, astrolabes, portolarios and what-not, it contains excellent portraits by Hogarth and Gainsborough, amongst others, fine shipping pieces by the Van de Veldes and Samuel Scott, and an enchanting Canaletto of the Queen's House itself.

In Camden Town is a small electronics firm which once had an order to make a radio-controlled stuffed duck capable of going forwards at two speeds, fast and slow, turning to the right and to the left, and sinking. The man who ordered it can occasionally be seen at the Round Pond in Kensington Gardens aiming it at real ducks as well as motor boats.

Watch any stretch of pavement in Oxford Street for ten minutes at rush hours. During that time you are bound to see at least three people topple over and fall down.

At the Hyde Park corner end of Knightsbridge there is a long island composed of rounded cobbles in the middle of the road. Watch the behaviour of any lady wearing high heels who makes her way on to it.

Junk Stalls

A minor art, a minor pleasure. But London's street markets and junk shops make London a junk collector's dream.

Junk is other people's left-overs, which they never usually wanted in the first place anyway. Junkards collect these left-overs, which they never usually know they wanted until they suddenly see them.

It might be bits of furniture, which turn out valuable antiques, or old biscuit tin lids, which will always be old biscuit tin lids.

Bad taste, unlike good taste, knows no limitations. It cocks a snook at the pundits and roams with uninhibited irreverence over every aspect of human creativity. When fresh, it may seem outrageous, but once its day is past, its original sin dies within it. It has gone beyond the boundaries of taste, good or bad. It acquires an interest, if any, peculiar to itself. This is junk.

Everybody gathers a lot of junk. It is the diversity of personal litter that gives a room its 'lived in' character. The junk-hunter recognises this phenomenon, and plays it. Instead of limiting his choice to beautiful things, he mixes them with objects that are attractive for other reasons. The skill is in the mixing, and the end product is a true expression of personal taste.

The good taste market has long ago been cornered by the antique dealers, the art-craft enthusiasts and the 'contemporary' Scandinavian designers. Their prices are as elegant as their goods. Junk is cheap: the problem is not how to afford it, but where to find it.

Modern junk abounds, particularly in the souvenir shops that cluster round the travel termini and the Places of Interest. You may occasionally find bits of new rubbish worth a niche in your scheme of things. They will mellow with time, and accumulate charm; but it is the old, démodé stuff that is most worth going after, because it is unfamiliar and has to be hunted for.

There are junk shops in the poorer parts of all the London boroughs. Most of them are small and cramped, and inspection is difficult. Some seem to be permanently shut. Others, more obliging, display small items on tables outside their shops, which the passer-by can look at and handle without embarrassment.

Any shopman, however, must be to some extent selective in

choosing what he offers for sale, and this is a deterrent to the dedicated junk-hunter, whose joy is in the chase, and whose triumph is in making his own discoveries unaided. The purist gravitates towards the market stalls, or looks for the here-today-gone-tomorrow vendors who dump a van-load on a vacant strip and destroy most of what they have not sold by the end of the day.

Market stalls can be deceptive. There is something about an open-air display that suggests cheapness and bargains. Dealers know this as well as shoppers. When a market has won a reputation among the connoisseurs, the pricey dealers join the bonanza and establish what are in effect branch businesses there.

This had already happened to the Caledonian Market before it was moved from Islington to its present pitch beside Tower Bridge Road. It has long been true of the Portobello Road, certainly at its southern end. When a dealer takes a stall in the Caledonian Market, he adds 20% to his prices, and in the Portobello Road 40%.

These places are nevertheless worth visiting, if only to look at the stuff on show. On a fine Friday morning the stalls of the Caledonian Market, standing close together and filled with bright things, make a delightful sight.

The same can be said of the Antique Supermarket in Barrett Street below Wigmore Street, though here the goods are displayed under the roof in partitioned alcoves. It has everything, from fine old furniture to toy trains by way of *objets d'art nouveau*, but the dealers know what they are selling.

Camden Passage, off Upper Street in Islington, now belongs to this class. It has become very sophisticated of late. A little enclave of boutiques has been built specially for the antique trade, where the dealers lead a friendly, fraternal sort of life, and seem to spend more time chatting than selling. At the week-end some junk stalls appear, though they would not admit to the title, nor would their prices match it.

London's unsophisticated street markets are legion. They are proletarian in character. The bourgeois would consider any such vivid manifestation of community life derogatory to the dignity of their own preserves, though they all sneak round to the nearest one to do their household shopping.

Most of these markets are open throughout the working week. They tend to thin out during the afternoons, leaving a residue of greengrocery and fish, but at the week-ends they are at their fullest and busiest. A few stay open on Sundays, and some take Mondays off.

You will usually find a junk stall or two on the busier days. It is always worth taking a stroll through a street market when you are passing. Even if you find nothing to buy, you can still enjoy the atmosphere and the crowds.

There are too many of these markets in London to attempt a complete list here. Ring any Town Hall, ask for their Information Department (failing that, the Market Inspector's office), and they will tell you where the markets in that borough are trading, and when they are open.

Some of the biggest and liveliest are in East London—Hoxton Street, Ridley Road, Dalston Lane, Mile End Waste in the White-chapel Road, to mention only a few.

North London has good markets in Chapel Street, Islington, and in Queen's Crescent, Kentish Town, and small ones in Inverness Street, Camden Town, and Seaton Place, off Hampstead Road.

South of the river are markets in East Street off the Walworth Road, and in the Cut, just south of Waterloo Station. Shepherd's Bush has an excellent market, Fulham has a big one in North End Road. Woolwich has a market in Beresford Square. The list could run on for ever.

Markets in the central districts are more metropolitan in character. Berwick Street, Soho, is probably the best known. Pimlico has a market in Tachbrook Street, and there is a small market between Seven Dials and Charing Cross Road. Leather Lane, off Clerkenwell Road, fills up with stalls for an hour or two at lunch-time, to catch the office workers. It has one or two junk stalls, but it does not trade at the week-end.

On Saturdays, the market in Church Street, Marylebone, stretches out the whole way from Lisson Grove to Edgware Road, and includes several junk stalls. Some of these are overflows from adjacent shops that are working their way up from junk to antique status. The smell of sophistication is already detectable.

Some of the old markets are falling now before the developers. Traders' licences are not being renewed in Strutton Ground. Only a fag-end remains of the once-flourishing book market in Farring-don Road.

There are markets, often specialist in character, that trade on Sundays only. A cluster of these can be found close together in the area northward from Aldgate. Club Row sells pets, Columbia Road, flowers. Cutler Street sells jewellery and diamonds. The diamonds are real, but most of the deals are made privately from hand to hand. In the famous Petticoat Lane Market that fills

Middlesex Street to bursting, you will find as much modern junk as you can stand.

Few market junkmen sell furniture, though you can find it here and there. Some people may be surprised to know that furniture going at junk prices can be worth having at all. But it is possible to get excellent wooden chairs at a few shillings apiece.

If you are looking for furniture, you should join the throng at half past nine on a Saturday morning at the Salvation Army depot in Spa Road, Bermondsey. Here you can choose your pieces from a large and varied collection, and buy serviceable and even attractive stuff for a song.

The man in charge says that one day a Victorian mahogany dining-table went for a pound. The next he heard of it was that it had changed hands in New York for three thousand dollars.

The Salvation Army also has a department for small junk. Here an *art nouveau* electric fire might be bought for five shillings.

There exists in London a migrant market devoted exclusively to junk. This is something not to be missed, if you can track it down. Until recently, it spread itself out every Sunday morning on a bomb site off Vallance Road in Bethnal Green, unofficial but winked at. Everything was there, from knick-knacks to wardrobes —junk at junk prices.

Unfortunately, the local population disapproved of this enterprise, and drove it off their ground. When last looked for it was clustering like driftwood in the indentations of Grimsby Street, not far from its original pitch. It may not be permitted to stay there for long. If it does, and people with money come to patronise it, it will soon go the way of the Cally and Portobello.

One small but favourite hunting ground of junk hunters is Reg's pitch in Camden Town. Reg appears in the Inverness Street Market on Wednesdays, Fridays and Saturdays, and might well claim to be the purest independent junk dealer in London. Unlike other junkmen, who commonly confine their operations to one small stall, Reg spreads himself over three or four large tables and part of the road as well. Each table is piled high with a mountain of nonsense, old, new, whole and broken, taken from the van as it comes, and displayed without a moment's pause for selection.

This is the real thing. All Gloucester Crescent goes happily treasure-hunting there every Reg-day morning. Reg himself takes no interest in the nature or history of his wares. He will quote you a price for anything without hesitation, but once quoted, that is his figure, take it or leave it.

You are unlikely to find anything of commercial value there, but it does sometimes happen. People have bought things from Reg for a shilling that have later been knowledgeably identified as worth a few pounds. This is immaterial, however. Commercial value is not what the junk-hunter is looking for.

A place like this calls for a special technique. When you approach the clutter of rubbish for the first time, it seems inconceivable that anything worth having could have got mixed in with it. This is where the joy of the chase comes keenest. You may stare for minutes at some half-buried item without seeing it, and when you do notice it, you may still feel doubtful. But sixpence or a couple of bob won't break you, so you take a chance. When you have got the thing home, and washed it, and examined it in isolation, its true merits reveal themselves. The very fact that you have picked it out and made it your own adds to it a quality that was not there before you bought it.

Perseverance is the secret, and penetrating eyes. You may find nothing to please you in several successive visits, and then one morning go galumphing home with half a dozen treasures tucked under your arm.

Sometimes you discover new kinds of things, things that until that moment it never occurred to you to like. One junk hunter chanced on a biscuit tin with pictures of the four seasons delicately printed in black on gold. It obviously dated from the last century. That set him looking for old tins. He had no idea till then there was so much charm in them. He must have thirty or forty of them by now, of which more than a dozen are currently in use. Reg sells them indiscriminately for sixpence a tin, but they come in all sorts. His collection includes one of the embossed tins in which on New Year's Day of 1900 Queen Victoria sent a gift of chocolate to every British soldier fighting in South Africa.

Another chance discovery started another junkard searching for children's games. There is a naivety about such things which becomes very beguiling once it is out of date. He has a game called 'A Race Through London', with leaden horse buses for pieces. Old packs of 'Snap' and 'Happy Families' cards are not uncommon. He has assembled thirteen different versions of 'Happy Families', ranging through successive periods from the well-known original Victorian set to the present day. Not long ago, he met another 'Happy Families' fancier. They swapped duplicates.

Junk is an all-inclusive medium. The scope is limitless, selection purely personal: what appeals to one junk-hunter may leave another cold. His eye may be caught by souvenir china, especially the gloriously gilded mugs and cups; by the gaily coloured glass furniture footings that were made to hold castors steady, and are useful now as paperweights and ashtrays; by blue enamel kitchen-ware; by the American clocks that were mass-produced from 1830 onwards, with paintings on glass below the face and exuberant manufacturers' labels on the inside woodwork; by trivia in glass, such as inkpots, particularly the larger and squarer kind, which may not have much practical value nowadays but are immensely satisfying in their transparent solidity.

Often it is the unexpected finds that make the greatest treasures. For five shillings, one junkard bought a brassbound box with two hinged sections and a secret compartment, the sort of thing that old sea captains used for office work on the voyage. It was made of beautiful wood, still in fine condition.

'If you had a chest like that made for you today,' an architect friend told him 'it could cost you anything up to a hundred pounds.'

For another five shillings, he acquired a model locomotive called 'Ajax', nearly a century old and built to work with live steam. Out of compliment to this delightful thing, he bought a group photograph from about the same period, showing a station staff on the old Great Eastern line, proud and very respectable in the uniform of the railways' heyday.

Once you become a junkard, you will find it hard not to amass more than you can use. When you see a pretty thing that will probably be destroyed if you don't buy it, it seems heartless to leave it to its fate, especially when the price of compassion is only sixpence or a shilling.

To collect is innocent: the sin is to retain. Unmake your collection as fast as you make it. It is always agreeable to have something by you to give to your appreciative friends. Unwanted surplus will make a good impression at a Christmas bazaar or even a jumble sale. They will call it 'bric-à-brac' there, or 'Victoriana'. If such Philistine language makes you writhe, trump it with 'folk art'. You can sometimes find good things for yourself at these throw-away functions.

Don't be afraid of taking to junk. It is a harmless addiction, and, *ex hypothesi*, the cheapest of them all. It would be miserly indeed to grudge a junkman his profit. On the other hand, you need not be anxious lest he is cheating himself. He may have already been paid for taking the stuff away.

London Churches, Part One

Is the same as London history. But you will not only learn history from London churches, you'll pick up architecture, literature, art and some exotic oddments of human vanities.

This first Church guide is basically about the buildings. A concise, but tight packed trip, from the Mediaeval to the Victorian. Telling you what to look for, how, where, why and when. From the sublime to the downright daft.

(The next section is about what happens inside some of these churches. From the sublime to the subliminal?)

OLD ONES, ODD ONES

Churchgoing is one of London's greatest and least-tasted pleasures. There are those who think churchgoing is a duty and that it is wicked to enjoy it. They must be warped puritans.

The great advantage of London churches is the variety of doctrine and ceremony and architecture which they have to offer. All tastes are catered for and the instinct to worship is strong in all of us.

All London churches are open on Sundays, except certain Guild churches in the City. More than half are open on weekdays and daily services are usual in Church of England and Roman Catholic fanes.

Those who recall the London of the 1920's will remember an even richer variety than there is now—the robed last angel sitting on his canopied throne by gaslight in the Catholic Apostolic Church in Gordon Square, where people used to speak with tongues. This was before that mighty Gothic Revival fabric (D. and R. Brandon 1853–5), which looks inside rather like Westminster Abbey without the monuments, was loaned to London University as a chapel.

Then there were the Peculiar People from Essex who used to have a Mission to London in Lambeth. During the fervent services in their humble building, which was reminiscent of the chapel described in Browning's *Christmas Eve*, one could read their hymn book and find these memorable lines:

> *Shall chapel doors rattle and umbrellas move*
> *To show that you'll the service disapprove?*

The Swedenborgians, supported partly by Mudie's, who ran the famous circulating library, had a Norman Revival church near King's Cross, with a bare table and an open Bible.

The church of Martin Luther in Hackney was all incense and vestments and its minister could remember when the carriages of rich City merchants crowded the Spelthorne Road.

Higher up was the strange spired church of the Ark of the Covenant on Clapton Common, with stained glass by Walter Crane. Here the Reverend Mr. Smyth-Piggot was first proclaimed as Jesus Christ before moving off to the Abode of Love in Somerset. Archbishop Nicholson is the present tenant of the Clapton Church and he it was who used to have services for people's pets in his church in Chelsea about ten years ago.

In the capacious arms of the Church of England, there was even more variety than there is to-day. Now the tendency is to have a family Communion at 9.30 and there is much less distinction between Catholic and Evangelical worship.

But in the neat Georgian Ram's Episcopal Chapel, Homerton, with its marble altar piece, the service was so low that the congregation objected to the Reverend Mr. McCarthy wearing a surplice for Morning and Evening Prayer, so that he took it off when entering the pulpit and preached in a black gown.

For this kind of thing today, you have to cross the river to the diocese of Southwark, where there are said to be over eighty clergymen of the Established Church who are fundamentalists.

At Christ Church, North Brixton—a dashing design in the Byzantine style of 1902 by Beresford Pite—the black gown is still worn in the pulpit and visiting preachers are supplied with the right sized black gown to fit them. The table is well out from the rear wall in the latest Roman Catholic fashion.

At St. Stephen's, Clapham Park, the Prayer Book service against gunpowder, treason and plot is still read on Guy Fawkes Day.

Before the war, the City of London had churches whose incumbents lived as far off as Bexhill and only appeared on Sundays to take the statutory services. What a joy it was to sit in a box pew while the gallery clock ticked and to hear the rolling 17th century English of the Prayer Book alone with the verger and the pew-opener and breathe in the hassock-scented dust of Dickensian London. The sole survival of City absenteeism today is the grand late Mediaeval church of St. Andrew Undershaft, Leadenhall Street, which, unlike the active churches of the rest of the City, with their weekday services, has been locked for years, except at 11 o'clock on a Sunday morning. Though it is on a crowded thoroughfare, there is still no indication of where the key is.

But it is worth visiting on a Sunday. St. Andrew's is a lofty East Anglian church with a 17th century stained window, removed from the east end to the west, and fine carvings, paintings and monuments and a tower with Mediaeval bells which are never rung.

St. Andrew Undershaft

MEDIAEVAL CHURCHES

The Mediaeval churches of London are not all that wonderful, if we except Westminster Abbey. The greatest of them was old St. Paul's Cathedral, then the longest cathedral in Europe. It was so much destroyed in the Fire that it had to be rebuilt (on a slightly different axis) by Sir Christopher Wren.

The most satisfying architecturally of the early churches of London is the little Norman chapel of St. John in the Tower of London, with its perfect Romanesque proportions. The next most satisfying with the same round-arched type is St. Bartholemew-the-Great, Smithfield, which is early 12th century, but much refurbished by the late Sir Aston Webb at the end of the last century. It is the choir and lady chapel of what once was a large priory building, and is now famous for its music as well as its architecture.

As for Westminster Abbey, it is three things. Architecturally, it is a French Mediaeval cathedral rebuilt by Henry III and belonging to the times when England and France were one kingdom. It is more like Amiens and Rheims than an English church. To its east end has been added the amazingly intricate Tudor chapel of Henry VII, the last and richest flowering of English flamboyant. Secondly, it is our greatest gallery of monumental sculpture from the Middle Ages until the Regency. It is thirdly the embodiment of English history, in stone and glass.

It is best enjoyed on a weekday Evensong in winter, preferably a windy, wet day when there are not many people about, and when choir and organ scoop out a heaven from London's central roar. One should sit in a stall in the choir and not outside in the nave.

The little Mediaeval churches of the City and Middlesex have mostly been so scraped and refurnished by the Victorians as to be more interesting to antiquaries than aesthetes—with the notable exception of Harefield, which has box pews and a wealth of coloured monuments.

WREN, AND AFTER

The grandest phase of church building in London was after the Great Fire of 1666, when Wren was busy on St. Paul's and the City churches. He rebuilt the bodies of the City churches first and added their spires and towers in Portland stone and lead after he had envisaged the dome of his cathedral. London must have had the most beautiful skyline in the world, before the Victorians and, more recently, modern post-war 'developers' ruined it with rent-collecting slabs.

No Wren church remains outside as Wren meant you to see it, with steeple showing above the chimney pots, except for a glimpse of St. Martin's, Ludgate, seen from outside Apothecaries' Hall, Blackfriars, and the tower and spire of St. Mary Abchurch as seen from Sherborne Lane. All else is blotted out by tall blocks, or stupidly cleared of the low buildings from which it was meant to rise, as has been St. Lawrence Jewry.

The Victorian and later bishops of London destroyed many of Wren's City churches and the Germans bombed nearly all the rest. Almost all post-war restorations have been spoiled inside by the introduction of stained glass which Wren never intended for his churches. Their colour and decoration was to be in the form of carved wood, plaster-work and wrought iron and painted altar pieces, with Moses, Aaron, the Commandments and Creed. St. James', Garlickhythe, and St. Mary Abchurch, the Welsh Church of St. Benet, Paul's Wharf, St. Margaret's, Lothbury, and St. Martin's, Ludgate are the most conservative and sympathetic post-war repairings.

Two Wren interiors survive near to each other, very much as they were before German visitation. St. Magnus the Martyr, London Bridge, is rich Anglo-Catholic baroque inside, though the westward position for saying the Mass would be physically impossible. The 17th century woodwork and ironwork is skilfully adapted to shrines and altars. As Eliot put it:

> ' . . . the walls of Magnus Martyr hold
> Inexplicable splendour of Ionian white and gold.'

Nearby, up a little alley smelling of fish, in a part which is as yet 'undeveloped' and therefore the real City of London, is St. Mary-at-Hill. It is plain brick outside, but Wren inside and richer in Dickensian atmosphere than any London church within. There are box pews, high pulpit, gallery and screen, carved balusters, carved altar-piece, sword rests and a sense of dead beadles and departed City pomp. The present Rector appreciates the atmosphere of his church and preaches shortly and well.

St. Paul's Cathedral itself is most splendid when viewed floodlit from its west front on a velvet night. From being impressively soot-blackened, it has been turned by cleaning into the cheerful Renaissance building its architect intended. It now has a smile like that which one sees on the bust of Wren. The interior was spoiled in its proportions in the last century, when the organ screen across the choir was folded back, so that the church does not look as long and mysterious as Wren intended. If there were to be a baldachino over the High Altar, it should have been under the dome and in front of a restored organ screen.

When London City burst its walls in the 18th century, and the richer folk started to live in red brick Queen Anne and Georgian squares and mansions in Middlesex and outside the river villages on the Surrey bank, there was much church building in Portland stone.

London's three most impressive churches of this time were those by Wren's pupil Nicholas Hawksmoor—Christ Church, Spital-fields (1723-9), locked and awaiting repair along with the meths drinkers who sit in its churchyard), St. George's-in-the-East (1715–23), which was bombed hollow and has a smaller new church inside it, and St. Anne's, Limehouse (1712–24), also in need of repair, but still open. These three churches sail like clippers over the wharves as one goes downstream to Greenwich.

Equally remarkable on the Surrey bank is London's most splendiferous baroque church, St. Paul's, Deptford by Thomas Archer. Its Rector, the Reverend Derek Brown, has turned the huge crypt into a boys' club and the grand theatrical interior of his church above is a club for worship. Deptford is now a tough part of London and its people have little official connection with the City and West End.

The other church of this date which everyone knows is St. Martins-in-the-Fields (1722–26), by James Gibbs. It was never meant to be seen as it is now, but was designed to rise up from narrow alleys, many of which were in what is now Trafalgar Square. Until Dick Sheppard became its vicar after the First World War, this church looked as though it might become 'redundant'. Since then, it has become a centre of Christian welfare, as has Chad Varah's glorious Wren church of St. Stephen's, Walbrook in the City.

The best restoration of a post-Wren Classical interior in London since the war is undoubtedly St. Giles-in-the-Fields (1731–33), now dwarfed by office blocks where once was Charing Cross High Street.

Four pretty little 18th century churches in the warm brown brick of Middlesex are St. Peter's, Vere Street (Evangelical and a Chapel of Ease to the Reverend Mr. Stott of All Souls, Langham Place, the cathedral of Low Church on the North bank), the Grosvenor Chapel (High), sumptuously restored by Sir Ninian Comper, and, in Middlesex, the unexpected country churches of Cranford and Littleton.

There was a brief, exciting phase of church building at the end of the 18th century, which produced some churches with Adam style interiors. The most original is All Hallows, London Wall, by George Dance junior (1765–67), with a coved ceiling lit by huge semi-circles and a delicate semi-dome at the east end. This is now largely an exhibition gallery for the Council for the Care of Churches, but such a use is better than pulling it down, an all too probable fate for any decent building, whether church, club, or Livery hall in the greedy city.

Another winner in this style by a follower of Dance is St. Botolph's, Aldersgate, which is at last open again to the public and is used for helping people who have come out of prison.

Far away in Wanstead, on the outskirts of Epping Forest, the parish church by Thomas Hardwick (1790) is a complete, light and elegant Adam-style interior with galleries, high pews and two-decker pulpit that looks like something in New England.

London is studded with Commissioners' churches which were built to save the new industrial and lower middle classes from atheism, after the Napoleonic Wars. Well known architects of the 1820's were employed and fixed sums were in most cases given for the building. The idea was to get in as many seats as possible at the lowest cost. The style of the church could be Greek or Gothic.

The three most splendid, on which rather more money than usual was spent, are New St. Pancras (1819–22) in the Euston Road, purest Greek without and within, but spoiled inside by inappropriate late Victorian stained glass; St. Luke's, Chelsea, by J. Savage (1820–4), in the Gothic style and the first church in London since the Middle Ages to have a stone vault; and St. James's, Bermondsey (1829), a classical building by the same architect. The future of this magnificent church seems to be still uncertain.

VICTORIAN CHURCHES

The most varied, extraordinary and numerous churches of the metropolis were built by the Victorians. They were put up in the slums and the suburbs, created by steam railways and later by electric tram cars. The old idea of driving atheism out was replaced by the more positive idea of bringing the Gospel to the slums. This was largely the work of Tractarians, the followers of Keble, Pusey and Newman. The last-mentioned went over to Rome. Tractarians who remained loyal to the Church considered that the Catholic Church in this country was Anglican and that the Roman Catholics were the Italian mission. They wanted to build in the slums churches for Catholic ritual which would be an uplifting contrast to their squalid surroundings. They were tall and cathedral-like in proportion and generally built of brick, London's most readily available building material. The west end let in the light, the east end, where the High Altar stood, was rich, dark and mysterious. Some of the earlier ones like St. Mary Magdalene, Munster Square (1849–52), by Carpenter, and St. Barnabas, Pimlico (1850), Cundy and Butterfield, are copies of the Mediaeval and very handsome ones in stone.

But then the Victorians 'went on from where Gothic left off' and the most amazing and richly decorated prototype of these is All Saints, Margaret Street by William Butterfield (1849–59). It is a

St. Magnus the Martyr

St. Martin's, Ludgate

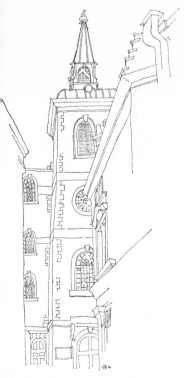

St. Mary Abchurch

St. Botolph's

brick building and inside it is decorated with coloured tiles, since brick does not admit of carving. The decoration becomes richer higher up the walls. In a small confined area it is amazing what a sense of lofty space the architect has created. There is a resident choir here and daily sung services and a large eclectic congregation on Sundays.

The architect G. E. Street, who designed the Law Courts, and founded the Arts and Crafts movement by means of his pupil William Morris, built a slightly less High Church answer to Butterfield in the brick Lombardo-Gothic masterpiece of St. James-the-Less (1858–61) near Victoria Station. Here the proportions inside are broad rather than lofty. In All Saints, Margaret Street, Prebendary Mackay, a former rector, used to say that the stained glass windows reminded him of a good hand at bridge, but the stained glass in St. James-the-Less is more like transparent pre-Raphaelite painting and there is a 'modified doom', that is to say one with not too much Hell in it, painted by G. F. Watts over the chancel. Both churches are perfect mid-Victorian period pieces, eminently practical and well adapted to High Church worship.

The grandest slum churches of this period are undoubtedly the three great brick buildings of St. Chad's, Haggerston, by James Brooks (1868) and St. Columba's, Kingsland Road (1867) by the same architect, and St. Augustine's, Kilburn (1870–80) by J. L. Pearson, which is derived from his earlier and fine brick church of St. Peter's, Kennington Lane (1863). Brooks went in for height and simplicity with a dark, tall east end and a light nave. Pearson went in for height and stone and brick vaulting and many mysterious vistas and little side chapels. St. Augustine's, Kilburn, has the highest spire in London. Dr. Pevsner describes it as 'one of the best churches of its date in the whole of England, a proud, honest, upright achievement.'

These churches were all built for Tractarian worship. They are often associated with devoted, gaunt priests, martyred and stoned for ritualism, who strode in their cassocks down dark alleys and by example brought their people to the pleasure of worship and lifted them out of the misery of 19th century industrialism.

There was also the Gospel to the richer suburbs, when wives of the wealthy tore off their jewels and gave them to be embroidered into vestments and hammered into altar crosses and left by will sacred pictures inherited from their families to decorate the church walls. A cathedral of this sort of thing is St. Cuthbert's, Philbeach Gardens, in what may now be termed the Australian quarter of

London and adjacent to Patrick Hamilton's 'Hangover Square', Earl's Court Square. It has now a different, though equally live congregation, from that of the 1880's when it was built.

The late Victorians produced more refined and equally original London churches. These were the times when 'artistic' was a favourite word and home handicrafts and folk music were popular, when the English Hymnal was better taste than Hymns Ancient and Modern, and sermons were more intellectual and less revivalist, and stained glass was greener and paler and pitch pine gave way to pale oak. Kensington and Chelsea and Ealing each have fine examples of this style. Holy Trinity, Kensington Gore, by G. F. Bodley (1902) is plain and uninviting outside. Inside it is a pale green many-vista'd twilight hung with mighty chandeliers.

Holy Trinity, Sloane Street (1888–90), by J. D. Sedding, has glass by Burne-Jones, electroliers by Bainbridge Reynolds, carving by Pomeroy and ironwork by Harry Wilson and Nelson Dawson and medallions by Armstead. It is the most elaborate Arts and Crafts church in London. It was built for High Church worship, but has gone rather Lower Church. To attend Evensong there is to fall back into the world of Pont Street, hansom cabs and Oscar Wilde.

'What are we to think of the man?'—one solemn denunciatory preacher said there recently—'who, buying a return railway ticket marked "not transferable" gives the return half to a friend? From small dishonesties like this, rise greater, until treaties are broken and there is war.'

The Church of England today is not usually so ridiculously out of touch as this. Its religion is not confined to Sundays as may be seen from the weekday work of City and inner West End churches, as well as those in the remaining slums and on the new housing estates.

One more of these late Victorian and Edwardian churches, which are plain outside and unexpectedly rich within, must be mentioned. That is the red brick church of St. Cyprian, Clarence Gate, by Sir Ninian Comper (1903). A low stone vaulted narthex opens to a wide expanse of polished dark wooden floor in which are reflected slender columns and a lace-like gold screen across the whole width of the church. The daylight is mitigated by bottle glass, the east windows contain Comper's stained glass and the altars are hung with his rose-pink hangings.

ROMAN CATHOLIC AND OTHERS

Outside the Church of England, the finest buildings are those of the Roman Catholics. They are all, with the exception of St. Etheldreda's, Ely Place, which is much restored Mediaeval, fairly recent. The best of all is the Cathedral of Westminster by J. F. Bentley (1895–1903), in his own Byzantine style: red brick and Portland stone without, marble and yellow London brick within.

The interior is immensely impressive, much more so than is now that of St. Paul's. When you are inside St. Paul's, you expect the dome to look bigger. When you first enter Westminster, you do not expect a central dome at all, until your eye is led by shallow saucer domes, along the nave, to the vast domed central space. The details of the cathedral vary in quality. The earlier chapels at the east end with their mosaics are perfect, and the light fittings are the best anywhere. Bentley and his assistant Marshall, instead of trying to hide electric light as something to be ashamed of, used the naked bulbs as pearls in compositions which are like hanging jewellery.

Brompton Oratory (1878) by H. Gribble is a faithful essay in Italian Baroque and excellent for music or ritual. The Cathedral of St. George, Southwark, a rather flimsy building by Pugin in 1841, was bombed, and the present rebuilt structure is most handsomely proportioned in the Gothic style, reminiscent in its loftiness of Maufe's Anglican cathedral of Guildford.

Methodists, Baptists, Congregationals and others have not built such fine buildings in London as they have in provincial cities. The best are Central Hall, Westminster (1905), by Lanchester and Rickards, Viennese baroque outside and rather plain, except for its main staircase, within, and the Congregational Church, Lyndhurst Road, Hampstead (1883–4), by Alfred Waterhouse, an original hexagonal plan in shiny brick and majolica.

The most historic building in London outside the Christian Church is the Synagogue (1701) in Bevis Marks off Houndsditch. It is like a City church inside, but spared Victorian accretions. Many 18th century brass candelabra twinkle in a forest of dark woodwork and you must keep your hat on if you are a man and sit in the gallery if you are a woman.

London Churches, Part Two

The story so far. Having built the churches, what then?

Well, in Roman Catholic churches, it's the ceremony that matters, not the sermon. In Nonconformist churches, it's the other way round. In the Church of England, as we shall see, anything goes.

But all of them, nevertheless, have their five star preachers. They are a bit thin on the ground, but well worth listening to if you can find them. Who is the best preacher in London? Now, read on.

The more elderly among devout Church people will always argue that there are no preachers today. They will hark back to the golden days of pulpit oratory, to the days of the great non-conformist spell-binding divines, or of Dick Sheppard of St. Martins-in-the-Fields, Cardinal Bourne at Westminster Cathedral, or to an earlier era in which Scott-Holland of St. Paul's reigned supreme.

Those were days in which, for three-quarters of a century, in fact right up to the end of the war, the *Church Times* published a sermon verbatim each week, selected from one or other of the London churches.

A revolution has occurred in the meantime, particularly within Anglicanism. The Parish Communion has gained an ascendancy undreamed of a generation ago at the expense and decline of the statutory order of Morning Prayer, where the emphasis was on 'the sermon'.

The very nature of the Communion service gives opportunity for only the briefest of expositions—generally pin-pointing some aspect of the Epistle or Gospel for the day—invariably from notes only or extempore. The long sermon of twenty-five minutes, or in some churches very much longer, has departed in all but a few places.

Nevertheless, the great exponents of 'the Word' have their successors, but for the most part they are practitioners with an entirely new technique.

Where to start? In theory you would expect the leading and most famous churches to have the best sermons and the best music—such as St. Paul's and Westminster Abbey in the Church of England or, amongst the Roman Catholics, that noted teaching church, Farm Street, Mayfair. Or one of the world famous

'Cathedrals' of Non-Conformity—Central Hall, Westminster, Bloomsbury Baptist Church or the City Temple, which cover the three main strands of Free Churchmanship. But it is really all a matter of luck.

St. Paul's, Westminster Abbey and Southwark Cathedral across the river, in accordance with their statutes, have residentiary canons, each of whom takes a month's duty in turn. Each Sunday of that month he will be responsible for preaching once. It is said, perhaps unkindly, that the total collections at any one will reflect the occupier of the pulpit.

Visiting preachers, often ordinary parish priests from the diocese, are also invited. They usually take the opportunity of the occasion to relieve themselves of their own particular theologies, which can be rather alarming for the casual visitor.

First of all then, to St. Paul's, with the finest music in England. The Archdeacon of London (the Ven. Martin Sullivan) once a Dean in New Zealand, is very much a contemporary, popular preacher with an attractive Commonwealth twang. As a direct foil, they have the Cathedral Chancellor (Canon Frederic Hood), who brings to his preaching ministry the Oxford voice with slurred R's. He was once the Principal of Pusey House, Oxford and is a master of the spiritual life. But he can be homely, sentimental, eloquent, well phrased, extremely polished and very adaptable.

At Westminster Abbey, Canon Michael Stancliffe, who is also Rector of the fashionable St. Margaret's, can be relied on for a meaty discourse of time-honoured standards. His colleague, Archdeacon Edward Carpenter, much in demand as a broadcaster on erudite burning topics of the day, is consistently stimulating. He is an ardent supporter of Chelsea Football Club, preaches in a rhetorical sing-song style and has some surprisingly radical opinions.

The urbane Dean of Westminster, Dr. Abbott, is also well worth hearing. He has a compelling style, although his soft, seductive thinking-aloud sermons don't appeal to everybody.

Over the river there is Southwark Cathedral, a Cinderella dwarfed by its more prosperous and familiar neighbours. The Provost, the Very Rev. Ernie Southcott, delivers great bursts of dramatic Canadian fervour like thunderclaps. The Bishop, Mervyn Stockwood, the Socialist controversialist, on the rare occasions that he preaches in the place where he has his official throne, is well worth the journey, for he is in the top flight of pulpit orators. The music at Southwark is also good—well into the four-star bracket.

Just across the river and into Billingsgate is St. Magnus the Martyr, where Fr. Colin Gill roars out bursts of old-style Anglo-Catholic fire in sermons short and full of instruction. In the opposite direction, at St. Cuthbert's, Philbeach Gardens, Kensington, another Anglo-Catholic 'hot-house', the unconventional Fr. Gerard Irvine has a sparkling style. He is an intellectual, but witty with it.

For those who need something above the ordinary in intellectual brilliance and interest, Prebendary Francois Piachaud of Christ Church, Chelsea is worth hearing.

At the shrine of the famous 'Tubby' Clayton, All Hallows, hard by the Tower of London, there is the Rev. Colin Cuttell (one of Clayton's own protégés). He also can be relied upon not to insult the thinking capacity of his congregation, and there aren't many you can say that about.

Another of Clayton's 'boys' is the Rev. Austen Williams, Vicar of London's most famous parish church—St. Martins-in-the-Fields. He has probably the largest following of all and is the Church of England's most popular broadcaster. He is very handsome, photographs well and is never boring.

Move east again, just for a quarter of a mile. Behind the massive Savoy Hotel is a gem of a church—the Queen's Chapel of the Savoy. The Rev. Roger Roberts holds sway with spellbinding oratory. The music is provided by a small professional choir, recently reinforced by a new organ, and is as good as many a cathedral. Going to the fashionable Savoy Chapel is certainly having the best of both worlds. Mr. Roberts, apart from being the Chaplain, is also editor of the *Church Times*.

Across the road, submerged almost by the great Covent Garden Market, is Inigo Jones's barn of a place, St. Paul's. The Rector, Prebendary Clarence May, is the most famous of London's clerical characters. To see him in his purple piping and lace is a splendid sight.

He was an actor with Ben Greet before he took holy orders and always looks the part. If you don't believe the vagaries of Anglicanism, pick a Sunday in June or July when he has a service for the blessing of animals. He does it very well and has been clawed by a lion cub before now. But don't interrupt, either for or against, or you will be speedily propelled towards the massive entrance doors. Clarence May preaches on topical subjects in a nice old fashioned romantic oratorical style, fast dying out.

Two of London's Suffragan Bishops might make a profitable Sabbath for the good sermon seekers. The scholarly young Anglo-

Catholic Bishop of Willesden (Graham Leonard) will reward you with an intellectual masterpiece. The Suffragan Bishop of Stepney, Evered Lunt (wrongly tagged 'the unready' by some disrespectful clergy), is a trifle posh but he can be an inspiring preacher with lashings of evangelical fervour.

So far they have been Anglo-Catholic or middle-of-the-road, so here are two Low Church parsons, both excellent. The Rev. John Stott, at All Soul's, Langham Place (near the B.B.C.), will amaze you with his hold on young people. He always has a church packed to the doors. Every 'mod con' is laid on in this comfortably furnished church. They even hand out prayer books in which one can 'point' the psalms correctly. Stott, one of the most brilliant Evangelicals of his generation, is in the top flight of preachers.

Holy Trinity, Prince Consort Road, Kensington, is now the headquarters of the College of Preachers (copied from an American pattern) and the benefice of its Director, the Rev. D. W. Cleverley Ford. He is a smooth Evangelical, with a handsome presence and a voice to match. It goes without saying that he wouldn't have got the job unless he could preach. And he does, superbly.

There is, perhaps, a New Testament precedent for keeping the best Anglican name until last. Without doubt the 'top of the bill' is Prebendary Gordon Phillips, a pocket sized Welshman. He is chaplain to London University and Rector of St. George's, Bloomsbury. He is unequalled for philosophy and sermons packed with intellectual substance.

Nonconformists, naturally, might not agree with this, as the sermon counts for more than the ceremony in dissenting churches.

Their big star has his following. Some say *he* is the best preacher in London.

He is of course Donald Soper—the Rev. Lord Soper, one of the life peers created by Prime Minister Harold Wilson. He is at the headquarters of the Methodists' West London Mission in Kingsway Hall, just up the road from Television House and Aldwych. He is humane, humorous and usually provocative. On weekdays he is often seen arguing out apologetics from the Christian Socialist viewpoint on Tower Hill. He has few equals at this game either.

For Congregationalists, the City Temple, Holborn Viaduct, now sumptuously rebuilt after war damage, is a place of special affection. Occasionally, the Rev. John Huxtable, the administrative leader of the Congregational Church can be heard here. For real drama nobody can beat the Rev. Martyn Lloyd-Jones at the Westminster

Chapel, Buckingham Gate. Old fashioned Calvinism preached at its best.

The great Baptist citadel is the Bloomsbury Church, at the top end of Shaftesbury Avenue, where Dr. Howard Williams is a worthy successor of many famous giants of Noncomformity.

These four Nonconformists make a powerful quartet—a combination even the Anglicans cannot eclipse.

Roman Catholicism, with its emphasis on sacrament rather than the Word, presents something of a problem. Its preachers are few and far between. There is certainly breath-taking music and ceremonial at Westminster Cathedral and Brompton Oratory. But for matchless intellectual sermons you must go to Farm Street, Mayfair, and listen to the Jesuits who preach regularly there. Eirenic in flavour, unparalleled for simplicity: you will certainly want to go again.

The times of sermons, incidentally, are given in the Saturday edition of the *Times*.

Sermons, music—now finally, bells. London reverberates with their sound above its traffic. Lovers of campanology will put the famous 'St. Mary le Bow', home of Bow bells, in Cheapside, top of their priority list. But they don't play nursery rhymes there, so go and listen to St. Clement Dane's in the Strand and really hear Oranges and Lemons come alive.

Visit the Flower Walk in Kensington Gardens on a Sunday afternoon after the nannies have been given a glass of port by the master; eavesdrop on some of the best gossip in Europe. In Holland Park at the same time they band together to throw rocks at the peacocks.

Food Buying in London

Can be a pleasure in itself. A sensual, heady pleasure. There are exotic shops flowing with the full-blooded South and markets ringing with full-blooded East Enders.

The best food shops are in Soho. When the night clubbers and the strippers sleep, the cheese shops and the wine shops come into their own.

The best food comes originally through Covent Garden, Smithfield and Billingsgate. So does the best atmosphere. You have to get up early to go there. And for Covent Garden, go early and quickly. They eventually plan to move the market. Covent Garden will never be the same again.

The lazy way to buy is to pick up a phone and dial SLO 1234 any time of day or night. Harrods will then send round one of their 105 green electric vans with anything from a pound of caviar (£30) to a packet of crisps (4d.).

But don't ring them. Set out on your own expedition into the jungle of London's foodland. Get up at dawn. Earlier. Better still, go to the markets at midnight.

AT COVENT GARDEN

This is the time that the first dark trucks slide into the market. Porters are stirring, drivers are drinking their fourpenny teas under the wide eaves of Inigo Jones' church, rubbing the sleep from their eyes.

A young man with searing red hair and a Jesus beard says he's going to sleep the night here. 'There used to be dozens of us spread out along the railings', he says. A girl of 20 says she sleeps out too. 'Usually in the backs of lorries. Sometimes I work as a waitress, but I always sleep here.' She looks rosy and healthy. 'It's the fresh air, i'n't it?'

Here are the loafers and characters who do odd jobs before the porters arrive. There's Stewart, hair down the collar of his coat, a man in his sixties. He used to be a fighter pilot. He rolls up to an older man in a flat hat and buttoned-up coat. 'What are you doing on my pitch? The brown from your sewer's coming over me. Move along or I'll get the Church of England Clergy to get you out.'

As dawn comes, Covent Garden emerges as an elegant lady of a place, pigeons flying, porters whistling, banks of flowers, vegetables in green stacks. Wimpled nuns are buying for their convents, early morning drunks steal up to take advantage of the pubs opening at five a.m., porters swap jokes with an all-night queue for Callas tickets.

'Characters,' says the man from Bermondsey, sipping his Black Ink in the Coach and Horses, 'My dad said there were more lunatics here than Bearstead. But it's not what it was.

'I've seen Ava Gardner come to this pub, no shoes, no stockings, it was pouring down. "Out", said the landlord, "You're not here on business". I've seen the Prince-of-Wales-that-was lying in the gutter, pissed as a pudding. You find all sorts in the Garden. Girl came here with nothing, on the game, left here in mink. In the back of vans, of course. But you're delving into masonic secrets, aren't you?'

You can buy a 56 lb. bag of spanish onions in the market for 12 bob, or get a tray of tropical fruit from Pouparts, the old-established firm whose site is a wire cage like a tennis court in the centre aisle. A brigadier-type in his seventies called Donald Ravenhill calls the business his 'little hobby'. He specialises in the exoticugli fruit from the West Indies, wild strawberries at Christmas-time, Chinese gooseberries for Mario Gallati's restaurants. 'People will pay anything for the best.'

BILLINGSGATE

It's only a number 13 bus ride from the Garden to the 'Gate', but there's no glamour about Billingsgate. The cobbled streets under the Monument run with fishy water and there's no delight in prosaic boxes of herring, mackerel and cod. Porters trundle by with boxes of fish on their heads, a trickle of icy water snaking out at one corner. The young porters wear hard bowlers, Dunn's seconds. 'The brim catches the drips', they say.

In Tubby Isaacs' place in Lovat Lane, there's Mr. Monty, a red-faced character in his fifties, chopping eels alive-o at the rate of 400 an hour. He's done nothing else for 40 years. He eats three pounds of them a day. 'My favourite nosh, never get tired of 'em.'

At Janssen's they have tanks of live trout brought from their Lincolnshire farms. They deliver them to hotels with oxygen tanks so that chefs can prepare Truite au bleu. Dead trout turn greeny-brown within hours and won't do.

At Tabor's they specialise in oysters from Cornwall and Galway. They also have very cheap Japanese oysters in plastic packets from

Hiroshima: 'Grown in the clean waters of the Inland Sea of Japan'. They aren't much bigger than mussels and taste cucumbery. Young Mr. Tabor, the boss's nephew, says oyster stall people put them in old shells and serve them as Portuguese. Madame Prunier buys them. 'Probably for her steak and kidney pies', says Mr. Tabor charitably.

SMITHFIELD

Now, that's everything a market should be. Large, impressive, orderly, bustling with activity.

It's a young man's place, and the youthful salesmen tackle the selling of meat as brokers might sell shares. Someone's whistling a phrase from Tannhauser, an assistant is practising a golf swing with a meat hook. Spirit is as strong among the bosses as it is among the union-minded pitchers, humpers and bummerees.

'It's a funny old place,' says David Andrade, who comes from the oldest Smithfield family. 'I often say it has the makings of a first-class social club. My great-great-grandfather came to Smithfield in the days when they drove the cattle through from the Angel and slaughtered them at the back of Newgate Jail where the Old Bailey is now. Before they built this market in 1868.'

They are sorry for the housewife, the dealers. One of them explained over a side of meat looking like a Henry Moore torso. 'This is topside of beef, 4s. 6d. a pound to you. When it gets into the High Street you'll probably buy it at nine or ten bob as a pound of rump.'

The trend, they say, is towards fatless, flavourless young beef. Douglas Rees, junior partner in one of the older firms, says: 'As long as it looks good on the slab, the housewife will buy it. She doesn't want flavour. Most people cover the meat with bloody sauce anyway.'

SOHO

Here, on the other hand, in the real hub of London's shopping, they may tell the customer what to have. In Roche's in Old Compton Street, see what you get from the owner, the nervous, bird-like Miss Kathleen Kennedy.

Shopper: I think I'll have a piece of that brie.

Miss Kennedy: I wouldn't have that cheese, it's not, ah, ripe.

Shopper: Then can I have a camembert?

Miss Kennedy: Ah, no, we're not selling camembert this week. It's too thundery. Turns them quicker than hot weather.'

She has 60 cheeses in her selection, from the goats' cheeses called banon, wrapped in chestnut leaves or rolled in rosemary, to melting Normandy cheeses in perfect condition, straight from the Paris market. She also sells expensive young vegetables, frogs' legs and snails. Once she had an assistant rush out to the back: 'A lady, miss, asking for pedigree snails.' She had asked for Petits Gris snails, so it turned out.

Roche's is a little bit of France. You have Spain down the road in the shop of Gomez Ortega, a happy muddle of paella pans, baccalao, hams, chorizo, tubs of olives and shelves of turron, the exquisite Spanish nougat from Jijona. Mr. Ortega is a fierce, likeable little man from Murcia where the poorest Spanish grow the best fruit. He was a fruit agent on the Paris market Les Halles, until he opened this shop in 1939. He still prefers his own version of English, and his catalogues will announce that he sells '*Bullsfighters, bullfighter postcars and postals, embroidered cards . . .*'

Italian shops are the oldest. The Parmagiani people came to London in 1890, now an uncle and a nephew run rival shops in Old Compton Street. But they have changed through the years from anxiously helpful family affairs to professional, air-conditioned stores. They stock some of the best cheeses in England, big wheels of gruyere and emmenthal, slabs of parmesan matured for three years, rich, creamy gorgonzola.

For British cheeses it's proper to go to Paxton and Whitfield in Brewer Street, who claim to have been top of the trade since 1741. In a nice old English grocer's shop with sawdust on the floor, they set out all the native cheeses, Stilton, Double Gloucester, Sage Derby, Blue Cheshire, in splendid condition. They stock French cheeses to the point 'where they get too dear and we drop 'em'. Frederick Archibald Moore, the boss, looks like Osbert Lancaster with a pricklier moustache and redder face. 'My father sold this place rather than give it to me. He didn't like me. I bought it myself later.'

Soho is full of characters. Like Benoit Bulcke, a 79-year-old Belgian who started continental butchery here 50 years ago. Old Benoit is a little man who wears a blue beret over a pair of enormous, bushy white eyebrows. 'It's not my meat which is the attraction,' he says. 'It's me.'

Across the road is Del Monico's, the wine store, where you find Old Dante who came from Switzerland as a young man without a penny. Dante is now 86, a chuckling little man with a boyish smile. Two grandsons run the shop, but some customers refuse to be served by anyone but Dante. Del Monico's is one of the busiest shops in all Soho, luring millionaire and pauper alike with its good cut-price wines, bankruptcy bargains, and brand name gin at 10s. a bottle cheaper.

'One bloke stopped his car, bought £200 worth of stuff, paid for it, drove it off,' said David, one of the grandsons. It's probably the only place where Mantovani is likely to bump into Sir John Barbirolli. 'We're strictly cash and carry,' says David, 'nobody gets anything till they pay, whoever they are.' (There was a well-known publisher signing a cheque because they wouldn't deliver his order until he did.)

Not like Christopher's, perhaps. Christopher's claim to be one of the last three independent wine firms together with Berry Bros. and Dolamores. They are in Jermyn Street behind a window as misleading as the front page of the *Times*. No wine, but a vase of flowers, and photographs of characters associated with the street, one week a bishop, next week a char. Inside it's like someone's drawing-room, people sitting about drinking sherry. Young man at a table behind a red screen in striped shirt, white collar and knitted tie, turns out to be one of the three partners. They are, respectively, Eton, Harrow and Winchester. 'But Eton, Harrow and Winchester tradesmen,' says senior partner Peter Noble engagingly.

If the Christopher people are tradesmen, ex–Parachute Sergeant Leonard McGarry boasts that his Brewer Street fish shop, Richards, is 'more like a club'. In eleven years he turned a white elephant into a sound commercial enterprise.

'We get them all,' says Mr. McGarry. 'Japanese who like raw fish, Burmese who have it for drying, the Chinese who won't have it prepared. I've sold a 301 lb. sturgeon from this shop. People stop their taxis outside for a pair of kippers.'

This shop is the sum of the experience of working in 68 fish shops in London. He has everything from live lobsters, and red and grey mullet, to octopus and oysters.

Of course, you don't have to stay in Soho. Explore the regional parts of London, West Indian shops in Notting Hill Gate, Jewish delicatessens in the East End.

Go out, if you like, to Balls Pond Road, to a shop called Xenos, one of 50 such Greek and Turkish shops to spring up in London in the last ten years. Amiable Cypriots sell black olive oil, pigstails in brine, hard, bitter goats' cheeses, broken meal for pilaffi, caper leaves in vinegar and many strange vegetables. Where, if you stay long enough, they will courteously serve you Turkish coffee.

If you should ever feel like rebelling against the antiseptic foods of the supermarket, there is a shop where you can buy dirty eggs, limp dates and scabby apples. This is the Wholefood Store in Baker Street, where unlikely girls wearing blue jeans and vocational expressions sell foods untainted by insecticides and artificial fertilisers.

The forbidding manageress, Miss Lilian Schofield, is likely to thrust improving tracts in your hand like *Mutilated Milk, the Menace of Pasteurisation*, or *Why Not Smoke?*

She sells 'raw' milk, flour from unsprayed crops, hand-churned butter. The eggs in the window are good and dirty from the farm. (The Egg Marketing Board bought two dozen here for a press demonstration.)

'We have a biochemist to analyse samples of all foods we sell,' says Miss Schofield. 'The usual dates you buy in a shop have been sprayed with insecticide, then washed in detergent, then coated in glycerine to make them look appetising. Not ours. We don't mind scabby apples with blemishes. It proves they haven't been sprayed.'

Some things you can't get out of a Harrods van.

If you're really hungry and penniless you can sit around most bars and cocktail lounges—keep looking at your watch as though you're waiting for someone to turn up—eating their nuts, olives, gerkins, pearl onions and crisps. Fu-Tong in Kensington High Street supplies five different varieties of nuts, but you're less conspicuous at the Savoy.

After all, half the population consists of them. Though you wouldn't think so, judging by every other book about London.

So here it is. The Female Scene. Not dishonest, in the way advertisements talk to women. Not sloppy and condescending, in the way the mass circulation magazines slop and condescend to women.

Just honest, racy, highly prejudiced informative stuff, which only years of living in London can give. Unless, of course, you read this . . .

Woman's London

London is the largest inhabitable city in the world for women. Tokyo is still positively feudal about women and New York does not count. Inherent frenetic energy and a kind of stoned madness are necessary if you want to live in New York for any length of time. It also has more unmarried women and divorcees per eligible head than is auspicious.

London is ideal—the multiplicity of choice and the variety of potential of friends, lovers, bosses, and husbands is dazzling. But a woman's life in London is fraught from morning to night with a need for swift, informed, and successful decision making.

Assuming, first of all, that you are unmarried and in London either to make your fortune, find a husband, or just to play the field, how should you best conduct yourself?

Domestic background is obviously of first importance, unless you just want somewhere to keep a change of underwear and eyelashes, somewhere to use as a recovery station after long periods of 'out'. In this case a 6 ft. by 4 ft. bed-sitter in Barons' Court will do as well as anything. Otherwise you should first consider:

WITH WHOM?

1. For unimpeded activity, you must obviously live alone in a self-contained flat. But remember that melancholics need an audience, and that the incurably gregarious are likely to begin talking to the wardrobe within a week.

2. If you need to be spoken to kindly first thing in the morning and last thing at night, cohabitation may be the answer. Living with a man is comparatively easy in the anonymity of London, provided

the landlord does not live on the premises. If he does he may return as 'not known at this address' mail addressed to you in your maiden name.

3. Do not live with relatives in any shape or form, or with friends of the family—although this may seem to be a good idea when you first arrive. Anyone who knew you as a child is bound to be demoralising, and to recall inhibiting memories of clean necks and rational behaviour.

4. If you cannot afford a whole flat to yourself, share one. Flat-sharing on a large scale, with as many as six or seven girls (or men) per unit, is a special feature of the London domestic scene. It occurs on a comparable scale nowhere else in the civilised world and has been made possible only by overcrowding, a native inability to convert old family houses into decent small flats, and British boarding school life, which trains the young from an early age to cope with the rigours of communal life.

Be sure that you have a room of your own, however small, and that the other occupants are not Moral Rearmers.

London flat-sharing girls fall into two main groups—(*a*) those who like cocoa on retiring, knitting patterns all over the living-room, and steadies in the kitchen brewing pots of tea; (*b*) those who never clean the bath, have sudden noisy and inelegant affaires, and abscond in the middle of the month without paying their share of the telephone bill. If you are the intolerant only child of rich multi-bathroomed parents—don't share a flat. Otherwise, get in touch with—

Share-A-Flat, *175 Piccadilly*, *W.1*, HYD 2545
Flatsharers, *11 Beauchamp Place*, *S.W.7*, KNI 0232
They charge a fee—usually the equivalent of one week's rent—but they do make some attempt to match up clients.

WHERE TO LIVE?
Mayfair, Belgravia, and Knightsbridge are permanently fashionable and impenetrably expensive, but if you can afford to live there, it can do you no harm.

Hampstead and Highgate are for politicians, Marghanita Laski, historians, expatriate Americans, successful actors and less successful film stars. They are a bit way out, and at that altitude can be offensively bracing.

Transalpine Fulham and nether Chelsea (World's End) are currently fashionable and still reasonably cheap. Chelsea proper has become a curious week-end and evening resort where people go to buy and wear extraordinary clothes, or to see who is buying and wearing extraordinary clothes.

Marylebone, Bloomsbury and Holland Park are all convenient, and not too violently expensive. Notting Hill Gate is suspect. North Kensington can be dodgy.

Islington is being colonised by a few interior decorators, journalists, television producers and property speculators. A brave attempt—but probably doomed to failure by the general indomitable scruffiness of the whole of this area of London.

South-west and West London, from Victoria to Olympia, is reasonably pleasant, with certain exceptions. Earls Court, for instance, is full of manic, rootless, fun-loving Australians.

Battersea, Greenwich, Blackheath, and Dulwich Village are now being opened up south of the river. But there is not much point in living in these places unless you mean to stay there most of the time. People who go to south London tend not to return. There are very few landmarks over there.

HOW TO FIND A FLAT

There is no painless way of acquiring a flat in London. Here are the four basic methods:

1. Buy the 10 a.m. edition of *The Evening Standard* as soon as it appears in the West End. In outlying districts it does not arrive until anything up to an hour later, by which time all will be lost. Rush with it to the nearest telephone, call all the numbers in the 'Accommodation Vacant' column that look at all feasible, and make appointments to view them in quick succession as soon as possible. The best ones are snapped up incredibly quickly so speed is essential in this operation.

2. You will notice, if you are observant, that the same telephone numbers recur in the accommodation columns of all evening and local papers. These numbers are those of accommodation bureaux. You will also notice that the entries accompanying these numbers usually look too good to be true. If you ring the bureau they will either tell you that that particular flat has just gone, or they will tell you to come round to their office immediately to make an appointment to see it. It will probably be gone by the time you get there—but, as it happens, they have another one just the same for a little more money. So, beware.

3. Notice boards outside shops such as stationers and tobacconists sometimes carry advertisements for flats vacant in the neighbourhood. But these are very often of the homely-digs-for-working-

man variety, and since there is no way of telling how long the advertisement has been there, you are likely to waste time and telephone calls on flats that went days ago. They might also turn out to be homely whores.

4. Estate agents in the area where you want to live are the best bet. They usually know the properties they are letting and they do the whole thing in a business-like fashion with an exchange of signed agreements and inventories.

HOW TO PAY THE RENT

London is a man's city when it comes to work. If you are reasonably intelligent and able to type you need never be out of a job typing someone's letters and answering his telephone. English girls are encouraged to be secretaries, typists, clerks, shop assistants, models, actresses, dress designers, librarians, nurses, social workers, and teachers, but not much else.

They are not encouraged to go into industry, political commentating, or economic advising. It is not exactly forbidden. If you are ambitious, you will need to be devious. American style go-getters and career girls are not popular, so never openly compete with men, always appear surprised at the least success, and be grateful for crumbs of praise. Unless you are the owner of some shining talent or glamour, you will be lucky if you make more than £20 a week. It is therefore important, if you are to enjoy the more expensive pleasures of London, that you should meet some of the people who earn more than this.

MEETING MEN

First read the chapter in this book devoted to the theory and practice of picking-up girls. Then you will know how the other half lives. What your half needs to know is when NOT to be picked up. Some of one's best friends are pick-ups, but accidents can happen. It is sometimes advisable to put him down very smartly because you don't know where he's been. Here are a few basic rules:

1. Always take care to be picked up in pleasant surroundings and, if outdoors, in the broadest of possible daylight. Best sites for the purpose are public parks (healthy), art galleries and museums (cultural), and expensive shops (rich). Play it cool. The man who has accosted you may have been wandering lonely as a cloud and just suddenly liked the look of you—or he may be a shameless and intrepid lecher. In either case it was not the beauty of your soul which attracted him to you.

2. Do not wander about in Soho at any time of the day or night with an available expression on your face. If anyone speaks to you it will be because (*a*) they think you are a prostitute (expensive, one hopes); (*b*) they are recruiting artistes for a strip-club; (*c*) they are a member of the editorial staff of *Private Eye* and have just nipped out for a breather from the Greek Street offices of that organ of opinion. All this is to be avoided unless you have a taste for low life.

3. Do not wander about unescorted anywhere in the West End at night. It is all right to walk briskly from point A to point B, but look neither to left nor right, and cross the road smartly if you are accosted. (Jay-walking is in theory illegal, but in practice it is an ancient British right.)

4. Do not go into pubs or licensed clubs alone. Some do not allow unescorted women on the premises anyway. You should not do this because it will LOOK as if you want to be picked up. No one will believe that you have just dropped in for a pint of mild and bitter. It is just permissible to go into a pub with another woman, but you should be careful to talk to one another intently, and not to stare about the place too much. Do not stand at the bar longer than is absolutely necessary to buy your drinks.

It is possible, of course, to meet the occasional man via an old-fashioned introduction. For instance, surprising numbers of girls meet remarkable numbers of men through their jobs. But make sure it is *through* rather than *at*. Office romances tend to be the Kiss of Death, either to the job or the romance or both. If you are one of ten girls in the typing pool of The National Association of Local Government Officers your scope is likely to be limited anyway. Other girls sometimes introduce one to the most exotic men—but it is not nice to poach, and a good girl friend is often harder to find than a man anyway. (If you talk to girls at London parties they will either think you are Lesbian or that you have original ideas about foursomes—or they will spend the entire conversation looking over your shoulder to see what the men are doing.)

Agony columns always exhort the lonely, jilted, or otherwise socially impoverished to join a club. This may be a good idea if you are actually interested in badminton or carpentry—you may indeed find a soulmate among the sawdust or solace through shuttlecocks. But generally speaking it is advisable to believe firmly, with Groucho Marx, that any club which will accept you as a member is not worth joining.

If you are in London for a very short time, and either need a partner for a particular function or simply cannot bear to go to the theatre alone, you might as a last resort hire a Paid Escort. Gigolos are unobtainable in London for love or money, but unemployed actors and male models may be had by the desperate for about £8 per evening plus expenses. Agencies who stock these gentlemen are: Cockburn's Agency—PAR 3515   Eros Agency—REG 0167 Piccadilly Bureau—HYD 7986   Courtney Bureau—HYD 5073 Ring them up first, then go round to their offices and look at photographs and specifications. Make sure you get one the right height.

PACKAGING

Clothes in London are very important—or so all whose livelihood depends on it would have you believe. At times of social disorder and upheaval, dress becomes bizarre because people are no longer at all sure of their respective roles in life. Clothes are supposedly an instant role-indicator, but at the moment they simply reflect prevailing British confusion. There are two principal possibilities— Hip or Normal—and any variations on these themes are up to you. *Posh Hip.* This category is catered for most lavishly. If you look reasonably sane in a buttercup-yellow satin gymslip and orange suede boots, you are going to have no difficulty at all. Girls with large striking features, small insignificant figures and long legs, do best at Boutiques. These have names such as Countdown, Blast Off, Top Gear, Change Down, Glad Rags, Clobber, Quorum, Ad Hoc, Palisades, Barricades and so forth. New ones open daily and there is no way of telling what will happen next. Most of their stock, designed by yet-rebelling fashion school graduates, is in limited editions and is therefore fairly expensive—£10 plus for simple shifts. Boutiques are to be found all over Chelsea and Fulham and in in the westernmost area of Soho behind Regent Street. Otherwise there is Mary Quant, who began it all at Bazaar (138a Kings Road, 46 Brompton Road, S.W.3). You need to be of above average height, and to have a figure which proceeds from shoulder to knee without intervening bulges to wear her more unusual designs. Woollands 21 Shop on the ground floor of the department store of the same name in Knightsbridge has a good, if expensive, collection of dresses, suits, and separates by young British designers. *Proletarian Hip.* Wallis Shops (13 Brompton Road, S.W.3, and 490 & 217 Oxford Street, W.1) have a good range (particularly in small sizes) of dresses, coats and suits in natty fabrics and designs. Neata-wear (328 Oxford Street, W.1, 78 Regent Street and 62 Shaftesbury Avenue) have, despite their name, a neat line in French imported trousers, suits, sweaters, and frilly underwear. Some of it looks better off than on, so be careful. Peter Robinson Top Shops at Oxford Circus and in the Strand have large fast-moving stocks of mass-produced dolly kit by Mary Quant, Gerald McCann, John Marks, Jean Varon, and Polly Peck. Fenwicks (63 New Bond Street) are particularly good for jewellery and all kinds of cheap and cheerful accessories, hats and handbags. Everything is stop press news and last weeks' Mondrian Helmet (remember?) is this week's broken range.

Normal. Jaeger (145 Kings Road, 26 Sloane Street, 204 Regent Street) is a wow for anything made of wool—sweaters that wash and suits and coats that go on for ever. The following department stores specialise in normal clothes for all normal occasions: John Lewis, and D. H. Evans (next to each other by Oxford Circus), Selfridges, Marshall & Snelgrove, Bourne & Hollingsworth (all in Oxford Street), Harvey Nichols (Knightsbridge), Debenham & Freebody (Wigmore Street), and Dickins & Jones (Regent Street).

Marks & Spencer (Oxford Street and branches everywhere) are justly famous for finish, quality, and superb value. A vest bearing the hallmark 'St. Michael' is a girl's best friend. They are unbeatable for underwear, sweaters, and stockings—but some of their dresses and larger garments are a bit basic and timeless in style.

Shoes for most people come from Mr. Clore's foot empire—Dolcis, Saxone, Manfield, and Lilley & Skinner. Minority shoes are to be had at Kurt Geiger (95 New Bond Street), Elliot (76 New Bond Street), Gamba (46 Dean Street), and Anello & Davide (Oxford Street) who will make shoes to your own specifications at no huge expense. A few boutiques stock shoes by individual young designers. Some of these are marvellous, particularly those designed by Moya. Some of them make you look like a lame goblin.

Now that all unmarried girls in London have been housed, employed, manned, and decently clad, it is time for honest married women.

PLANNED FECUNDITY

Or what every young girl should know.

1. The Family Planning Association. This worthy charitable organisation supplies information and contraceptives to all married women and imminent brides at a cost of from 5s. to £3 depending upon your ability to pay. The Association also carries out pregnancy tests, investigates infertility, and gives advice on marital difficulties. Central London Clinics are at:

The Public Services Building, *Milton Court, Moor Lane, E.C.2,* CLE 7086

St. Stephens Hospital, *Fulham Road, S.W.10,* FLA 8161.

Province of Natal Centre, *Guildford Place, W.C.1,* CLE 7086.

North Kensington Marriage Welfare Centre, *12 Telford Road, Ladbroke Grove, W.10,* LAD 2532

Health Centre, *217 Lisson Grove, Marylebone, N.W.8,* PAD 8244

Westminster F.P.A. Clinic, *1 Bessborough Street,* TAT 9560

Times of clinics vary, so it is important to telephone before you go along.

2. At one time obvious deceits were practised on the Family Planning Association by the desperate. This is no longer necessary because unmarried girls are catered for by the good old Marie Stopes Memorial Clinic at 108 Whitfield Street, W.1 (EUS 4628). Believing that prevention is absolutely better than cure, they even equip the most alarmingly precocious teenage girls.

3. Doctors. National Health Service doctors are not DIRECTED to give contraceptive advice to anyone other than women whose health would be endangered by pregnancy. Some doctors are therefore not properly trained to give such advice, but there are many enlightened practitioners who both are and will. The usual fee is about 2 or 3 gns., plus the cost of the contraceptive prescribed. The best procedure is to get the telephone number and address of a doctor with a practice in the worldly West End, ring him up and make an appointment to see him as a private patient. It is as well to announce your purpose in coming to see him at that stage since he may be morally against the whole business or not qualified to advise you. Registers of doctors in all areas are kept by Public Libraries.

ABORTION

Abortion is, at the time of writing, absolutely illegal by statute law, though several precedents have been established in test cases for the abortion of pregnancies which are the result of rape, or which would seriously endanger the physical or mental health of the mother.

Abortions are therefore occasionally performed by doctors who think their action justifiable and who are prepared to face prosecution if necessary. But this is very rare. It is estimated—though quite how is not clear—that between 10,000 and 100,000 illegal abortions take place annually in conditions of varying safety.

The cost can be anything from £20 to £300 plus, depending upon whether it is a dangerous back-street operation performed by an unskilled para-medical exponent, or a proper surgical operation with good after-care.

In London anyone who wants an abortion can get one—provided they can face the round of enquiries necessary to locate an abortionist. There must be at least thirty practising abortionists in London, including one who offers a special students' rate. Most of them do it simply for the money, but there are a few who risk their livelihood occasionally in the belief that no woman should be obliged to bear a child which she does not want and which she has conceived involuntarily.

The most expensive kind of abortion is the sort where two or more doctors get together with two or more psychiatrists and jointly vouch for the necessity of the operation. Such abortions require the co-operation of successful or distinguished doctors and usually take place in hospitals or nursing homes. Debutantes traditionally go abroad, usually to Switzerland, either for an appendectomy or a rest.

ADOPTION

The demand for adoptive children is always very much greater than the supply. In London the best ways of setting about finding a child to adopt are through the Greater London Council Children's Committee, or through one of the following adoption societies:

(1) National Children's Adoption Association, *71 Knightsbridge, S.W.1*, BEL 6436

(2) The Church Adoption Society, *4a Bloomsbury Square, W.C.1*, HOL 3310

(3) The Crusade of Rescue Catholic Adoption Society, *73 St. Charles Square, W.10*, LAD 5305

(4) The National Children's Home, *85 Highbury Park, N.5*, CAN 2033

All these societies, particularly the religious ones, require that the child be brought up in the religion specified by the natural mother. Attempts are being made at the moment to set up an agnostic adoption society. Enquiries about this should be made to The Hon. Secretary, The Standing Committee of Societies Registered for Adoption, Gort Lodge, Petersham, Surrey.

SUCCESSFUL SICKNESS

National Health doctors are, by definition, underpaid, overworked, disgruntled and disenchanted. If you intend to make a practice of being seriously indisposed you should therefore find yourself an expensive Harley Street quack without delay. Unfortunately, since doctors are not allowed to advertise except inadvertently when treating Prime Ministers or royalty, no information can be provided here as to who is best for spleen and who for dyspepsia.

The only way to get undivided attention on National Health is to go down to the East India docks and contract a really obscure tropical disease. There is a danger of course that you may then languish undiagnosed in surgeries all over London, but there is a good chance that you will be transferred with your interesting symptoms to a Teaching Hospital. Here you will be feted and medicated, dieted and photographed within an inch, or possibly less, of your life.

If you really have got something wrong with you teaching hospitals are always best because these are where the top specialists are stationed. They are:

Middlesex Hospital, *Mortimer Street, W.1*
St. George's Hospital, *Hyde Park Corner, S.W.1*
University College Hospital, *Gower Street, W.C.1*
St. Thomas's Hospital, *S.E.1*
St. Bartholomew's Hospital, *W. Smithfield, E.C.1*
King's College Hospital, *Denmark Hill, S.E.5*

Ordinary citizens who go to hospital are usually put into wards with other citizens. If you want to be ill by yourself you can pay for a private ward at most hospitals, and some also have 'amenity wards' where you pay less and share with just one or two other people.

Undemocratic though it may appear, the private ward business does subsidise the National Health end. Private wards are specially posh at the Middlesex Hospital. Ultra posh is King Edward VII's Hospital for Officers, which has only 12 patients per doctor. There are fifty beds and forty top medicos in attendance. But you can only get in if you have been a *bona fide* officer *and* are a private patient of one of the forty doctors. The Queen Mother has been a patient here —because she is, for a start, commander-in-chief of sundry Highland regiments. A satisfied client of the Edward VII recently called it 'a very comfortable annexe to White's'.

The top nursing home is undoubtedly the London Clinic. You don't go there necessarily to get better—simply to recover in solicitous peace or decline gracefully in comfort. But it is much smoother, one understands, to die at Claridges. The London Clinic has 150 beds—a number that will be doubled when current re-building and extension is complete. Then even more film stars and deposed monarchs will regularly be featured in the press entering or leaving the clinic. When it was opened in 1932 The Duke of Atholl explained 'We are catering for the type of patients who would not go into hospital if they could possibly help it'.

HELP!

To avoid hospitalisation you may well need domestic help. This is hard to come by in London, and as hard to keep since competition for the services of good daily cleaners, housekeepers and cooks is keen.

Au pair girls are an answer of a sort, but it is important to make sure that no one takes advantage of anyone else in this rather loosely defined arrangement, the basis of which is that the girl should live as one of the family, if she can stand it, and should do no work that the mistress of the house would not undertake herself. Therefore, if you cannot run your household unaided, there is no reason to suppose that an eighteen-year-old Swedish girl, who has been seriously disturbed by a series of films about free love in her native land, will be able to do so. Allow your au pair girl a reasonable amount of free time before midnight, and do not tell her about The Rheingold Club 'where the unescorted girl can feel completely at her ease . . .' (361 Oxford Street, W.1—MAY 5343). Find her either through the personal columns of newspapers or from:

(1) Au Pair International, *195 Greyhound Road, W.14*, FUL 0469
(2) British Continental Domestic Agency, *27 Old Bond Street, W.1*, HYD 2711

For cooks, cleaners, butlers and bottle-washers try:

(1) The Belgravia Agency, *35 Brompton Road, S.W.3*, KNI 4343
(2) Mrs. Lines, *165 Kensington High Street, W.8*, WES 4165
(3) The Mostyn Bureau, *52 Beauchamp Place, S.W.3*, KEN 5936

If you want living-in staff you haven't a hope unless you can provide them with their own TV set. Male cleaners are either a bit dainty or exceedingly thorough—try Domestics Unlimited, 426 Harrow Road (CUN 0461). Their men cost 6s. 6d. an hour (sixpence above par) and work for periods of not less than four hours at a stretch.

In cases of emergency or idleness, food can be delivered to you, pre-cooked and ready for consumption, by the Chicken Delivery Service, 50 Pembroke Road, W.8 (dial CHICKEN or CHI 2536). Cook and Butler will also cater for you, either cooking on your premises or their own at 75/77 Church Road, Teddington, Middlesex (TED 3932).

If you cannot find a soppy girl to do some free baby-sitting for you, you will need either:

(1) Babyminder's Babysitting Service, *88 George Street, W.1,* WEL 3515

They charge 5s. the first time you use them, plus 5s. 6d. an hour in the evening, or 5s. during the day.

(2) Universal Aunts Ltd., *36 Walpole Street, S.W.3,* SLO 9834

This stalwart body of women will provide all kinds of help, from baby-sitting (3s. 6d. per hour for a minimum period of three hours, 4s. per hour in the evening, and 5s. per hour after midnight) to finding you a cook or to doing your mending.

Now that your household is fully equipped with au pair girls, male cleaners, and Universal Aunts, you will need to find something to do. You could go out and spend some money.

SHOPS EVERYONE SHOULD KNOW ABOUT

1. *Snob Shopping.* Harrods and Fortnum & Mason are the two smartest shops in London and a certain amount of lifemanship is necessary in broaching them successfully.

Do not attempt to buy anything more than a small jar of beef extract or a packet of hairpins at your first visits. Shop assistants at both are either very snotty and offhand, or staggeringly servile and obliging.

It is vital to establish at the outset that you are not someone to be trifled with. It is sad, but true, that to get any kind of service you will probably have to transform yourself into a Grande Dame. Unless you have the sheer moral courage and dramatic talent to try on half-a-dozen 'model gowns' at Harrods and then sweep out of the department announcing that it really has deteriorated beyond belief in recent years—you are not in quite the right league for this kind of shopping.

However, both Harrods and Fortnums have excellent greed-food halls where you can buy, should occasion arise, brandied peaches and tinned whole pheasants in aspic. Fortnums has a jolly restaurant where you can have tea without being kicked to death by the populace, and Harrods has a superb assignation centre in their Banking Hall—a lot of back-to-back leather sofas occupied by mysterious people reading *The Listener.*

2. *Wine.* The Army & Navy Stores were founded in 1871 by a group of Army officers who formed themselves into a co-operative to buy wine more cheaply. The Army & Navy is today the largest retail wine store in Britain with over half a million bottles in stock. Should you feel a need to order intoxicants, or anything else, in the

middle of the night, you can telephone your instructions to their ever-open recording machine (VIC 1234).

3. *Household Equipment and Furniture.* Selfridges (England's answer to Macy's) has a household basement where you will find every conceivable aid to doing-it-yourself. If you want luminous plastic tiles for the boudoir ceiling, they've probably got them.

The best shops in London for contemporary (for lack of a better word) furniture are Heals (Tottenham Court Road) and Habitat (Fulham Road). Habitat tends to be pricey—a couch constructed on the same general lines as a treble deck-chair can set you back something horrible.

Heals are super for modern foreign furniture in particular, and for incidental furnishings, linens, kitchen equipment, glass and china.

Libertys (Regent Street) are marvellous for all kinds of fabrics, furniture, china and glass. Specialised kitchen stuff—precision-built saucepans and stainless steel garlic crushers etc.—are best found at Staines (Victoria Street) or at one of the caterers' suppliers in Soho.

Peter Jones (Sloane Square) is where people go to buy not-too-vulgar gilt and marble-topped Italian occasional tables. Maples are best for beds and made-to measure-curtains. They are also excellent dexterous house-movers, and will pack and move every stick of furniture with a minimum of agony.

4. *Tweedy/Sports.* Simpsons, Lillywhites, Aquascutum, and Moss Bros. (who also hire clothes for special occasions) are the shops to patronise for sports equipment and clothing. They tend to be expensive, but everything is well made and top quality for staying power. Burberrys make deathless British mackintoshes for traditional continuous rain.

5. *Children's Clothes.* Unless you believe in buying real camel hair coats for children who are growing at the rate of at least three inches in all directions per year, Marks and Spencers are as good as anyone. Their children's clothes are often much prettier than those for adults, and they are just as well made and have good deep hems. Daniel Neal (Kensington High Street) have provided for generations of warmly lagged babies and young children. Kinch & Lack (Artillery Row) are the school uniform experts—but most schools specify exactly where your child's monster-gear is to be bought.

6. *Toys.* Harrods and Hamleys have between them got everything that any child, however acquisitive, destructive, or spoilt,could want. James Galt (30 Great Marlborough Street, W.1) have everything that any design-conscious progressive parent could want. Their toys tend to be made of wood and very educational.

CHOOSE YOUR CLUB

Men's clubs were first invented to provide an escape from the dim female domestic circle. They were then perpetuated as places where civilised men might do nothing at all in decent obscurity. Women can do nothing at home all day in private, so women's clubs have no real raison d'être other than their members' need to be sociable and busy—which is what makes them so alarming to the unclubbable.

Clubwomanship is by no means as developed an art in this country as it is in America. The American Woman's Club, 1 Cadogan Gardens, S.W.1 (SLO 2033), provides for professionals in exile.

In country areas of Britain there is, always, The Women's Institute, which tirelessly organises jam-making competitions, whist drives, jumble sales and garden fetes until no one has a blank date in her Women's Institute Diary.

The Townswomen's Guild (2 Cromwell Place, S.W.7—KEN 8817) is the urban equivalent of all this. The Guild was evolved from the Kensington Ladies Society in 1929 and had then as its immediate object the education of women as citizens. Evidently there were then, despite the suffragettes, a lot of women who did not realise that they were not obliged to vote as directed by their husbands, fathers or brothers. The Townswomen's Guild is fairly earnest still, but intelligent and even sophisticated in educational matters. If you ever see a large party of women in hats going round a museum en masse do not be alarmed—it is probably just the Guild improving its collective cultural awareness.

If you would rather do something less cerebral, try The Women's League of Health and Beauty. They meet weekly in all parts of London and leap about to music in order to keep the body beautiful. Telephone STR 3577 or PER 9524 for details. Mums can join the country-wide Mother's Union (Mary Sumner House, Tufton Street, S.W.1 (ABB 4087). This Union is very concerned with the sanctity of marriage and matters of that ilk, so you can't join if you are divorced.

A club with its own premises and residential 'overnight' facilities is The Forum (42 Belgrave Square, S.W.1 (BEL 7383). Membership is 18 gns a year, with reductions for country and evening members. It is largely for professional women and has very active art, literary, archaeological, photographic and dramatic groups.

There is a Lady Golfers' Club, 3 Whitehall Court, S.W.1 (WHI 3160) and a Women's Press Club, 52 Carey Street, W.C.2 (HOL 5437) and a University Women's Club, 2 Audley Square, W.1

(GRO 2268), but women have really nothing at all to equal the White's and Boodles.

You can sometimes become an 'associate member' of these strong-holds of St. James's—but you have to stay in your own annexed quarters and, as second-class citizens, receive directives of this nature: 'Wives of members may entertain guests in the ladies' annexe paying by vouchers signed by their husbands'.

In its clubland heart London remains determinedly masculine.

You get into less trouble with your illicit parking if you obtain (from any car hire firm) a Union Jack sticker inscribed 'Visitor to Britain'. Place it on your windscreen and assume a heavy Australian accent whenever challenged.

If you wish to avoid the expense of taking a nephew and his sixteen small friends to the Zoo in Regents Park (though possibly this could be accomplished by having previously made an appointment with the Head Keeper to discuss your donation of an elephant to the establishment) try them on Harrods (3rd Floor), the Battersea Dogs' Home and the Regent Pet Stores, Parkway, Camden Town.

You can send live bees, 'if in a suitable container', by post.

London has gradually become THE PLACE for men's clothes—even in the eyes of continental glossies and Time Magazine. *Although elegant ex-monarchs have always come to London for quietly hand-made clothes, it is only recently that the exploding teenage market and the world of pop have injected the necessary vitality and unabashed dress-consciousness to make London the shopping centre, too, of the youthful gods of today. While new shops open every week with startling displays of extravaganza (and only a few close), the older firms watch and slowly incorporate the more lasting innovations.*

The following can be no more than a rough guide to a rapidly changing scene where, surprisingly, quality is still considered to be as important as style.

TAILORS (listed in order of expense)

H. HUNTSMAN & SONS, 11 Savile Row, W.1
London's most expensive tailor still specializes in country wear. Basic riding breeches about £45, nylon from £35, buckskin about £110 (a collector's item). Three-piece Town suits cost about £100, jackets £70, trousers £30, dinner jacket and trousers about £150. A very traditional tailor. Huntsman also make shirts.

KILGOUR, FRENCH & STANBURY, 33a Dover Street, W.1
Traditional, but they pride themselves on their modern outlook. Suits from about £80, jackets £55, trousers £26. Dinner jacket and trousers about £100.

BLADES, 25 Dover Street, W.1
A young man's tailor. The more unusual your demands, the more they will like you, but everything is beautifully cut. Suits from about £70 gns., jackets 47 gns., trousers 22 gns., dinner jackets (without trousers) from about 57 gns.

LESLIE & ROBERTS, 16 St. George Street, W.1
Traditional. Don't like publicity of this sort.

D

DENMAN & GODDARD, 31 Sackville Street, W.1
Another traditional tailor who is prepared to experiment. Responsible for Lord Snowdon's plus-twos. Considerable discount for prompt payment. Suits from about £63, jackets £30, trousers £19, dinner jacket and trousers from about 75 gns.

G. WELCHMAN, 25 Sackville Street, W.1
The winner in 1966 of both the Silk and Terylene Trophies. Suits from £54, jackets £30, trousers 8 gns., dinner jacket and trousers from about £60. Recommended even by other tailors.

N. H. CHAPMAN, 54 Piccadilly, W.1
A reliable tailor, who will make anything you ask for at a more reasonable price than most. Suits from 50 gns., jackets 35 gns., trousers 16 gns., dinner jacket and trousers from about 55 gns.

TAILORING CHAINS

LEW ROSE, 39 Savile Row and branches throughout greater London
Specializes in hand tailoring at modest prices. For people in a hurry they operate a 48 hour service. Nothing ready-made. Will try anything the customer wants. Suits from 22 gns., jackets from 16 gns., trousers from 8 gns.

NEVILLE REED, Strand and branches
Pierre Cardin designs for Neville Reed, both ready-made and styles for made-to-measure suits which start at about £20.

HEPWORTH, branches throughout London and England
A chain of ready-made stores with large tailoring departments. Suits from £12 15s. 0d., jackets from £7 9s. 6d., trousers from £4. For Hardy Amies styling on a suit you pay about £3 more.

MONTAGUE BURTON, branches throughout London and England
Another ready-made chain, but the largest of their business is made-to-measure tailoring. Recently, *Which* Consumer Guide decided that for value for money the customer should go either to one of the established 'Savile Row' tailors or to Burton's. Suits from about £10, jackets and trousers from £6.

SHOPS AND SPECIALIZED TAILORING

DOUG HAYWARD, FUL 6179

Mr. Hayward comes to you for fittings. His clients are well-groomed actors and socialites. Often he is too busy to take new customers but, if you hit a lucky day, you can be sure of having one of the smartest suits anywhere beautifully hand-tailored from about 60 gns.

JOHN MICHAEL, Old Compton Street and branches

Suits from 55 gns., jackets from 38 gns., trousers 18 gns.

SIMON SHOP, 341 King's Road

Designed and fitted at the shop, made in Savile Row, suits are from 40 gns., jackets from 28 gns., trousers from 8 gns. Highly individual dinner jackets and trousers from 80 gns. Simon Boyle also plans to make shoes and shirts.

ALAN SIEVEWRIGHT, BAY 2820

A theatrical designer who was commissioned by P. J. Proby to make a set of clothes for his American tour. You can go to him at 19 Hyde Park Square, or he will come to you. Severe styles in exotic cloths. Day suits from about 35 gns., evening outfits from 70 gns.

HUNG ON YOU, 22 Cate Street
Michael Rainey or Christopher Lynch will design you a suit in olive velveteen or forties stripes which will be made up in ten days. Also more conventional materials. Mick Jagger and others buy their suits from 35 gns., jackets from 20 gns., trousers from 8 gns.

JOHN STEPHEN CUSTOM BUILT, Carnaby Street
Dormeuil suits from about 37 gns., jackets 18 gns., trousers 8 gns. Dinner jacket and trousers about 50 gns. A gold lame leather jacket, worn with suede trousers, costs 50 gns.

MARC SAVILLE, 2 Wetherby Place, Hereford Square, S.W.7. FRE 5909
Make suits for about £30 for anybody from M.Ps to pop singers. Like particularly people who know exactly what they want, whatever it might be.

PAUL'S MALE BOUTIQUE, Carnaby Street
Suits from 27 gns., jackets from 12 gns, trousers from £5.

OFF THE PEG (alphabetically)
Several of the following shops have tailoring departments. Some sell exclusively men's clothes: some are menswear departments in large stores. The standards in all are high and the prices for articles of the same quality vary little from shop to shop, though some have a wider price range.

AQUASCUTUM, Regent Street
Stock all menswear. The widest price range. (Also manufacturers for many of the following.)

AUSTIN REED, Regent Street and branches
Stock all menswear.
On the third floor at Regent Street is the *Cue Shop* for younger tastes.

BURBERRYS, Haymarket
Stock all menswear. A famous name but on the dull side.

CECIL GEE, Shaftesbury Avenue and branches
Stock all menswear. Continental flavour.

FORTNUM AND MASON, Piccadilly
Stock all menswear. Expensive. Small selection.

HARRODS, Brompton Road
Stock all menswear. Uninspired department for small boys.

HECTOR POWE, Regent Street and branches
Stock all menswear. Cheaper than the rest of Regent Street.

JAEGER, Regent Street and branches
One of the best shops in London for trousers, jackets and suits. Also
sell shirts, woollies and ties.

JOHN MICHAEL, Savile Row and branches
(Also own SPORTIQUE and GUY shops)
Stock all menswear including fancy underpants and fur-lined suede
coats. Smart but not cheap.

JOHN STEPHEN, Carnaby Street and branches
(Also own HIS CLOTHES, ADAM W.1, MALE W.1, DOMINO MALE,
THE MAN'S SHOP, VILLAGE STORE and TEEN STORE)
Lower priced. The accent is on style rather than durability. Excellent
for trousers, summer and winter. They stock everything the young
in taste could want.

LIBERTY, Regent Street
Stock all menswear. Amusing ties.

LILLYWHITES, Piccadilly Circus and Sloane Street
Specialize in sportswear. Occasionally have unusual suede coats.

MARSHALL AND SNELGROVE, Oxford Street
Stock all menswear. Good English suits for teenagers.

MILORD, Denman Street
All imported. Stock everything except suits.

PAUL'S MALE BOUTIQUE, Carnaby Street
Again for a younger market and cheaper. All clothes, well-made
and imaginative.

SIMPSONS, Piccadilly
Stock all menswear. Good ski clothes. TREND department keeps an eye on new developments.

SMART WESTON, Coventry Street and branches
Stock all menswear. Continental-looking and a little cheaper. Vast selection of trousers.

WOOLLANDS, Knightsbridge
Stock all menswear. Excellent woollies.

WAY OUT
GRANNY TAKES A TRIP, World's End
Design their own shirts and trousers. Small selection of cleaned and darned exotica.

HUNG ON YOU, Cale Street
Messrs. Rainey and Lynch design shirts, trousers, jackets and suits. Probably the most original ready-made clothes in London.

JUST MEN, Tyron Street (off the King's Road)
Shirts, trousers, jackets and suits moving towards the way-out. Pretty watch straps.

WOOLLIES
Burlington Arcade
Between here and BILL, in Bond Street, the lushest display of cashmeres, etc., in London. Conveniently near for checking colours and prices, which vary little, try NOBLE JONES and FISHERS.

WESTAWAY & WESTAWAY (29 Bloomsbury Way, W.C.1) are cheaper. The largest selection of woollies under one roof. Frequently 'discovered' by French magazines. Cashmere sweaters from £6 15s. 0d., Shetland from £3 10s. 0d., Lambswool from £2 19s. 6d. Westaway and Westaway are also the Scots Specialist. Men's hip length tartan shirts (pure wool) at £2 19s. 6d. Tartan socks, scarves, ties and full dress kilts from 14 gns. If they don't have what you want, they'll send it.

MARKS & SPENCER. Sometimes worth a visit, but they have their drab periods. New lines are tried out in their Oxford Street branch (Marble Arch end). Long-lasting pullovers from about £2, cardigans from £3.

JOHN MICHAEL shops have fairly expensive imported Italian sweaters. So do MILORD.

SIMPSONS and LIBERTY are good places for the January sales.

WOOLLANDS have a wide selection, some imported.

SHIRTS
Made-to-Measure

Made-to-measure shirts start from about £6 in poplin, £9 in silk at JOHN ERICSON, TURNBULL & ASSER and HARVIE AND HUDSON, all in Jermyn Street. HAWES & CURTIS in Burlington Gardens is a little more expensive. All three shops have ready-made shirts at about £2 less.

AUSTIN REED have a shirt-making department at their Regent Street and Knightsbridge branches where poplin shirts are from £5, silk from about £10.

A small plaque in a doorway near the Flamingo Club in Wardour Street betrays the whereabouts of PHILIP STEVENS, formerly the STAR SHIRT CO.—prospective clients should be, somehow, stars.

Ready-made

All the recommended stores have shirt departments. The most interesting are JAEGER, LIBERTY, AQUASCUTUM, and WOOLLANDS. The CUE SHOP at Austin Reed has an American-Nordic flavour. LILLYWHITES for sporty people.

In Carnaby Street, the JOHN STEPHEN shops and PAUL'S MALE BOUTIQUE have bright young shirts at most prices. ROGER ROGER (corner of Brewer Street and Wardour Street) specializes in eye-catchers. Not too expensive.

JOHN MICHAEL has its own range of shirts at and from 4 gns. Italian evening shirts are from 13 gns. This firm is also the sole agent for Gant's American button-down shirts.

MILORD (Denman Street) have a large selection of imported shirts —mainly Italian. (Here you can have coffee and look at the antiques while you shop. Everything is for sale.)

THE WESTERN SHOP (owned by John Michael, in Old Compton Street). Denim and flowered shirts by Levi. All western gear.

If you must have a shirt that is really different, the following shops are recommended:

HUNG ON YOU (Cale Street) about 6 gns. Exotic evening shirts from 11 gns.

JUST MEN (Tyron Street, off the King's Road, Chelsea) £4.
GRANNY TAKES A TRIP (World's End) 4-5 gns.
All three firms design their shirts against, or in excess of current trends and have them made up accordingly.

SHOES
Made-to-Measure
JOHN LOBB, St. James's Street
World-famous shoemakers. Plain Town shoes from 33 gns., brogues from 34 gns., riding boots from 56 gns. More expensive are crocodile or ostrich from about 60 gns.

NIKOLAUS TUCZEK, Clifford Street
Will undertake to make any shoe you ask for although they feel happier with more traditional footwear. Town shoes from £26, riding boots from £50.

ANELLO AND DAVIDE, Charing Cross Road
Theatrical shoemakers who will make you boots in any style, starting from about 8 gns. for a plain boot to the knee.

MR. CLEVERLEY, HOW 5932
For the exclusive services of Mr. Cleverley—he comes to you—it is essential to have a personal introduction.

Ready-made
More expensive English shoes are found in JERMYN STREET or CHURCH in the Burlington Arcade.
RUSSELL AND BROMLEY (they have a branch in Bond Street) also have an English look.
Most shops who import costlier shoes have a branch in BOND STREET: BALLY are Swiss and smart; for the rest the influence is mainly Italian, some French—ELLIOTT, JOHN MICHAEL, RAOUL and PINET.
The cheaper shoe chains have branches in OXFORD STREET. Try DOLCIS or MANFIELD.
Younger and more unusual shoes are found at TOPPER, RAVEL and (again) RAOUL, who all have branches in Carnaby Street and Soho.
Excellent BALLET SHOES are made by GAMBA at the corner of Dean Street and Old Compton Street.

MISCELLANEOUS
Camping and Tough Outdoors
MILLETTS (Victoria) Ltd. Wilton Road and branches.

Wide selections of rougher clothes in denim, oilskin, corduroy etc.

WARD, BRANDON AND SONS (see under Jeans).

Fancy Dress
M. BERMAN (ring first to find which branch you need) and L. AND H. NATHAN in Drury Lane hire costumes by the week.

Hats
JAMES LOCK in St. James's Street is probably the best known London hatter.

For pop, leather or fur, try Carnaby Street or MILORD in Denman Street.

Hermes
In Jermyn Street. Expensive ties and cufflinks.

Hire
ALKIT of Cambridge Circus and MOSS BROS. of Covent Garden have large hire departments to cover most occasions.

Jeans
Levis—blue, white and otherwise—are stocked by John Michael shops: GUY, SPORTIQUE and THE WESTERN SHOP. Also WARD, BRANDON AND SONS at 571 Kings Road (past World's End). Large selections, too, of donkey jackets, tough shirts and trousers.

Leather
CECIL GEE have a LEATHER SHOP in Shaftesbury Avenue. Most of the department stores have a few leather and suede coats—particularly try AUSTIN REED and LILLYWHITES. CARNABY STREET and ROGER ROGER have coats, jackets, and trousers.

For motor-cycling equipment try MILLETTS.

Trusses etc.
The largest display of this type of paraphernalia is to be found in the CHARING CROSS ROAD.

Pyjamas, Socks and Underwear
For silk pyjamas and socks try the more expensive hosiers—in

MEN'S CLOTHES

JERMYN STREET, BOND STREET and the BURLINGTON ARCADE. MARKS AND SPENCER have sensible and hard-wearing pyjamas, socks and underwear.

JOHN MICHAEL have flannel nightshirts and brightly coloured Eminence type underpants.

CARNABY STREET, too, offers briefer underwear in most colours.

WESTAWAY AND WESTAWAY have tartan socks and stockings.

Western

THE WESTERN SHOP (Old Compton Street) has most western gear, including a range of suede trousers.

Innocent Pleasures

Innocence is a matter of opinion. Pleasure is a matter of taste. But there are everyman pleasures which everyone, some time, some day, feels like enjoying. Like a walk in the park, or a day at the sea.

Sunday is the day for innocent pleasures, for that is the day most people want to get away, to the countryside, to a stately home, to an amusing entertainment, to an open park, or just to somewhere nice.

There's Sunday in London at the Maritime Museum. Or Sunday out of London at a Benedictine Monastery. Do pleasures come more innocent than that?

How to travel on Sunday. What to look at, listen to or take part in. What to do with children. Where to eat. And for the big day-out, where to go.

Transport

Travelling at the week-end, especially on a Sunday, can be a delight. It can also be a pleasure in itself.

BUS TOURS

Buses gad about at the week-end with a life of their own, a *joie de vivre* springing from the end of a week's tension in City jams. Return to childhood and for six shillings have a day's unlimited travel on a red bus. You ask for a Red Rover. Children 3s. A book called *London from a Bus Top* can be got from London Transport, 55 Broadway, Westminster, S.W.1, free.

SIGHTSEEING COACHES

For 5s. you have a two-hour trip, leaving from Buckingham Palace Road, Victoria, near Eccleston Bridge. Every hour from 11 a.m. to 5 p.m. but not at one o'clock because that's lunchtime.

USE BUSES

to tour the City on your own. So much to see and do if you love old London. City of London Information Centre, St. Paul's Churchyard, E.C.4, give it to you straight. Obvious place to see, the Guildhall, where even in this day and age people like de Gaulle are entertained with unthought-of pomp and splendour. No wonder foreign heads of state have such a funny idea about us. Climb the Monument, standing on the site where the Great Fire of London started.

A BUS OR TUBE

will take you to London's enormous Sunday morning market. Firstly, Petticoat Lane, which includes the roads around Middlesex Street, a noisy chaos of stalls and shops, with Pearly Kings and Queens parading. Other streets nearby are equally exciting and should be looked for. Club Row in Bethnal Green Road for pets of all kinds. Cheshire Street for junk and bedding. And further away, East Street, E.17, with its 'Lanes', a quieter, more characterful place than Petticoat Lane.

TIME TO TAKE TO THE WATER

The best thing to do is to get British Travel and Holidays' booklet *London from the River*, MAY 9191, or write to them at 64 St. James's Street, S.W.1. There are trips up and down the river from many points—to Greenwich downriver, and Richmond upriver are the more popular ones. See where the servants of the king chained the prisoners at low tide and other amusing historical places.

GO IN A BOAT TO THE SEASIDE

Yes. All the way to Southend on Eagle Steamers (MIN 4451), sailing from Tower Hill, E.C.3. Day return—a guinea. Or go barging about through canal backwaters in secret wooden ways from Little Venice (back of Paddington Station) past the Regents Park Zoo. Ring CUN 3428. Four bob a nob. Children two bob.

Sunday Entertainment

Because of people like the Lord's Day Observance Society, pleasures *have* to be pretty innocent on a Sunday. But there are many to choose from. So why not . . .

WANDER ROUND THE ART GALLERIES

on a Sunday. Apart from the obvious ones, the National Gallery and the Tate Gallery (which house the most representative selection of national treasures) there is the National Portrait Gallery, which is just round the corner from the National Gallery in St. Martin's Place, W.C.2. Not the paintings but the painted are of interest here (2 p.m. to 6 p.m.).

Courtauld Institute Galleries, Woburn Square, W.C.1 contains many famous impressionist paintings, including Van Gogh's self-portrait with ear cut off.

The Queen's Gallery, Buckingham Palace Road, S.W.1, has changing exhibitions of paintings belonging to the Queen but merely to visit the place is of interest. Open 2 p.m. to 5 p.m. (2s. 6d. admission).

Royal Academy in Piccadilly, 2 p.m. to 6 p.m. from May to August for their Summer Exhibition, which improves every year, but still has some way to go. That is to say, when all the top British artists consent to be hung there.

Whitechapel Art Gallery, High Street, E.1, 2 p.m. to 6 p.m., is an enterprising, modern gallery for special exhibitions.

London's first public art gallery was *Dulwich College Picture Gallery*, College Road, S.E.21, 2 p.m. to 6 p.m., May to August, and makes a nice day out because of the setting and the walk through the park to get to it.

Hampton Court Palace recreates an era of history with its collection, notably Sir Peter Lely's portraits of Charles II's friends, mostly female.

OR WONDER AT THE OPEN-AIR ART

At Hampstead from 10 a.m. to 8 p.m. June, July and August. Unkind comments are usually overheard by the artists standing near. They find therapeutic satisfaction in talking about their work, and don't mind if you don't buy their paintings as long as you like them. At the top of Heath Street, by Whitestone Pond.

For a fortnight in May, Victoria Embankment Gardens. And on Sundays there are ad hoc exhibitions on the railings in Piccadilly by Green Park, and in Bayswater Road near Notting Hill. Like Speaker's Corner, they just happened, but they are not officially approved of by police.

LISTEN TO CONCERTS

A magazine called *This Month* in London is necessary equipment. Available from British Travel and Holidays Association, 64 St. James's Street, W.1. The Royal Festival Hall is an acoustical pleasure and Sunday is a good day to go. Two concerts usually, 3 p.m. and 7.30 p.m. There's always something on in the Albert Hall, but the cheapest seat may put you in a block of warped sound reception. The ticket people know, so ask them. Kenwood open-air concerts are delightful, though the fact that they play from across the water gives an optical illusion that they are farther off than they are. Holland Park is a lovely setting for the occasional symphony. The G.L.C. booklet *Open Air Entertainments* gives details of these and other concerts.

TRY TO LISTEN TO POP MUSIC CONCERTS
Prince of Wales Theatre, Coventry Street, W.1. A spot for the socially curious. If you can get in. And if you can bear the noise when you do.

TAKE IN JAZZ
Ronnie Scott's, 39 Gerrard Street, and the Marquee, 156 Oxford Street. From 7.30 p.m.

OR JUST LISTEN TO THE BAND
Traditional afternoon pleasure, musical wallpaper to a walk in the Park. Don't go specially to find them. Let them happen on you, strains beyond the trees. Walk closer, but not too near. The Royal Parks perhaps have a higher standard of playing (times on a notice-board at the entrance) but does the standard matter, filtered through half a mile of woodland?

GET YOUR KNEES UP TO MUSIC HALL
Sunday evenings at Windsor Castle, 309 Harrow Road, W.9 (CUN 1063). Relics from the old Metropolitan Music Hall in Edgware Road give authentic flavour.

GO TO THE THEATRE
Royal Court Theatre, Sloane Square, where the English Stage Society put on new plays (SLO 2273). Membership a guinea a year. Or the Unity, Goldrington Street, N.W.1 (EUS 5391).

WATCH A FILM
National Film Theatre, South Bank, S.E.1 (WAT 3232) is worth joining as a member. Get their programmes sent to you. Shows at 4 p.m., 6.15 p.m. and 8.30 p.m. for enthusiasts, because you have to queue for anything good. Arts Theatre Club (3 gns. a year membership) is at 6 Great Newport Street, W.C.2 (TEM 7541). They show films from 2.30 p.m. on Sunday which have not been censored by Lord Cobbold.

GO DANCING
Hammersmith Palais and the Empire Ballroom, Leicester Square for students of the social scene. A session at 3 p.m., another one at 7.30 p.m. Or a tea-dance at the Linguists Club perhaps, 20 Grosvenor Place, S.W.1. (But it's 7 gns. a year.)

GO FISHING
You need *Fishing for Londoners*, 2s. 6d., with lists of reservoirs, rivers, etc. for details. Pleasant spots at Pen Ponds, Richmond, Osterley Park, Bushey Park, Hampton Court, Battersea Park.

PLAY SPORT
List of London activities from Central Council of Physical Recreation, 6 Bedford Square, W.C.1. There are 200-odd organisations they can put you in touch with.

With Children in Mind

VISIT THE DOLL'S MUSEUM
and Hospital, 114 Glenthorne Road, Hammersmith, W.6, 12 p.m. to 6 p.m. There are 500 dolls in Barry Elders Museum and Hospital. A place of extraordinary devotion.

TAKE THEM TO MADAME TUSSAUD'S
Marylebone Road, N.W.1, by Baker Street tube station, 10 a.m. to 7 p.m. Lifeless heads in wax of lifeless people? Size is the extraordinary thing. Can Shastri be so small, de Gaulle so tall? Intimate insight into Royal Family.

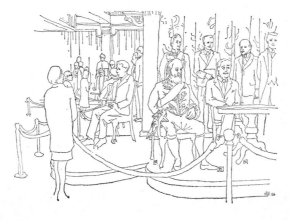

SPEND AN AFTERNOON AT THE MARIONETTE THEATRE
Friends of the Little Angel Club, 14 Dagmar Passage, Cross Street, N.1 (CAN 1787). Membership 5s., Sunday shows at 3 p.m. Show costs 3s. 6d. for children, 5s. adults.

TAKE SOPHISTICATED CHILDREN TO THE PLANETARIUM
Next to Madame Tussaud's, by Baker Street tube station, 10 a.m. to 7 p.m. Sends you into a reverie about the vastness of things as the different night sky changes above your head. Same effect on some people as a very tragic play. But jolly good and instructional for children, they say.

TAKE COUNTRY CHILDREN
to see sophisticated London pigeons in Trafalgar Square. Hitchcock's film, *The Birds*, could have germinated here. The fat, plump birds can hardly get off the ground as you walk through them. You can find more normal pigeons in Sloane Square. The difference between battery birds and free-range.

IF YOU HAVEN'T
any children perhaps you could borrow some from Dr. Barnardo's Houses (STE 3400). But they need to get to know you. Start by helping about the place at Sunday tea-time.

Eating on a Sunday
can be a problem, if you don't know what's open.

BREAKFAST
Victoria Station's Chicken Inn opens at 5.30 a.m. Sunday morning. Not early enough? West London Air Terminal, in Cromwell Road, a quiet triumph in modern architecture, is open round the clock.

LUNCH
You'll see a few faces that seem vaguely familiar if you go to Lyons Carvery in the Strand, near Trafalgar Square, for lunch. Television stars? Yes. And isn't that the whole Charles Greville column. All six of them. Help yourself and eat as much as you can but Lyons will still show a profit. The George and Dragon in Southwark is corny, and you may be stared at as typical Britons, but it really is very nice.

Bishop of Southwark sometimes turns up in his beautiful robes after matins or wherever it is he's been. Steak Houses are open on Sunday from 12 p.m. to remind you that anyone can cook a steak, but its nicer if someone else does.

DINNER

This calls for a trip to Soho. No need to name the dozens of Italian restaurants, and their veal and lasagne dishes must be tasted. A fine night for curry, preferably at the Star of India in Old Brompton Road, the Punjab in Monmouth Street, W.C.2. Chinese: the Lotus House, in Edgware Road, is where some of the famous go, and Fu Tong, 29 Kensington High Street, which has given birth to a cookery book on Chinese Food by Helen Burke. Chelsea is strong on the Oriental. No one needs to be reminded of the Savoy, White Tower, Tiberio and the Caprice, where the stars are patients to be nursed in Mario Gallati's bedside manner. Quentin Crewe in *Queen* magazine is a sure guide to the top places, often rude, usually just, with an infinite capacity for pleasure.

SUNDAY MONEY

on the other hand, may well be a bigger problem. If you can't get in on a bank raid, most of which take place early on Sunday morning, it's worth knowing that Dorfman's Bank, 70 Park Lane (GRO 1891) has a 24-hour service, and will actually cash cheques if you have the suitable identification. But in advance first fill in one of their forms which they will clear with your own bank. They change travellers' cheques, foreign money, too.

For the Real Bumper Day Out

here are some of the places you must visit. Unlike any other British city, London itself is packed with parks, all with excellent facilities. But there are scores of other parks, stately homes, museums and places of interest not far away. Most of them for free.

ALEXANDRA PALACE

Here are 280 acres of parkland on high ground, near Wood Green. Entertaining on a Sunday evening with plenty of life. A lake to fish in all day. And Britain's best roller skating rink which doesn't open till 7 p.m. (until 10.30 p.m.).

AVERY HILL
Tropical and sub-tropical plants second only to Kew Gardens. Hibiscus from Asia, red-hot cats' tails from Guinea, Australian acacia and wattles, South African humming bird flowers. 11 a.m. to 5 p.m. in April to September. 1 p.m. to 4 p.m. rest of year.

BATTERSEA PARK
Does the idea of the Fun Fair put some people off? And the gas works. A pity, because the Park has a natural English-style beauty with a rocky, winding walk under hanging trees round a waterbird lake. Botanical garden and a wild garden.

BEACONSFIELD MODEL VILLAGE
sheer wonder for children.

BETHNAL GREEN MUSEUM
Cambridge Heath Road, E.2 (ADV 2415), dolls' houses and dolls as you never knew existed, in interesting metal and glass building of Crystal Palace vintage, 2.30 p.m. to 6 p.m.

BRITISH MUSEUM
Great Russell Street. It's not the place for half an hour's stroll, but a week's gaping. The *British Museum Guide* lists some of the more impressive objects they have cunningly acquired. Sir Frank Francis, the head, is a bibliophile, and has his eye on future collections he hopes the Museum may inherit. That's how it works. And he can justify our keeping of the Elgin marbles, a part of the Parthenon you won't see when you go to Athens. Houses the Magna Carta. Surprising how many people haven't been there and it's fun for all the family. 2.30 p.m. to 6 p.m.

BROCKWELL PARK
A mile west of Dulwich Park. Great natural beauty. It has an Old English Garden, very Stratford-on-Avonish with its clipped yew hedges. It was the former kitchen garden of the mansion.

CLIVEDEN
Near Maidenhead. A branch of the Astors lives in Palladian-style in a home in a beautiful setting by the Thames. House and Grounds, August 17th to September 22nd, 2.30 p.m. to 5.30 p.m. A swimming-pool here, the scene of one of the most famous parties of the 'sixties.

COMMONWEALTH INSTITUTE

Kensington High Street, W.8, is a superb modern building and not a modern matchbox on its side. Its pleasing outside lines are continued roomily inside, and all the countries of the Commonwealth have their own exciting displays, and a gallery with splendid examples of Commonwealth art.

CRYSTAL PALACE

The park is the headquarters of the National Recretaion Centre. They have a ski-ing slope made of nylon brushes. (Crystal Palace Southern Region Station.) The children's area with zoo, rock and water garden, boating and fishing lake is also home for giant concrete dicynodonts, ichthysauruses, iguanadons, petrodactyls and a giant sloth. The life-size portrayals of early Crystal Palace don't quite satisfy the academicians in all respects, but they are pretty effective. The actual Crystal Palace burnt down in 1936, and one Fleet Street photographer late getting there got a picture of Winston Churchill in carpet slippers rushing out to see the fire, which was a great scoop.

DEVIL'S DYKE

Brighton. Brighton itself, of course, should not be missed. Only an hour from London, station to station. Afterwards, take a bus into the Downs, and then walk on the country's springiest turf, with a clean wind blowing up from the hazy blue sea.

DULWICH PARK

Acres of rhododendrons and azalea beds, and a rock and water garden. Late spring is the best time to see it.

GEFFRYE MUSEUM

Kingsland Road, E.2. 2 p.m. to 5 p.m. A look at real craftsmanship in furniture. Separate rooms trace the history of furniture from 1600 in every detail.

GOLDER'S HILL

A short walk from Golder's Green underground station. See the deer in natural setting of a typical English park. Other animals in pens. Charming flower garden with blossoming wisteria.

GREENWICH PARK

One of London's most beautiful views is from the Observatory.

down across a deep green wooded slope to the National Maritime Museum, a splendid white pillared palace of a place. Then, beyond it, the crowded river of the East End, and London roofs rolling away to St. Pauls. Exceptionally attractive flower garden to wander through. Bandstand, and the Observatory itself with astrolobes which are pure works of art in themselves, though mariners actually plotted courses by them. Stand with one foot in the Western Hemisphere, one in the Eastern. The Greenwich meridian line runs through here. The Maritime Museum is open 2.30 p.m. to 6 p.m. The *Cutty Sark* is at Greenwich, open 2.30 p.m. to 5 p.m. Blackheath itself is no more a heath, but a number of large greens bisected by toads. But you can stop your car to watch cricket on your weary way home.

HAINAULT FOREST

This is a fragment of the old Forest of Essex, Royal hunting ground. You get to it by tube to Hainault, then bus. Two golf courses occupy about a sixth of the total area, which gives you an idea of the size. You can see cross-country running here, fish in the lake (pike are numerous) or simply find a quiet undisturbed spot to picnic. About a quarter of it is thick woodland.

HAMPSTEAD HEATH

A marvellous piece of countryside contained by an affluent area of London, rolling hills and vales, and what appears to be a little hamlet nestling in one fold, The Vale of Heath. There is a lake here, a small one, where the Albert Brothers tried to fly a machine heavier than air. The year—1965. They failed. If you approach the Heath from Hampstead tube station, walk up the hill to Whitestone pond, where model enthusiasts sail their boats, and children have pony rides. You can fish in Hampstead Ponds, on the south side. Swim in Highgate Ponds on the north-east side. The traditional Hampstead fairs are at Easter, Whitsun and Bank Holiday weekends, and in spirit are closer to the pagan festivals than the Christian ones.

HAMPTON COURT

One of the country's loveliest show places, with gardens, palace and maze. Henry VIII hunted from here, but the Royal Palace was started by Cardinal Wolsey. May to September 11 a.m. to 6 p.m. March, April and October, 2 p.m. to 5 p.m. Rest of winter, 2 p.m. to 4 p.m.

HATFIELD HOUSE
Hatfield, Herts. Severely right-wing Lord Salisbury's home, June to October, 1 p.m. to 7 p.m. Henry VIII had it, and it's very beautiful. What more could you ask?

HEVER CASTLE
Edenbridge, Kent. April to October, 1 p.m. to 7 p.m. Ann Boleyn's former home, passed into the hands of the Astors. Castle, large lake, Italian gardens.

HOGARTH PRINTS
Where better than Hogarth's own house, Hogarth Lane, Chiswick, W.4. May to September, 2 p.m. to 6 p.m. Rest of year 2 p.m. to 4 p.m.

HOLLAND PARK
Kensington. Former estate of Holland House, and the charming layout of the garden is in Dutch style, full of secluded alcoves. Best in spring with the rhododendrons out.

HORNIMAN MUSEUM
London Road, Forest Hill, S.E.2, 2 p.m. to 6 p.m. A boy's encyclopaedia come to life. Birds, musical instruments, tribal costumes, weapons.

HYDE PARK
Speakers Corner starts from first light on a Sunday. Fun once, boring thereafter. But the park, with the Serpentine, riding in Rotten Row, gives it an amiable Sunday mood.

IMPERIAL WAR MUSEUM
Lambeth Road, S.E.1. War weapons right up to the last war, including flying bombs and submarine. Whatever your views on peace, a healthy, war-like boy should not be deprived of a visit here.

IVEAGH COLLECTION
Kenwood House, Hampstead Lane, N.W.3. A beautiful, much-looked-at house with library and orangery, and a touch of Adam. A Rembrandt self-portrait here. Poetry readings, Sunday concerts.

KENSINGTON GARDENS

The Round Pond to see some of the country's finest model boats. And sometimes in the distance, a little Royal child or two out with Nanny. You'll know when they're coming when you see their detective chasing a *Paris-Match* photographer with a telescopic camera.

KEW GARDENS

Britain's largest botanical gardens with huge houses of tropical and sub-tropical plants, rolling gardens with rhododendrons, and every sort of tree ever grown. Chinese pagoda. Kew Palace is a 17th-century Flemish-style building with some of George III's paraphernalia. April to September, 1 p.m. to 6 p.m.

LUTON HOO

Sir Harold Werner's home near Luton, Bedfordshire. Mid-April to end of September, 2 p.m. to 6 p.m. Impressive art collection in Adam house, worth revisiting.

MONKS

Most monasteries and nunneries welcome guests, for the day or to stay as long as you like, but it's best to write first—nicely—and ask if they will have you. No money necessary, just pay what you can afford.

The Association for Promoting Retreats, 23 Victoria Grove, London W.8, KNI 8952, will give you a list of Anglican places to stay at throughout the country.

Best and jolliest Roman Catholic monastery near London is Aylesford Abbey in Kent. Accommodation for up to 100 guests, family parties catered for.

Nashdom Abbey, near Slough, Bucks., is a very select, small C. of E. monastery. Good food, absolute peace, but accommodation for only ten guests at a time, until they build additions. Write to Brother Cuthbert, the guest master.

NATURAL HISTORY MUSEUM

Cromwell Road, South Kensington, S.W.7, 2.30 p.m. to 6 p.m. Everything to do with natural history, beautifully and clearly displayed. It has everything, including some impressive prehistoric skeletons.

PECKHAM RYE

Camberwell. American Garden, English Garden and Japanese Garden (red-hot pokers, roses and bamboos are the flags of the nations). Pleasant stream and water garden.

REGENTS PARK

The Zoo is all right, but a bit crowded on Sunday. Everyone comes to gape and criticise Lord Snowdon's birdcage ('That doesn't look like a birdcage') and to look with admiration at Sir Hugh Casson's elephant house. Having done that, it's off to the monkey house. But there is the Queen Mary Rose Garden and a boating lake. It's the best sizeable chunk of educated countryside in Central London. Splendid view of the Nash Terraces.

RAVENSCOURT PARK

Pensioners have formed a Rose Garden Club in honour of the displays. Pretty little place divided by hedges.

ST. JAMES'S PARK

The view from here towards Whitehall evokes Moscow and Turkey, and you feel proud it's British. It's a lovely park, with an enormous range of water birds. They can be watched at feeding time, 3 p.m.

SCIENCE MUSEUM

Exhibition Road, South Kensington, S.W.7, 2.30 p.m. to 6 p.m. With vintage cars, steam engines, a Glasgow tram, coaches, earliest electrical apparatus, telephones. Look for Shepherd's space capsule.

SYON HOUSE

at Brentford in Middlesex. Belongs to Duke of Northumberland. July to September, 1 p.m. to 5 p.m. Set in parkland near the Thames where you can repair to the London Apprentice afterwards. Interiors by Robert Adam at his best. Severely-cut lawns, stark in simplicity.

THE ROOKERY

Streatham Common. A rookery with a rockery, and miniature waterfall. Big grass lawns and stately cedars. Open-air theatre here in the summer, framed by a vast cedar.

TOWER OF LONDON

Tower Hill, E.C.3, 2 p.m. to 5 p.m. Crown Jewels, Bloody Tower, dungeons, miles of mailed armour, cutting swords and pikes. This symbol of awful power for centuries would today be described as a maximum security prison. In several centuries time, Durham Jail may enjoy similar reputation.

VICTORIA AND ALBERT MUSEUM
Cromwell Road, South Kensington, 2.30 p.m. to 6 p.m. In spite of its title which does sound forbidding, it is a very great place, stuffed absolutely full of historic works of art from all over the world. How we plundered those Indian and Burmese temples for the mighty Indian collection. Some of the figures are huge. The museum ranges all over the fine and applied arts.

VICTORIA PARK
Hackney. Greatest range of open-air sports north of the Thames. Speciality is the nursery, with 200,000 plants bedded out a year, and fine chrysanthemum house—a must for lovers of the bloom.

WALLACE COLLECTION
Manchester Square, 2 p.m. to 5 p.m. An interesting collection from a single family, strong on 18th-century French artists. Collection of priceless snuffboxes.

WATERLOW PARK
Not far from Hampstead Heath, the Highgate side. Buses from Archway tube station up the hill. One of London's pleasantest and least-known parks with its ponds, varieties of water-fowl, aviary, gardens, with a grass theatre in the summer. Twenty-six acres of beautiful trees on undulating ground.

WELLINGTON MUSEUM
Apsley House, 149 Piccadilly, W.1, 2.30 p.m. to 6 p.m. All the trappings of England's most-honoured leader. It was his house too. Number 1, London.

WEST WYCOMBE'S HELL FIRE CAVES
set fire to the imaginations. Nice to revel in the memories of orgies long-past.

WOOLWICH ROTUNDA MUSEUM
All the guns the Royal Artillery ever fired, and masses that they captured. Many of these oriental captures could take their place in a museum of art.

Statues

THE OLDEST STATUE in London is of King Alfred. For five centuries he occupied a niche at Westminster Hall. He now stands in marmoreal tranquillity in the centre of Trinity Square, Southwark, where he has been continuing his pale and ancient dreams since 1825. One of the most recent is Epstein's 'Pan', in Knightsbridge (above).

CHARLES I's statue by Hubert le Sueur on the south side of Trafalgar Square is not only artistically successful, it is also the earliest equestrian statue in London. During the Civil War the Roundheads sold it to a brazier, John Rivet, to break it up. The clever Mr. Rivet buried the statue instead and then set about making his fortune by selling souvenirs ostensibly cast from the bronze of Charles I. At the Restoration of the Monarchy he made himself a few more pennies by producing an undamaged monument to the late king and sold it to His Majesty's Government to be re-erected.

GEORGE I was not popular with his people, and his statues suffered for it. As fast as statues of the king were erected, the populace tore them up. One in Leicester Square was dragged from his horse and lynched (the horse was left untouched, for who in England would hurt a horse?). Another effigy in Grosvenor Square was destroyed. Therefore the King had himself hoisted out of reach—and almost out of sight—on top of the steeple of St. George's Church, Bloomsbury. Or perhaps he wanted to identify himself with the English dragon-fighting saint to improve his image.

A COMMENTATOR on London in the mid-nineteenth century complains bitterly of the absence of statues to poets, artists, musicians and philosophers. Evidently the authorities took this to heart and the rest of the century was a period of fervent poet-building. Soon there appeared Robert Burns on the Victoria Embankment, Byron in Park Lane; Leicester Square was populated with Isaac Newton, Hogarth, Joshuah Reynolds and Shakespeare. Milton arrived at Cripplegate, Doctor Johnson in the Strand. The pace quickened and in the hurry to erect more monuments to more artists they were commemorated in groups like communal weddings or war memorials; thus we have three poets in the poets' fountain and no less than fifty-two on the Albert Memorial in Kensington Gardens—plus similar numbers of artists and philosophers and musicians.

WILLIAM HUSKISSON, whose nearly naked form adorns Pimlico Gardens, owes his immortality to the fact that he was run over and killed by a train. Naturally, it was the first train, Stephenson's Rocket, that killed him, in the first railway accident. He was also a politician and mortal enemy of the Duke of Wellington, who chanced to be present when it happened.

A BEAUTIFUL STATUE and unique of that monarch is the one of James II near the National Gallery. It is the work of Grinling Gibbons and is an excellent example of the Roman-Emperor image which was the royal fashion in statuary and kingship in the seventeenty century. There is a companion statue of Charles II before Chelsea Hospital.

IN THE CHURCHYARD of St. Mary's Church, Aldermanbury, E.C. there is a memorial to John Hemyntes and Henry Cundell. To these two gentlemen, one theatre director, the other actor, William Shakespeare bequeathed 26s. 8d. 'To buy them rynges'. Their monument is surmounted by a bust of the bard.

THE MONUMENT to the Machine Gun Corps at Hyde Park Corner
has nothing to do with machine guns, it is a beautiful work by
F. Derwent Wood. The nude figure represents David leaning on
Goliath's sword.

THE STATUE OF GEORGE II as a Roman Warrior in Golden Square was originally at Canons, the seat of the Duke of Chandos. When this residence was demolished in 1747 and the contents sold, the auctioneer cunningly disposed of this cumbersome work at the tap of a hammer to an unwittingly nodding member of the crowd: 'Thank you, Sir. The statue of that excellent monarch is yours.' What else *could* the poor man do with such an immense work but give it to the public?

MRS. SARAH SIDDONS, immortalized in marble in Paddington Green was an actress of the eighteenth century. After her failure to make any impression on the London public, she went to play before provincial (and more naïve?) audiences, found herself fame, with which she returned to London, and fortune too.

WHY IS THERE a statue of Napoleon at the Royal Military Academy, Woolwich? (of all places!) Of course, it is Eugéne, Louis Jean Joseph Napoleon, the son of Emperor Napoleon III. The Imperial family came to England to live in exile when the young Prince, and heir to the French throne and Empire, was 14. He had a military training at Woolwich and was killed by Zulus on June 1, 1879 while in the service of a British expedition to Africa under Lord Chelmsford.

OPPOSITE THE SMITHFIELD Meat Market stands ancient St. Bartholo-mew's Hospital, founded in 1102 by Rahere. Henry VIII refounded the hospital in 1546 (perhaps in the event of 'one man's meat being another man's poison'). Over the splendid new (1702) gateway perches this promiscuous sovereign looking rather nervous and not at all virile . . . Or is he waiting for one of his wives to have a baby?

THE RATHER MYSTERIOUS and defaced statue in Soho Square, thought by some to be of Charles II, by others to be of James II, is probably of the Duke of Monmouth, bastard elder brother of James II. The square was once owned by and named after the Duke. After the defeat of his rebellion the square was renamed King's square. Later the name changed again; this time to Soho Square (Soho being the password used by Monmouth's supporters), popular arguments about the name evidently were the cause of the statue's mutilation.

WHAT HAS WATERLOO in common with Castor and Pollux? It is the immense figure of Achilles in Hyde Park, erected to the honour of the Duke of Wellington at the expense of his 'countrywomen'. This work sculpted by Sir Richard Westmacott is in fact a copy of one of two magnificent specimens of ancient art which now stand before the Papal palace in Rome. The Emperor Constantine had them brought from Alexandria for his bathroom. The works are attributed to no less a sculptor than Phidias. Neither of the statues represents Achilles. They are Castor and Pollux.

WHICH QUEEN is represented by the statue of a plump and portly lady in Queen's Square? Is it Queen Anne, after whom the square was named? Or it might be Queen Charlotte or Queen Caroline. It is certain that the statue was placed there long after the square was founded. Perhaps the statue is a synthesis of all three queens.

'*Peace in her Quadriga' by Adrian Jones, 1912.*
At the top of Constitution Hill

Speciality Services

Where and how to hire the simple sounding things, like butlers, baby-sitters, bagpipes, boy friends or boats. Or perhaps you want a nude, a juke box and a helicopter?

What do you do if you want to ski, to practise archery or go sailing? Which is the best Maternity Hospital or taxidermist?

Naturally, there eventually comes the time when you want to see some incunabulae, or tersichore and of course, find out about Xzit. You don't want to be caught short, do you?

ALLIGATORS
And other unusual pets from Harrods, Knightsbridge, S.W.1 (SLO 1234).

ANIMAL-CARE
Ring the Royal Society for the Prevention of Cruelty to Animals, WHI 7177, and they will advise on care of tortoises or giraffes and tell you what to do with them. The Blue Cross have an excellent emergency clinic in Victoria where you can take run-over pets at night. You have to sign an alarming document absolving them from responsibility if you leave them there, suggesting Dickensian sawbones treatment, but it's just a formality (VIC 5556).

ANSWERING SERVICES
How many times have you been given WEL 6655 as someone's number? Sort of familiar. Their answering service costs eight guineas a quarter, and they will accept calls for you over 24 hours. Specially good at dealing politely and firmly with people who are polite and firm in their efforts to get you.

ARTIST'S THINGS
It's the little things that stump you. Where to get a quill. Answer, Lechertier Barbe Ltd., 95 Jermyn Street, S.W.1 (WHI 2938), They are also the oldest artists' colourmen, established 1827. Pay a visit to Dryad's, 22 Bloomsbury Street, W.C.1 (MUS 0234) for country handicrafts equipment, weaving materials, pottery tools, coloured leather hides, miles of cheap, coloured hessian for dashing curtains.

BAGPIPES

From Henry Starck, 12 Kentish Town Road. Nice and old-fashioned so that you think of Queen Victoria's faithful servant Brown and *his* pipes.

BABY-SITTERS

You might take pot luck and go and look on the notice board of your nearest launderette. But to be sure of first-class nannies (who will soon inform you of the *important* people's children they have looked after) try Babyminders (WEL 3515), who charge 4s. 6d. an hour. Universal Aunts are highly polite and efficient, and not only supply baby-sitters but find secretaries, maids, home-help shoppers, and are interested in any sort of inquiry. What is comforting is that they have a doctor's scheme to cope with emergencies (SLO 9834). You could get an actress to baby-sit for you from CUN 0461 if you want to put your daughter on the stage.

BARREL ORGANS

Why not take one on a cruise down the Thames instead of a pop group? From Antonio Tomasso (PAL 4198). Cost two guineas a day. Ten tunes.

BICYCLING

The only way to beat rush-hour jams. So why don't more people hire them? Try Savile's Stores, 165 York Road, Battersea (BAT 4279). Cost 15s. a week.

BILLIARDS

There are 18 Temperance Halls, superbly equipped with dreamy squares of lawn green, where you can play. Ring MAC 3960 to find the nearest. Oh, life membership is 1s.

BINGOING

There is a Bingo Casino at the Lyceum in the Strand—you can play from 7.50 p.m. But you have to join it 24 hours in advance before you can play. Membership free.

BOOKWORMS

Around the British Museum in Bloomsbury is the traditional stalking ground. Ask to see their incunabulae and they will be flattered (books which were in at the birth of printing). Also Maggs Bros., 50 Berkeley Square, the most famous antiquarian booksellers in Europe. If people really do want to read political stuff they must go to the Fabian Society Bookshop, 11 Dartmouth Street, S.W.1 to see what the Labour Party will be up to in 20 years time, the C.P.C. bookshop at Abbey House, 6 Victoria Street, S.W.1, to see what the Conservatives intend to do about it.

BOOZING

Thorough boozers will not only have a round-the-clock timetable of pubs and clubs which are open (like early morning opening in the Markets) but a well-thumbed address book of breweries to visit round the year in suitable changes of disguise. Write to Guinness at Park Royal, N.W.10, for a conducted visit, explaining your academic interest. Or Charrington's (this is the best beer, isn't it?) at Anchor Brewery, Mile End, E.1. And Booth's, the gin people, at 57 Clerkenwell Road, E.C.1. Once you've got the hang, write to anyone. They'll be delighted to have you singing their praises the rest of your drinking life. The telephone number of Alcoholics Anonymous is FLA 9669. For (Pubs, see pages 33-40.)

BREAKDOWN SERVICE

Any motorist who hasn't joined the Automobile Association or Royal Automobile Club is mad. The first is bigger, but the R.A.C. is more of a real club. In any case ring them when you're stuck because they are the most helpful souls in the world and oddly enough enjoy giving service. The A.A. is WHI 1200. For two guineas you get the lot, a handbook to the whole country with towns and populations, maps. They give you lists of almost anything. A tourist plan? 'The fastest way or the prettiest, sir? Ah. You'll arrive Monte Carlo Wednesday at 2 p.m. allowing for the wine festival in Beaune.' R.A.C. telephone number, WHI 4343.

CAR-CLEANING

Drive in, don't book, to St. George's Garage, Brompton Road, S.W.3, and they wash and clean you in five minutes for 12s. 6d. On rainy days, it's cheaper, 7s. 6d., because they don't dry it. At Melbury Garage, 282 Kensington High Street, they clean your car for 7s. 6d.

CAR-HIRE

Paddy Barthropp will make you feel like a lord and put you into one of his fleet of Rolls. He's at Clifton Place Gardens, Sussex Mews East, W.2 (AMB 1101). Alternatively Roy Price Car Hire at REN

3555. And chauffeur too? No problem. Any make of car any hour from Travelwise (SLO 6151).

CHARS

An especially high quality char who may end up on your television screen like Elke Sommer can be obtained from Domestics Unlimited, 426 Harrow Road, W.9 (CUN 0461), where resting actors and all sorts sign up. 25s. for four hours.

CHOCOLATES AND GOODIES

Hand-made chocolates from Prestat, 24 South Molton Street, W.1, Bendick's, 46 New Bond Street, W.1, and from Charbonnel and Walker, 31 Old Bond Street. Cheaper in London than the continent.

CLANMANSHIP

Clobber yourself up with a mixture of the clans at The Royal Scotch Warehouse, 14a Clifford Street, W.1. Why don't you try a Stewart dress tartan, Mr. Polonius T. Bernstein? It's better than anything Mondrian ever did.

CRICKET

Cricket nets at Alf Gover's school, 172 East Hill, S.W.18 (VAN 1796) through the day till 11 p.m.

CLUBBING

Not night or gentlemen's clubs but places where overseas visitors are made welcome. If you worship the Union Jack, and think of the Queen as Mother, you must go to the Victoria League who have very pleasant premises at 38 Chesham Place, S.W.1 (BEL 2201). They do lunches, and have a licence. Membership is £1 for the under-30's, 30s. for over-30's. The English-Speaking Union is helpful at Dartmouth House, 37 Charles Street, W.1 (MAY 7400). You don't have to be a member to go along and meet people (lovely Indian girls in saris, for example), but full members can book bedrooms (they have 100) from 30s. a single room per night. Wednesday is the big social night. Or try the All Nations Social Club, all races welcome, at 83 Chiltern Street, W.1 (EUS 1792). It costs 10s. a year and membership limited to over-19's. Exciting prospect of tea 4d. and coffee 6d.

COFFEE-BUYING

Very important, this. Markus, whose shop you can smell all the way down Connaught Street, W.2 (PAD 4020). Also good value at the Algerian Coffee Stores, Old Compton Street, Soho (GER 2480).

COOKING LESSONS

Cusine Mondiale, 4 Somers Mews, Radnor Place, London W.2. Mrs. Rina Hands will come to your own kitchen to show you how to cook for your guests.

CREEPING UP ON THE STARS

With information from Celebrity Service (GRO 8511), you can arrange to be hanging around in the foyer of the right hotel when Zirus P. Schfokapper comes down and, who knows, he might instantly sign you up for one of his films. Handy for agents, journalists. It costs 7 gns. a month for which you receive their steady stream of bulletins on who's staying where. But look, if it's really important to know where the Beatles are, lie and say you're the *Daily Express*.

DAILY EVENTS

ASK 9211 gives you a brief resumé, including the changing of the guard, popular theatres, exhibitions. The amusing thing to do is to dial ASK 9411 and pass the phone to a friend—'It's for you, long distance.' He'll get the same thing but in German. In Spanish dial ASK 9511. French ASK 9311.

DINING AT HOME

Madame Prunier (HYD 1373) will let you have a superb meal to impress your dinner guests (*My dear*, this turbotin à l'amiral is better than Prunier's). She has an 'On Prendra' list. Or ask Knightsbridge Kitchens, 5 Walton Street, S.W.3 (KNI 3429), who specialise in this sort of thing. Meals work out about £2 a head, or you can order separate dishes. They need 24 hours' notice, and will provide specimen menus.

DOG-BUYING

Unless you want a pedigree, there are lots of sad, appealing and lost dogs at the Battersea Dogs' Home, Battersea Park Road, S.W.8, open Monday to Saturday 9.30 a.m. to 5.30 p.m.

DOWN AND OUT

Betty James, the admirable author of several books on London which you ought to buy, says you must ring her friend Joy at HUNTER 4041 (Temporary Staff Ltd., 64 George Street, W.1), and if you can type, file, clerk, scrub floors, serve beer, or do anything, she will fix you up. It's a very informal set-up.

DRUG-ADDICTION

Strictly illegal, unless you have a doctor's prescription and join the queue on Saturday nights, at the all-night Boots in Piccadilly Circus.

DRY-CLEANING

Most expensive and best, because it is all done by hand, Lilliman and Cox, 4 Hanover Square, W.1. Achille Serre do fast work, while you wait sometimes; at 48 South Molton Street, W.1, and 19 Jermyn Street, W.1, in particular.

EATING UNUSUALLY

Apart from the millions of off-beat eating places, from pitch black steak houses to kaleidoscopically-lit Golden Eggs (24-hour service), it's worth mentioning Vega, off Leicester Square for veg' and two veg'. The Cordon Bleu place at 31 Marylebone Lane (WEL 3880) give you some good stuff the students have been cooking in the day. A lesser known version of this is Westminster Technical College's catering school restaurant at 76 Vincent Square, S.W.1 (VIC 4221), but you must get there about 12.30 p.m. and start queueing.

ELOQUENCE

Trafalgar Square gets the big flag-waving stuff, with stars of stage and screen in attendance. Plenty of police specially trained to be as impartial to Hitler's followers as the movement for World Peace. British democracy. They are not so evident at Speaker's Corner, Hyde Park, where passions are expressed less intelligently but with more feeling. Lord Soper still soap-boxes in his husky voice. He says more people in public life ought to do it. Atheism, Roman Catholicism, and the Irish are main topics, which shows you it's a slice out of another era.

ESCORTS

It seems very sad that anyone should need an escort service, or that it should matter whether you went to some function without a partner. Perhaps you wonder if the name doesn't hide some other function? You'll get a thick ear and a writ wrapped round your neck if you suggest it. For genuine inquiries try Norman Courtney Guide Escort (HYD 5073) and someone will turn up wearing the right gear and take care of things very nicely.

FANCY DRESS
You can't do better than go to Nathan's, the oldest theatrical costumiers, at 141 Drury Lane, W.C.2. If you haven't any ideas you soon will have after stepping inside but resist temptation to hire a suit of armour.

FLOWERS
—that are perfect (unlike real flowers) from Fleur Décor, 97 Baker Street, W.1. Biggest artificial flower people in the country. Best value in ordinary flowers from Woolworths, Oxford Street. Or hang about Covent Garden at dawn. Flowers until 9.30 p.m. at the Savoy Hotel stall.

FLYING
Hire a plane with instructor at Elstree Flying Club (ELS 3070) for six guineas or so. Depends on the plane. If you go by train to Edgware the steward meets you at the station. That's nice.

FOOTBALL
Nicest atmosphere is at West Ham, one of the smallest First Division grounds. Chelsea gives you a good view because you are set back further from the game by the dog track. Spurs and Arsenal are strongly partisan and give their teams good vocal support. In the lower divisions Millwall, at the Den, sit almost on top of the crowd and provide terrific atmosphere.

FOREIGN MAGAZINES
Parisian papers in time for breakfast from The Baker Street Bookshop, 70 Baker Street. Soho is centre of the trade; Hungarian comics, Spanish weeklies, French satire. For example, Librairie Parisienne, 48 Old Compton Street, and Solosy, 53 Charing Cross Road. They will take an order for the *Malta Times*, or anything you want.

FREE ENTERTAINMENT

Write three weeks in advance to the Ticket Unit, B.B.C., Portland Place, W.1, for B.B.C. programmes you want to see. Or Viewers Correspondence, Rediffusion, Television House, Kingsway, W.C.2, sending a stamped addressed envelope. For Radio Luxembourg write to 38 Hertford Street, W.1. You'll meet that man who always seems to be there, guffawing his way through the unfunniest shows.

FREE NOSH

Not so easy to come by, free nosh. But the *Daily Mail* Ideal Home Exhibition is a good eating place for six weeks beginning in March.

FUN

London is full of funfairs from 'appy 'ampstead to H'ealing. But Labour gave the country the only Government fun and you can find it at Battersea Park Festival Funfair.

FURNITURE

Heal's, 195 Tottenham Court Road, W.1, are still exciting and still the best, though not as good as they were. At the Design Centre look up the catalogues and get the addresses of firms making things you'd like to have. Very satisfying. But wouldn't it be great to ring up the Royal College of Art (KNI 5020) and get one of their design lads to have a go? Or the lively people at Hornsey College of Art (FIT 1761). Become a patron of the living arts.

GARAGES AND CARS

Park in the world's largest underground car park, at Hyde Park, by Marble Arch. Takes 1,000 cars. Also all-night service and petrol. All-night service and petrol also at Hertford Hotel, Bayswater Road, Cumberland Hotel Garage, Marble Arch. Driving lessons from British School of Motoring branches (see phone book) and disabled drivers accommodated at WES 3222. Further information on night service from A.A., who have a special booklet. A.A., Fanum House, Leicester Square.

GETTING CLEAN

If you adopt the Boy Scouts' motto, Be Prepared, you should be able to spend a night at the Turkish baths. It's not the people who run them, who are above suspicion, but the steam has a peculiar effect on some chaps. Maybe the towels suggest togas and Roman

baths and Nero's parties. But they are splendid places. The Savoy
Turkish Baths, 91 Jermyn Street, W.1, is open 24 hours a day, all
week. It's 10s. 6d. daytime, or a guinea after 9 p.m., when you
get a single cubicle to sleep in. Ladies' baths at Dorchester Hotel
(MAY 8888). Finnish sauna (birch sprigs optional) at Finland House,
56 Haymarket S.W.1 (TRA 2601), gives you a relaxed, silly, peace-
with-the-world feeling which may be the answer to international
tension. One in the City, too, at 22 Finsbury Street, E.C.2 (MOO
8921).

GLOVES
The Glove Shop, 138 New Bond Street, W.1, have nice expensive
gloves. Also Regent Glove Co., 239 Regent Street, W.1.

GOLF
Golf Illustrated (1s. a week) tells you where to go. Public Greens at
Addington Court, Surrey; Beckenham Place Park, Kent; Brent
Valley, Hanwell, Middx.; Coulsdon Court, Surrey; Haste Hill,
Northwood Hills, Middlesex; Richmond Park; Royal Epping
Forest, Chingford; Hainault Forest, Essex. Wentworth is an O.K.

club to join if they'll have you. Eisenhower played there. Or, for a penny a ball, bash it about at Finchley Golf Centre, High Road, North Finchley (HIL 0411), any time round the clock.

GUIDE TO GUIDES

People who know don't usually trust guide books. It's not that they're wrong (though they date pretty fast)—just that they're usually only half right. *The Penguin Guide to London* (7s. 6d.) has a chapter on the Tower of London which tells you that George V wore the Imperial Indian Crown at the Delhi Durbar in 1911. It doesn't tell you that you might have to queue two hours to see it.

The Penguin Guide is full, informative and cheap (five bob cheaper paradoxically than Betty James' otherwise splendid *London on £1 a Day*). But it has bad maps. This doesn't matter too much as any tube station will give you a bus and tube map for free and most garages will give you a road map. The *A to Z Atlas of London* is a good investment at 3s. 6d. and the best Kultural guide is probably David Piper's at 30s.

For modern London the best guides are the ones the natives use. *The Times* will tell you where the Queen is going to be every day, the main social and public functions and church services. Every paper will tell you what's on at which theatre and cinema and what sporting events are taking place.

What's on in London (weekly 1s. 3d.) tells you just that in some detail. *London Life* (weekly 2s. 6d.) does the same with more panache and less accuracy. Most glossy magazines give details of how and where to spend money eating, dancing or gawping. *The Good Food Guide* and Egon Ronay both produce reliable accounts of what to eat and where to do it. But don't trust the A.A. British handbook which concentrates largely on the ratio of baths to beds and doesn't include London anyway.

If in doubt ask a policeman. That's what they're for.

If you can't read you can always hire someone. Guild of Guide Lecturers do summer work, ring HYD 6888. From two guineas, specify language. Take-a-Guide Ltd. send out a car for two or three, the driver is the guide. He'll go where you want, but has his own ideas too.

GYMNASIUMS

Edward Bolton, a rowing Blue, runs a fashionable gym where John Osborne limbered up between Look Back in Anger and Tom

Jones (PAR 4011). Have a punch-up at Stan Baker's gym or keep-fit classes (BER 4817). Or have a fling with the British Judo Association who will give you nearby thumping-grounds (ABB 6697).

HAIRDRESSERS

Harold Macmillan is a Charles of the Ritz man, where they used to get his side pieces flying to keep Vicky amused. That may be a reason for not going there. Topper, 17 Old Bond Street, W.1. Trumper, 9 Curzon Street, W.1, Truefitt and Hill, 23 Old Bond Street (who sound as if they might have been fags at Eton) give gentlemanly short back and sides. Vidal Sassoon does men's hair, and gorgeous it looks (MAY 9665. 171 New Bond Street, W.1, and MAY 2463, Grosvenor House, Park Lane, W.1). For women, well, Sassoon again. Princess Margaret has Rene of Mayfair, 66 South Audley Street, W.1, GRO 3227, and her hair always looks nice. Mind it's Rene of Mayfair when you look it up, there are so many Renes. For a youngish swinging style, try John Cornel. A dozen branches, see phone book. Richard Conway has a go-ahead salon at Caltex House in Raphael Street, S.W.7, with decor by Nicholas Jenkins from the Royal College of Art. They even make fun of themselves by getting people like the scathing *Private Eye* cartoonist Ralph Steadman to do publicity drawings (KNI 6303).

HAMPERS

You drive your Rolls from Jack Barclay to Stanley Spencer's Cookham and take a girl in a summer dress on a punt, suitably provided with champagne and a hamper from Fortnum and Mason's, Piccadilly (REG 8040). But first you make sure she knows how to punt.

HARPS

More with-it than guitars, and you can grow ivy in the strings. J. G. Morley, 56 Old Brompton Road, S.W.7.

HATS

Do people still wear hats? Dunn's desperately wish they did and they try hard enough. A bowler to have as a fetish should be lovingly bought from Lock's *near* Lobb's at 6 St. James's Street, S.W.1. (Lock and Lobb always sound like a Surrey bowling pair.) Fishing hats from Burberry's, 18 Haymarket, S.W.1. And other sporting hattage.

HELICOPTERS

Try Rentacopter (BEL 6477). But you have to stick to the river so you don't fall on people's houses. Just drown. Or Westland Heliport, BAT 0181 for a pleasure flip.

HIRING SUITS AND DRESSES

Meet the nobility on equal terms in the hire-clothing section of Moss Bros. The fitters will charm the pants off you. But they are very, very good. Find them among the cabbage leaves of Covent Garden, 20 King Street, W.C.2.

HORSE RACING

Nearest courses at Alexandra Park, N.22; Sandown Park, Esher, Surrey; Kempton Park, Sunbury, Mddx; and Epsom of course, for the Derby.

HOTELS

In an emergency ring Hotel Accommodation Service Ltd., 93 Baker Street, W.1 (WEL 2555), for rooms from 30s. (*See* 'Hotels', pages 19-27.)

ICE-SKATING

Streatham is the place. The Silver Blades, 386 Streatham High Road, S.W.16. Skates cost 2s. to hire. The West End's handiest rink is at Bayswater—The Queen's Ice Club, Queensway, W.2. Hardy Amies once held a party there.

INFORMATION

British Travel and Holidays Association, 64 St. James's Street, S.W.1 (MAY 9191), give you wads of stuff to take away. London Tourist Board at West London Air Terminal are good too. For general knowledge, ring the *Daily Telegraph*. Other newspapers do. They have a bureau at FLE 4242 in office hours. Citizen's Advice Bureau at TRA 2825 tell you about mortgages, legal problems. Look in telephone book to see if there's one more local.

JAIL-VISITING

Apply to the Home Office to see if you can visit or entertain Her Majesty's guests (WHI 8100). Ideal chance to get a captive audience—and the poor folk do appreciate it.

JEWELLERY HIRE
Robert White and Sons (TEM 8237). Look like a Duchess for a special occasion—the only time she wears hers, too.

JELLIED EELS
Best river eels jellied as only the British can jelly them from Tubby Isaac's near Aldgate tube station.

JUKE-BOXES
Coin Machine Exchange (SHO 2203) hire them out for £7 10s. a day, arranging delivery and collection.

KITCHEN DESIGN
A firm of interior decorators specialise in doing up kitchens stylishly on the cheap. John King and Associates at REG 8308.

KITCHEN POTS AND PANS
The most respected cookery writer of them all has a dream of a shop at 46 Bourne Street, S.W.1, Elizabeth David. Things sell so fast you may be unlucky enough to go on a day when it's been completely emptied. Go down to Smithfield Market to the trade shops for butchers' aprons, knives, chopping blocks. Woollands in Knightsbridge is an Aladdin's cave for the home cook.

KOALA BEARS STUFFED
Or lions and tigers, at Gerrard's, 61 College Place, Camden Town. They stuff anything.

LAVATORIES
Peter Wolfe publishes the *Good Loo Guide* by Jonathan Routh, with humorous drawings by John Glashan. The Piccadilly Hotel is a five-star loo, and the great thing is that hotels are generally the best places to pee in. Watch out for Hatchett's new loo also in Piccadilly, where the new management intend to make it the most talked-about loo in Europe. Being purely practical and public, there is a 24-hour loo at Victoria Embankment Gardens, near Charing Cross tube.

LEATHERY HORSEY THINGS
Swaine, Adeney Brigg and Sons in Piccadilly next to Fortnum and Mason for a perfect flagellation set. Tom Hill's shop, 26 Brompton Road, for riding boots and such.

LETTER-HEADINGS

Typographical work, like brochures, advertising and books by Charles Crawley, a painstaking craftsman (PUT 6483). Repro-prints give you printed type work to your specification at 19–21 Goswell Road, London E.C.1. Cheaper and quicker than the big boys.

LINEN

You can hire this from Advance Linen Services (MAY 8886).

LITTLE THINGS THAT PLEASE

Like diamonds, rubies, emeralds. Garrard and Co., 112 Regent Street. Garrard's would alter your crown if you were becoming Queen. They fixed Queen Elizabeth's. Costume jewellery and marvellous belts at Paris House, 41 South Molton Street. Jewellery repairs, Herring, Morgan and Southon, Berwick Street, W.1.

LOST

We mean you. Ring ABB 1234 and be patient because they handle millions of calls a year. Any time of day and night they will give you travel advice, bus or tube. It is the London Transport Travel Enquiry Office. They are splendid at helping blind people and hospitals, even take calls from the States asking for Mr. Murphy who works for London Transport. But if you ask them why the Number Elevens pile up in Whitehall, they'll refer you to the P.R. London Transport Board, 55 Broadway, N.W.1.

MARQUEES

Better than messing up a house for a party. Ring MAN 0814 and ask Benjamin Edginton.

MARRIAGE

Humourist Stephen Potter's wife Heather Jenner has a marriage bureau at 124 New Bond Street (MAY 9634), and isn't too dead serious about it all, thank goodness, but she does it very well.

MATERNITY HOMES

Nicest place to have a baby is at Queen Mary's Maternity Home, Hampstead. Beautiful situation, devoted staff, intelligent pre-natal classes for fathers as well as mothers. More modern than this, however, is University College Hospital, Queen Charlotte's, Hammersmith or Charing Cross Hospital, all practitioners of natural childbirth, with some of the best gynaecologists in the country. Fathers are invited to watch the birth. Which is why some people prefer Hampstead.

MINK
Calman Links do minks from home-grown. 33 Margaret Street, W.1. Hire one from Twentieth Century Fur Hirers, 10 Princes Street, W.1 (MAY 2711).

MODEL EVERYTHINGS
Railways, ships and so on. Bassett Lowkes, 112 High Holborn, W.C.1. Model-making materials, A. W. Hambling, 10 Cecil Court, W.C.2.

MONEY-MAKING
Conducted visits round the Mint (no free samples) by writing to The Royal Mint, Tower Hill, E.C.3 (ROY 8261).

NAPPY SERVICE
Baby Ward Laundry Service (VIC 6776) collect dirty nappies three times a week for a reasonable charge depending on number of nappies. Prompt and efficient service throughout London. Minimum charge 11s. 6d. a week.

NEWSPAPERS
As old as yesterday's newspaper. And you can find out how old yesterday's newspapers are by taking a trip round one. First editions are bound for the London stations well before midnight. *The Times* and *Daily Mail* are rather proud of their particular papers and like to take you round, usually at 9 p.m. when the papers are going to bed. You must write to them (Printing House Square and North-cliffe House, Tudor Street, E.C.4, respectively). Last edition is a collector's item you only find at Fleet Street tube stations at 8 a.m. and includes news other papers scooped in their first editions. For a more reasonable hour, ask to go round the *Evening Standard*, from 2 p.m. Shoe Lane, E.C.4.

NUDE MODELS
Getting one is harder than becoming one. Art schools are reluctant to pass on names to any but other bona fide art schools. So how do they get them? From people who ring up offering to pose. If you wanted to pose in the nude you would earn 8s. 9d. an hour and be

much appreciated as they are in short supply. Try Royal Academy Schools (REG 7981), St. Martin's School of Art (GER 0058), Central School of Art (FLA 4846). The thing that is essential is not beauty but the ability to keep still.

NUDITY

West London Sun and Health Club invite you to take your clothes off at 177 Ladbroke Grove, W.10.

OLD-FASHIONED COACH AND HORSES

People who hire out coaches for films (*Wicked Lady* sort of stuff) at Glebe Farm, Ruislip (VIK 2044). Some of their horses are television stars.

OLD SILVER

Tiffin catering company (AMB 1081) will provide it. From an ice bucket to impressive dishes.

ON LONDON

Can't recommend too highly two books by Betty James, *London on £1 a Day*, 12s. 6d., published by Batsford, and companion volume, *London on Sunday*. Also Denys Parsons' compilation for BP., *What's Where*, full of oddities you might expect from the compiler of newspaper misprints. In the same category, *London Night and Day*, edited by Sam Lambert (6s.), where the day is divided into hours so you turn to the appropriate time. *Geographer's A to Z*, book Atlas of London at 3s. 6d. is a must, the most worn book in any Londoner's household, with information on London places to visit. The G.L.C. do *Open Air Entertainment* which is really useful (Greater London Council, County Hall, London S.E.1, price 1s. 6d. inc. postage). The City of London Information Centre, St. Pauls Churchyard, E.C.4 (MON 3030) do a monthly diary of events, and this is only 3s. a year post free. *What's On In London* is an invaluable guide to general entertainment, which you can get at any bookstall (1s. 3d.).

OPEN-AIR THEATRE

The place you have to go is Regent's Park in the Inner Circle, beginning in June, throughout our stormy, chilly summer. If you take blankets you will be about ready to exchange Shakespeare for Clement Freud at the end. This gastronome runs the catering side and provides dinners afterwards. Which pay for the acting. Clement weather drives them to Clement's place, they say.

ORCHESTRAS
From the Orchestral Association (GER 5027).

OUTDOOR PARTIES
Tents, barbecues, what-have-you. J. Cross and Co. Ltd., 18 Gleneagle Road, Streatham, S.W.16.

PAGEANTRY
Changing of the Guard at 11 a.m. at Buckingham Palace and St. James's Palace nearly every day. It's not the ceremony so much as the splendid sight of the fellows marching in full colour down the main streets while traffic is put to a halt (WHI 4466 to get details). The Whitehall guards on horseback are beautifully got up from the plumes of their helmets to leather breeches and boots. Such young lads as well. They change the Guard at 11.30 a.m., Sunday at 10 a.m. Write to the Resident Governor at the Tower of London for the marvellous gibberish of locking the Tower at night, from 9.40 p.m. They were doing this when the Bloody Tower really was Bloody. He's very sensitive about it. Put your son down for Eton at the same time.

PAINTINGS FOR HIRE
From A.I.A. Gallery (GER 4846), 15 Lisle Street, W.1, at 15s. a month, pictures that cost hundreds to buy. They also sell them.

PAVEMENT ARTISTS
A transient art because the Law says they must be rubbed out frequently. High art in this field is naturally outside the National Gallery where passers-by put money in the hat out of respect to the trade practised by Botticelli, Turner and Constable.

PAWNBROKERS
T. M. Sutton, 156 Victoria Street, S.W.1 and E. A. Barker, 1 Court House, E.C.3, are the smart places to take your grandfather's gold hunter.

PERFUME
For men as well. Floris at 89 Jermyn Street, W.1 (notice the Royal Warrant—they made George IV smell the way he did). Toilet waters, bath essences and so on, and especially English flower perfumes. Heavenly.

PERIOD FURNITURE

Hire it from The Old Times Furnishing Company (PUT 3551) who do a lot for the stage and television.

PHOTO-COPYING

Professional Service from H. Erenberg (HUN 1115).

PHOTOGRAPHS

Unless prompted by personal vanity you need only get yourself a passport picture from the 24-hour service by the Passport Office, Petty France, Westminster. If Cecil Beaton consents to take your picture and you can pay for it, he'll make a royal job of it (KEN 4351). Archie Parker (KNI 1744) and Tom Hustler (MAY 9921) make passable images of debs to their mothers' breathless pleasure. Any Snowdon picture lifts you into a near-Establishment niche. For something modern, showing your hairy armpits, for example, young David Bailey (PRI 9955), 100 gns.!

PIANO-HIRING

A grand for four guineas a month, plus the cost of delivering it, from Wigmore Hall and Piano Galleries (WEL 1789).

PIPE-SMOKERS

They understand about pipes at Inderwick, 45 Carnaby Street and Dunhill's, 30 Duke Street, St. James's, W.1. Also at the 100-year-old Charaton's, 14 Panton Street, S.W.1.

PLUMBERS

One Number (ACO 8741) deal with emergencies, plumbing or electrical, and any general household dramas. There is a membership fee of two guineas, and they have a brochure of a wide range of other services, which include discount buying. Emergency Roofing and Plumbing Service (REN 1405) take calls day and night.

POTTERY AND CHINA AND GLASS

The Craftsman Potters Association behind Liberty's, a London show place for a hundred or so real English potters is great (GER 7605). Primavera, 149 Sloane Street, S.W.1, has a decent selection and lots of new continental ornaments which obviously were a real pleasure collecting. Modern glass at Peter Jones, Sloane Square and Heal's, Tottenham Court Road. Wedgwood china at 34 Wigmore Street, W.1.

PREHISTORIC ANIMALS

You can get models of them at Gregory Bottley, 30 Old Church Street, S.W.3, and other remnants of prehistoric life, fossils, lumps of rock, minerals. Very smart today.

PORNOGRAPHY

One of the best collections in the world is at the British Museum, but you have to prove that you are a *bona fide* student before you can get at it. In the seedier areas of Soho and the Charing Cross Road, if you look sufficiently furtive, you can 'buy' a scrofulous book for anything from £2 to £25, but you get half the price back when you return the book to the shop.

PROFESSIONAL ADVICE

Owing to professional etiquette there is no way of knowing when you're on to a bum steer when you try to get a doctor, dentist, solicitor, stockbroker, estate agent, banker or insurance firm. Professional bodies won't tell you who's good and who's bad. They merely offer you the Law List, or Medical Register. All you need is a pin. So the rule is this. You ask your doctor for the name of a good dentist, your dentist for a good doctor. A stockbroker for a banker. An estate agent for a solicitor, and so on. Professional etiquette only restricts them to reserving comment about their own business.

QUEUEING

Obviously a pleasure for the queuers, and the greatest cameraderie is to be found among the kit-bags, camping stools, thermoses, etc., at any Covent Garden Opera House queue. You should start at least 12 hours before a performance. During the England tennis championships, there is a great outdoor air of heartiness among Wimbledon queues. In either case you're too dead tired and stiff to enjoy the show afterwards. But you queued. Queues for January Sales rubbish not recommended to any but rugby wives.

RECORDS

Best selection of classical records at Discurio, 9 Shepherd Street, W.1. And highly-informed staff to advise.

RIDING

There are stables near all the London Parks. Richmond Park and Wimbledon Common are particularly attractive. If you ride in Rotten Row people presume you must be Someone, though that's not so. Anyone can get a horse from the Knightsbridge Riding School, 11 Elvaston Mews, S.W.7. The magazine *Riding* gives a list of schools and stables. Out of town, go to Epsom Downs. Or a bit further afield Windsor, but the Queen rides here, and she expects proper dress from would-be riders. The Duke in polo togs can be seen here too, knocking a ball about on Smith's lawn.

RIVER-TRIPPING

The thing to do is hire yourself a boat, not a motor boat, but a Thames passenger steamer, and have yourself a party on it. Glide down the Thames on a summer evening, jazz band playing. Ring POP 5255. Otherwise make do with the usual river trips. In the summer they leave every 20 minutes from Charing Cross Pier and Westminster Pier and go down to Greenwich. Same telephone for information and sailing times.

ROOF-GARDENS

Derry and Toms, Kensington High Street, have $1\frac{1}{2}$ acres of delight on their roof in Spanish, Japanese and Tudor styles. Morning coffee, salad lunches, and of course, tea. It's really beautiful.

ROWING

For half a crown an hour you can row yourself away down enchanting willowy waters at Maidenhead and Windsor. Or row the length of the Serpentine. Regent's Park has a small lake for rowing and you can take out a little dinghy with a sail.

SECOND-HAND BUYS

The Nearly New Shop, 5 Dorset Street, W.1. Buy or sell, proceeds to Y.W.C.A.

SECRETARIES

Lots of agencies, but T.I.P.S.—The Individual Personal Secretaries— can do you very promptly and efficiently. Ring LAN 7011, 310 Regent Street, W.1.

SHIRT-MAKERS

The Duke of Gloucester gets his from Dare and Dolphin, 90 Piccadilly, W.1. Hawes and Curtis at 2 Burlington Gardens, W.1. Merryweather Ltd., 19 Ryder Street, W.1. Oh heck, they are too nice. Back to Cecil Gee in Shaftesbury Avenue, and Carnaby Street. John Michael Shops for a chi-chi effect.

SHOES

Traditionally Lobb of 26 St. James's Street, S.W.1, or McAfee, 38 Dover Street, W.1. They make them for you. The trek down Clore's Oxford Street Empire always seems utterly despairing. Ballet shoes from Gamba, 46 Dean Street in Soho. The world's best.

SKELETONS

Not English ones, perish the thought, but from abroad. Get one for your cupboard from Adam Rouilly, 18 Fitzroy Street.

SKI-ING

The Crystal Palace park ski-ing slope of nylon brushes is a great place to get bruised in preparation for breaking a leg in Switzerland (SYD 0131).

SLEIGHT-OF-HAND

Foyles Entertainments, 125 Charing Cross Road, W.C.2 (GER 5660), put on children's shows, and provide cartoon films.

SLEUTHS

Victor Q-Men are ex-Yard birds. Ask for Doughy Baker (TRA 1661). Ace Detective Agency have several branches. Ring WIM 1908 or GER 3387. One of the best games in London is to get together a party, and each person is to be tailed all day. The one who manages to keep tailed longest is the winner. If only it wasn't so damned expensive.

SPEEDWAY

Wimbledon, New Cross and Hackney Wick are the places to go for this dirty, noisy and exciting sport. Refer to the *Speedway Star and News*, 1s.

STOCK CAR RACING

Careering smash after smash, just like the M1. Drivers get bonuses for turning their cars over, win or lose. Ring ALB 2441 to find out when they are having the next one at West Ham Stadium. About six meetings a year, summer months.

SUICIDE

Before taking this drastic step ring the Samaritans, MAN 9000, who enjoy talking people out of it. Politicians should ring this number before committing the country to equally drastic steps, there's a lot of common sense on the other end of the line.

SWIMMING

Smooth place to go is the Oasis in Endell Street, W.C.2, where the *Daily Mirror* photographers take pictures of big-bosomed beauties. They also take the girls (who don't look half as good out of the picture) to Roehampton's pleasant but small outdoor pool. They also go to the Serpentine where you swim in chill brown mud, spiced with eye-smarting chlorine. One of the most pleasant outdoor pools is Lordship Lane, N.17, with decent water slides and diving boards. Gospel Oak Lido, N.W.5, also very good, although outside it looks like something from a People's Republic. Get up early to go to Chelsea Baths to swim with Lord Longford, before he goes off to the office, but leave him alone (he once toppled a photographer into the water who wanted to take his picture). High diving in the open air at Highgate Pond, Hampstead Heath, for men only. Behind wooden fences here they sprawl in the buff. Women only at Kenwood pond, on the Heath. White House, Albany, indoor pool, in Albany Street, N.W.1. Membership 3 gns. a year. Very comfortable with handy bar. Or hire your own from Purley Pools (BYW 1322).

TAILORS

You can't ignore Savile Row, but you won't find the endless credit they are so famous for. They may ask for money. Cecil Gee in Shaftesbury Avenue clothes a lot of the famous very efficiently and unfussily, but pretty expensive. Anywhere in Carnaby Street will dress you as a talking point. Simpson's, Piccadilly, for ready-to-wear, and have the satisfaction of knowing that the chairman bought Sir Winston Churchill's Hyde Park Gate house.

TAXIS

The telephone book under Taxicabs tells you the nearest rank, though you can ring till you drop dead during rush hours. The Owner Drivers Radio Taxi service is TER 6444 and Radio Taxis MOU 3232. You can get what are still called Minicabs, but turn out to be big Zephyrs and Zodiacs from 24-hour Minicabs (VIC 3961) who are decent enough to pass you on to another smaller firm if they can't do it for you. Two bob a mile. Minicab war over—'We get on very well with the big black'ns.'

TELEPHONE

Tells you the time, of course, dial TIM. But it will also wake you like an alarm if you dial 100 and ask for a call. They will also remind you of appointments if you want. Capital operators, too.

TEN-PIN BOWLING

Golders Green, Top Rank Bowling (SPE 9803) is the go-ahead place. But also at Excel, Shaftesbury Avenue, W.1 (GER 1580). Acton's ABC Bowl (SHE 4591), London Airport (SKY 1396).

TENNIS

Real tennis costs 22 gns. a year at the Queen's Club, West Kensington, W.14 (FUL 3421). And ordinary tennis. Holland Park Lawn Tennis Club is ten gns. a year. So you can guess what they mean in Durham when they talk about your lawn tennis accent. Ordinary people play in ordinary London parks and thoroughly enjoy it, turning out in jeans and brown plimsolls if they want.

TERPSICHORE

Dance floors from Campbell Marson and Co., Maxwell Road, Fulham, S.W.6 (REN 3635). Floors from about £7 for 15 square feet.

TIES

The trade's moving too fast. Paris designers to be found in Jermyn Street. And lots of dead square stripey ties too. Hardy Amies fancies himself. They're not bad at all.

TIPPING

In most continental countries, tipping is a matter of psychological warfare which only the toughest customer has ever a chance of winning. In Britain things are a bit more gentlemanly, but it still pays to know what the accepted rate is, unless you fancy a slanging match with a taxi driver.

Taxis. You don't have to tip of course, and you're unlikely to get the smallest scrap of extra service worth paying for, but it's still customary to give a taxi driver a shilling tip for a ride up to ten shillings. Above that ten per cent.

Hotels. In most London hotels a service charge is now automatically added to the bill. It's been creeping up in the last few years and now varies from ten to fifteen per cent. The Savoy adds 12½ per cent for food and 15 per cent for rooms. The Berkeley and Claridges charge 15 per cent for everything. The Hilton charges 12½ per cent. Nothing else is required, but porters still hope for a shilling a piece for carrying baggage, cloakroom attendants for at least sixpence, and commissionaires half a crown for getting a taxi. If you're staying at the hotel for any length of time, it's worth tipping at least the first time.

Restaurants. Unless there is a special arrangement on the menu, ten per cent is the normal tip. Some, like Simpson's, have a cover charge of two shillings just for sitting down, and it is left to you to decide what else to tip. Stone's Chop House have a cover charge of half a crown and also add ten per cent service. In both these places, as in others where joints are carved in front of you, it is customary for the person ordering to slip the carver half a crown for himself.

It is all a con trick of course. But when porters have been conned into doing the job in the first place for little more than the promise of tips, it seems churlish not to fork out. And when a hairdresser whispers in your ear, 'Oh yes sir, we get a lot of distinguished people in here, but you're the first this morning' he's probably worth two bob just for his cheek.

If you feel really strongly against tipping, you can always join the Anti-Tipping Campaign which prints cards saying: 'Thank you. I appreciate your services, but I have not left a tip. I believe tipping is a patronising habit and that you should receive a proper wage without having to rely on charity. Please pass this on to your employer or union.'

As the recipients of tips don't feel at all patronised, why should you worry? The money spent on the cards might just as well go to them.

TOAST-MASTERS
Society of Toastmasters and M.C's will help you. Ring Mr. Maurice Lewin, secretary, at VAL 7834.

TOURS
Tourist season buses to a circular tour of London for 5s., leaving from between Buckingham Palace Road and Eccelston Bridge, Victoria. They leave at 11 a.m., 12 p.m., 2 p.m., 3 p.m., 4 p.m. and 5 p.m. On foot, get to know the Know London Society by writing to the Treasurer, 10 Chaffinan Avenue, Sunsley, Croydon, Surrey.

TOXOPHILY

British School of Archery principal, Frank Bilson (TER 7804) has details of competitions. Highgate and Regents Park are match sites. County of London Archery Association, 14 Clore Road, Barnes, S.W.13 for further help.

TOYS

Paul and Marjorie Abbatt, at 94 Wimpole Street, W.1, are devoted to educational, sensible toys as a life-work. Heal's give a lot of chances to bright young toymakers in Tottenham Court Road. Don't take a boy or girl into Hamley's, 200 Regent Street, because there will come a time when you must take them home, and there will be tears. It's a children's idea of paradise, and the biggest toy shop in the country.

UNDERGROUND

First trains in the week are at 5.30 a.m., last trains are at about 12 p.m. But you can get connections in central areas of London up to 12.15 p.m., sometimes till 12.30 p.m. if you're very lucky. An hour later starting on Sundays, an hour earlier stopping. Hampstead tube station is the best place to be in event of nuclear attack, being as deep as Nelson's column is high. The Northern Line is the longest continuous tunnel in the world. And some fool holds a record for travelling all the way round the underground's 273 stations. It's still the best service in the world.

UNIVERSITY OF LONDON

Great number of external courses. Write to Senate House, W.C.1, or ring MUS 8000 for details.

VENDING MACHINES

A marching army of them is beginning to occupy London. Some of the most elaborate in the Earls Court Road. monsters with 100-odd compartments for the things you didn't have time to buy in the day. Your dinner. Or the dog's dinner. Razor blades, soap etc. Dairy stuff at Express Dairies, 51 Abingdon Road, Kensington; 204 Earls Court Road, Earls Court; and 4 Thayer Street, Marylebone.

VILLAGE CRICKET

Spend a Saturday or Sunday afternoon as the players do in country surroundings near some nice old pubs. Kew Green, Ham Common, Stanmore Green, Chiswick Park, for example.

VILLAS

If you quickly want a villa in Spain ring PYT 6051 for Villa Sales and Rentals.

WATER-SKI-ING

British team train at Ruislip Lido, RU4 3831. Nearby is Prince's Club, near London Airport. Lord Snowdon is president of the Federation. David Nations at ROY 8271 will advise enthusiasts.

WEATHER

The London Weather Centre (TEM 4311) give a 24-hour forecast. Home counties news from WEA 2211, London. WEA 3311 for Essex. WEA 4411 for Kent. WEA 5511 Sussex coast. Winter road conditions dial ASK 6611, the A.A. report.

WEDDING PRESENTS

Princess Alexandra placed her wedding list with Harrod's when she married Angus Ogilvy. It was a surprise because a lot of people went to the General Trading Company, 144 Sloane Street, S.W.1, expecting to find the list there. They do a lot of that sort of thing. More the sort of present for people who have got everything,

WIGS

Hire one from De Marco Hair Creations at WEL 1500.

X-FILMS

The good films that the big distributors can't be bothered with can best be seen at The Academy, Oxford Street, Cameo-Polytechnic in Regent Street, Paris-Pullman, Drayton Gardens; the Everyman, Hampstead; Cameo-Royal, Charing Cross Road. They don't bother so much with the nasty foreign films.

X-RAYS

St. John's and Red Cross Mobile Unit, 12 Grosvenor Street, S.W.1 (BEL 2646).

XZIT

Should you want Xzit, you must ring HYD 1875. Wait a minute. What is Xzit? Xzit is the trade name of a firm with American connections who make refractories. Coatings for tanks. Well, it might come in handy.

YACHTING
Buy *Yachting Monthly* or *Yachting World*. They can answer queries (HOL 5327 and WAT 3333). Try your hand on Regents Park Lake, or go down to Putney where there's a flourishing club—it's the spot where the Oxford and Cambridge boat race starts. And model yachts. Ring the London Model Yacht Club, STR 5351.

YEOMAN OF THE GUARD
i.e. Beefeaters, the thing that Americans believe so typical of England. There is only one spot in the British Isles where you can find these Gilbert and Sullivan fellows. And you should know this is at the Tower of London with the ravens.

Y.M.C.A. AND Y.W.C.A.
Two never-to-be-forgotten organisations which thrive on Christianity, communal living and table tennis. Y.M.C.A.'s headquarters, MUS 8954, Y.W.C.A.'s headquarters, WEL 6951. Women are better catered for than men.

ZOO PARTIES
The Regents Park Zoo allow parties on their premises given justification (academic rather than orgiastic) and bring live animals to the party. Disconcerting after a few drinks to shake hands with a boa-constrictor.

ZOOLOGICAL SOCIETY
They answer animal questions which is very nice of them (PRI 3544).

Best free range of cosmetics in any London cloakrooms: the Mayfair Hotel, for gents; and for ladies, BOAC Departures in Victoria, where there are also free showers for gents.

PRIVATE

PLEASURES

Gambling, Part One

London is now the gambling centre of Europe. Perhaps the world. Even American gamblers come here by charter plane, rather than go to Las Vegas.

The reason is that the 1960 Gaming Act made gaming legal. Since then, a new gaming house opens about every second week. (Every first week there's a new betting shop.)

The British are born gamblers, but up to now they've had their instincts suppressed, or directed elsewhere. Now, they make the Chinese look like amateurs. Drink was the Victorians' vice. Today it's gambling. This is how, why and where they go about it.

There was a woman in the London Bankruptcy Court not long ago who claimed she had lost more than £15,000 in a gambling club.

It all started, she said, because a friend persuaded her to go to a club for a quiet game of bridge. On the night she first went there, there was no bridge game in progress—and she fell under the spell of chemin de fer.

She found it a simple and fascinating game and on the first night she won several hundreds of pounds. She became one of the club's most regular players and her winnings went up and up. At one time she was £32,000 ahead.

There was champagne and caviar and £20 tips for the croupier and in only a little over a year more than £100,000 passed through that woman's hands.

When she appeared in the bankruptcy court she said that the final result of her gambling spree was the loss of two mink coats, her jewels, her money, also her husband's money—and an outstanding debt of £4,500.

She said: 'I have learned my lesson.'

She had, of course, become a compulsive gambler. There is no excitement, no glamour, in fact no pleasure attached to compulsive gambling. It is a disease, a drug. And a little bit of this disease affects all gamblers.

They make the game sexual, emotionless, pathetic. The pathos is in the tired, flat, worn faces of the regular gamblers, sitting from dawn to dusk, losing plastic money because there is nothing in this world they would rather do.

Why do they do it? Some are sadists, enjoying it best when other losers squirm; others are masochists, squirming with pleasure when they themselves lose.

'In one's childhood,' says Simon Raven, the novelist, 'Mummy and Nanny said it was wrong to get something for nothing. Obsessive gamblers have a subconscious desire to be punished.'

Tim Holland, chairman of Crockford's, has a simpler explanation. He says it gives people something to occupy their time. 'It's a relaxation which can be exciting, win or lose.' He admits that gambling has little appeal for people with any intellectual interests. 'People who haven't the intellect to read a book, or get bored with TV, go gambling. Take myself. If I have an evening off, I don't go and watch Brecht. I want to be amused, so I back horses.'

Simon Raven maintains there is some sexual excitement in excessive gambling. He believes that a gambler when he is losing becomes sexually excited. But of course, that's a theory which is going to take some proving.

The gambler lives in a fantasy world, on a wavelength he can't control, beyond all reason and emotion. This is why he tends to be suspect. There is a question mark over his head. For outside the gaming room, who knows what he will do?

This is one of the reasons why the exclusive clubs try to remain exclusive. If it were known which chairmen of which public companies were spending their nights gambling, their shares would soon fall. Many chairmen have themselves fallen, but up to now the scandal has been kept quiet. But it has been the real reason behind many dramatic stock exchange tumbles.

Tim Holland says that he knows two chairmen who are regular gamblers. One knows when to stop. The other does not. The one who does not has become unbalanced. Mr Holland, for one, would never ever invest in his company, even though to the outside world it is an eminently sound investment.

Of course, these are the excesses of gambling. And who, after all, should decide what anyone should do in his own time and with his own money?

It is excellent entertainment, a pleasant escape, for those who can afford it. And the majority do get a harmless pleasure out of it all. But the beginner should remember to treat it just as *entertainment*. The chances of making money out of it are nil. In fact, the chances are against it.

Nor is this really unexpected, because the people who run the clubs—the good ones as well as the bad—are in the business for one purpose only: to take money.

Tim Holland never makes any pretence about it. He is in business to make a handsome profit.

So are all the rest, but every one of the club bosses is quick to point out that this does not mean that their patrons can be played for mugs. Indeed it would be very difficult to find any business organisation in London which is as meticulous about the way in which it treats its 'customers' and in which it keeps its accounts as the top gambling clubs.

But the profits are still very handsome. In 1964, the shareholders of Crockford's were handed a 200 per cent dividend and in 1965 they got a free bonus issue of three shares for every one held.

To reach that stage of financial success, Crockford's has ridden the crest of a high-class gambling wave which was started on its way by the Act of Parliament passed in 1960. Crockford's has also had the advantage of Tim Holland in control.

His first rule for the would-be player at the gaming tables is this: Be perfectly clear in your mind that there is all the difference in the world between luck and chance.

Luck may give you an early and very good win. Chance will ensure that if you go on playing the tables, night after night, the wheel of fortune will turn, sometimes with disastrous results.

All club bosses know that even the most successful player will lose all his winnings, provided he goes on playing long enough. No one is ever rich enough, or brave enough, to *increase* his stakes when he starts losing, which is the only way to get out of a losing streak when it inevitably comes.

So the clubs have spared nothing to make their establishment both plush and sophisticated. Nothing is too good for the patron at the tables.

But if all things evened out, there would not be enough to meet the overheads, let alone provide the bountiful profits which have come with the spread of the gaming urge.

The clubs, first of all, take table money—the sum you pay for sitting down and having a game.

In theory, they should make no money from the game itself. For under the 1960 Act, every player must have an equal chance of winning and an equal opportunity to take the bank.

But the club operators work on a principle of having the odds on their side, if this is humanly possible.

The easiest example of how this can be arranged—all above board —is roulette.

The top pay-out is 35 to 1, yet with zero there are 36 possible holes into which the ball can finally drop. This gives the bank an advantage of slightly less than three per cent. It doesn't sound much, but when many thousands of pounds can be staked on a single table within a week it can mount up.

The fact that the clubs can make use of this three per cent advantage spotlights one of the curiosities of the English gaming laws. Its apparent legality is the outcome of an obscure blending of the 1960 Act, an amending Government measure of 1963 and case law built up through a number of recent High Court actions.

The present position is that the clubs are not being stopped from taking advantage of this three per cent, although it can be argued that the 1960 Act intended just the opposite.

Lawyers differ in their views, but some of London's top-ranking police think that a prosecution against one of the clubs could be started to show that the three per cent advantage cannot be accepted by the clubs.

Any legal action could change the whole future of London's gaming clubs. But for the present the clubs go merrily on, with the club owners taking every possible step to enjoy the advantages which differing interpretations of the 1960 Act allow.

How this is being done is shown by the roulette affair. There is really not much room for doubt now that at the time Parliament passed the 1960 Act the majority of members believed that it would mean that in such games there would be no built-in advantage for the bank—which in clubs would normally be the club owners.

In roulette, this could be easily assumed to mean that zero made the game illegal and that is just what was assumed. So a new game, named Legalite, was invented. In general this was roulette without the zero, so the chances of any one number coming up became 35 to 1 instead of 36 to 1. The certain long-term profit for the bank had gone and the operator was, therefore, in a much more precarious position.

But this was put right as far as the club operators were concerned by a decision in the High Court in 1962. Strictly speaking this decision was concerned with bingo, but a number of lawyers soon found justification for extending its implications to roulette and as yet no one has challenged their right to do so.

The lawyers, and therefore the clubs, have taken this High Court decision to mean that in roulette, if it is possible for every player to take over the bank if he should so wish, then even with zero it can still be said to be a game of equal chance for all concerned with no built-in advantage for the house.

Every London gambling club goes to great lengths to ensure that somewhere and somehow the information is made available to all the players that they can have a go at the bank. In some, the chef de table will call out after every five or less spins: 'Qui veut la banque?' Crockford's have it printed on the player's ticket. Most have it displayed in large notices. Almost all make sure it figures prominently in their rules.

In fact they could well afford to shout it from the house tops because very few players ever take advantage of the offer. In some of the lesser clubs it is an almost unheard of happening. This is not surprising because the three per cent advantage can be reckoned on only in the very long run. To take over the bank for only a few spins can be a disastrous experience.

But the fact that they have had to offer the bank around has opened up for the clubs another possible legal headache. Who satisfies the understandable anger of the players if one of their number who has taken the bank goes broke and can't pay out?

It doesn't often happen. Some of the clubs say it has never happened with them, but it is not unknown and steps have been taken to meet the possibility. There is a rule which most clubs have now introduced which says that any player taking the bank must cover all of the stakes before he spins the wheel. Some others have introduced a rule by which a player taking the bank need accept only the bets he wants to accept. A combination of these rules is also in operation in at least one club.

Together they have produced an effective 'stopper' for what could otherwise be a potential cause of a lot of trouble.

There are now at least 100 gaming clubs in London. They bring in lots of tourists and lots of foreign money. In a good week, they handle 10 million pounds.

To become a member of many clubs, all you have to do is arrive wearing a tie and they'll make you a member straight away. But clubs of this sort are opening and closing all the time. They are not interested in laying on facilities. (All *good* clubs give first class meals, much better than ordinary night clubs.) These former—both the legal and the illegal—are not worth naming. They will con you if you are not careful—and in any case, their names are likely to change overnight.

But there are a few dozen clubs well worth visiting. Some are very exclusive, some cater for the man in the street—like the

Golden Nugget in Shaftesbury Avenue, or the Victoria Sporting Club at Marble Arch. In these, you don't need to spend much money.

To become a member of the top four exclusive clubs—Crockford's, the Clermont (or Aspinall's), Quents, and Curzon House—is very difficult. You have to be nominated by several members, then you are socially and financially vetted before you are elected.

'What we're looking for,' says Tim Holland, 'are people who are nicely behaved and who have some money. By nicely behaved I mean they don't pick their noses or swear at the table. What we want is a first-class chap.

'As for money, it's no use anybody earning say £2,000 a year wanting to join. In fact, we don't really want *anybody* on a salary. Someone on a fixed salary only gets into trouble when things go wrong.'

The exclusive clubs are very gentlemanly. Members tend to know each other and the decor is extravagant and luxurious. Anyone opening a new one spends most money on decor. The Pair of Shoes and The New Casanova, both smallish clubs in Mayfair, spent £80,000 each on furnishings and decorations alone.

Even compared with a fairly large club like Crockford's, at 16 Carlton House Terrace (next to bits of the Foreign Office), the Victoria Sporting Club at Marble Arch (next to Woolworths) is a different world. Their £250,000 building is brand new and contemporary. They have forty-five gaming tables, fifty-five croupiers, a total staff of 290 and on a good night they have 2,600 people gambling.

The Victoria set itself a target of 10,000 members in three years. After one year in business, they have now made it. The average stakes are lower than at Crockford's (who have 3,500 members, paying 8 guineas a year membership fees) but both are taking roughly the same amount of money every night—£25,000.

Crockford's last year made a profit of £258,000 . . .

The highest sum lost by one person in one session at Crockford's is £25,000. At the Victoria it is £10,000. The present-day London record for any club is held by Les Ambassadeurs where a famous peer lost £125,000 in one evening.

As gaming debts are not recoverable at law, most clubs reckon to be done out of up to 10% of their profits. 'One well-known man won £1,300 at my club one night,' says Eric Steiner of The Pair of Shoes. 'The next night he lost £3,000, and paid for it with a dud cheque.'

At all the exclusive clubs you usually get free drink and breakfast.

At the others you have to pay for it. But all clubs try to lay on special attractions for members. Crockford's are fond of giving banquets. The Olympic in Bayswater once offered a free Rolls-Royce to whoever got the most consecutive wins at chemin de fer.

The Victoria, to attract Americans, runs a monthly charter plane from New York. This brings across 160 gamblers who get a week at the Hilton plus food and drink at the Victoria, all for just over £250 each. It costs the Victoria much more than £250 to provide all that, but of course they make on the actual gambling, and in publicity. American, German, Polish, Canadian and French TV teams have been asked especially to do features on the gambling-crazy Americans pouring off the planes on to the Victoria gaming tables.

But they are now finding that only 20% of each plane-load actually spend their time gambling. The rest go and look at Buckingham Palace, or go straight on to Paris. As gaming men know, you can't win all the time.

In all clubs the games are much the same as in the big clubs—chemin, roulette, and, at an ever-increasing rate, black jack.

This is an American version of pontoon and its popularity in London, especially in the smaller legitimate clubs, has undoubtedly been due to its success in provincial gambling clubs.

Businessmen from the cities of the North and the Midlands, in London for conferences and exhibitions, make up a large part of the 'floating' membership of gambling clubs. They are content to pay over their annual membership fee just to get in for a few nights. And it is to them that the Londoners have to give thanks—if that is the word—for the extensive spread of cheaper gambling.

Previously, if the man bent on a flutter at the tables couldn't get into Crockford's or its like, his only alternative was something only slightly less—Quent's in Hill Street, Mayfair, where the annual subscriptions are £2 2s. Now the whole picture has changed, and changed so remarkably that one wonders just how long will elapse before the organisation and rules of gambling are reconsidered.

In the meantime the spread is sure to go on and more and more night clubs and restaurants are likely to go into the gambling business. The owner of one small club which has now installed roulette and black jack puts it this way: 'We started to get people coming in here for a meal and then they would ask us to cash their cheques, just so that they could go off to the gambling club up the road with plenty of playing money in their pockets.

'Then it got even worse. They started to go to the gambling

club for their dinner as well and they came in here only to cash their cheques.'

Perhaps he was stretching the point because he was rather peeved. But the fact remains: if, when in London, you want a flutter at chemin, at roulette, at black jack, even at bridge, you will not have to look very far.

And the age-old rule of London applies: Ask any taxi driver. Unless he is a religious man with a hatred of gambling, he will know enough addresses to cover all the possible requirements, from Curzon Street down to the back streets of Earls Court and the Chinese gambling dens of Soho and the East End.

These last are where you would see real gambling. But you will not be invited to join. The Chinese consider a European in the gambling schools a sign of bad luck.

If you want to turn up at some address in a Rolls, any West End car showroom selling new models of the car will be pleased to give you a trial run.

Most disgusting free exhibit in London: plaster model of bad food covered in flies: ground floor of the Natural History Museum.

Gambling, Part Two

Some confessions of another gambling man. Not the red plush of the gambling clubs this time, but the sad suburban streets and the betting shops.

Their growth has been sensational. Yet saturation still seems centuries away.

More of an essay than a guide. For, as every betting man knows, a betting shop is a betting shop is a betting shop.

Let us consider the horse. It is firm and warm and good to look at. It has a leg at each corner and a head and a tail. It's wide enough on the top to carry a little man and it's likely to be as intelligent and far less vicious than those who breed it, buy it, train it or ride it.

Let us consider the gambler. He is a lonely man, single-minded and poor company. He is stupid, illogical, vain and no better-looking than the rest of humanity. There is very little risk in his day-to-day life and no doubt at all about his ultimate death. It's long odds against his immortality, he realises, but no true gambler was ever disheartened by the length of the odds. Whatever he has not, he covets. Whatever he has, he claims the right to throw away.

Let us consider money. It either crinkles or it chinks. It may be exchanged for most things, except immortality. Most people like it for itself alone. Gamblers do. They like the look of it and the feel of it. Most of all, they like the thought of its easy acquisition.

Let us consider the betting shop. These are places where the gambler (q.v.) puts his money (q.v.) on the horse (q.v.) in the belief that the fastest horse will pass the post in front of all the others. The vanity of this belief is childlike.

There are 16,000 betting shops in Britain—1,188 of them in London. They are particularly concentrated around the periphery, in such areas as Shepherd's Bush, Clapham, Shoreditch and Kilburn.

A betting shop reflects its locality. Where there are markets, there are betting shops full of market people. Where there are professional gentlemen, the betting shops contain professional gentlemen. Behind Broadcasting House there are betting shops full of broadcasters. In the West End there are establishments for shoppers; in Soho, shops which cater specifically for the waiters; in Hampstead, there are betting shops for Socialists (who should know better); and in Denmark Street, there are betting shops for vocalists.

Church Street, Kensington, has at the last count turned up its nose at them. The royal parks are also still chaste—unless you count the Exchange Telegraph commentary system which the Queen Mother is said to have installed at Kensington Palace.

There are some whose clientele is almost totally West Indian—the West Indian is inclined to fancy dark horses. One in the Hammersmith Road opposite the Cadby Hall bakery has a clientele all floury white, like angels.

There are even family betting shops. There are few sadder sights than a row of round inquisitive faces, peering from their prams through the plastic strips of curtains, as if they know only too well what is happening to next week's supply of Cow and Gate.

Within a normal betting shop there are the following furnishings. Item: two or three battered stools, used to carrying overweight and amateur riders. Are they shining at the sides from the tight knee-grips of gamblers vicariously riding their nightmares in a tight finish?

Item: pages from the sporting newspapers pinned to the walls. These are useful, for do they not give the names of the winners and the reasons why? 'Yashma (3.45)', says the stable correspondent, 'has done well since her good but unavailing effort at Goodwood and should go too fast for her rivals in the Leas Nursery at Folkestone.' Alas, she didn't.

Day after day, these same assurances, confident predictions, rational arguments, all to such little purpose. What a resilient race are racing correspondents. Like unsuccessful surgeons who watch day after day as their patients subside under the knife. 'The going was too heavy, should have worn blinkers,' murmurs the anaesthetist, shaking his hoary head sorrowfully.

Raise your eyes from these gospels to those printed above where the light doesn't catch them. What do they say? 'When favourite odds-on Limit 3-1 to a place' and 'Place Bets only at Tote' and so forth.

These are to be studied with care, for they may hurt. '£10 limit horse forecast' can hurt a lot. Indeed the word 'Limit' is the one which should be emblazoned in letters of amber as a warning.

The rules of each house vary. If you have a pretty face, lady, you may get special odds at Kevin St. John O'Brady on Notting Hill. But try that in Joe Coral, and see where it gets you. Jack Swift's branch just off Kensington High Street has a special room for clients betting £5 or over. They are wise to the truth that the railway companies tumbled to years ago. People will pay extra to mix with people who will pay extra to mix with them. It has something of the feel, this room, of the prefects' common room. All mugs together.

Other notices on the walls might include extracts from the relevant betting and gaming acts, or warnings against pickpockets (an ironical touch that). Perhaps even occasionally a sop to aesthetics, a picture of a horse, a framed copy of a winning yankee bet—very aesthetic, that one. Or even, very rarely, a touch of fantasy. One little betting shop has a home-made picture of the 'oozlum bird' which makes up for the fact that they never seem to have as many winners there as at other more pretentious shops.

Item: the paying-in counter and Item: the paying-out window. The fact that the one is a whole counter and the other just a window is a fair comment on one's chances of winning.

Item: a back room. Here the settlers work. Settlers are not indigestion tablets, but a bespectacled race of gnomes who eat pencils and decree who shall lose how much how fast.

Item: the loudspeaker. This is the Pandora's box, from which, when all the winds blew out, hope at the bottom lay. You see, even after the announcement of the result there *could* always be an objection.

That is about all the items, except for the board with the 'blower' prices. This, the cynosure of all eyes, contains the names and current odds of all the horses in the imminent race or races. Some board-writers are true masters of their arts. G. Breskal of Circus Road, St. John's Wood, boasts the most handsome script, but the competition is fierce. If only those monk/copyists could be got out of their cells and produce a board with full illuminations. Now, that would be something.

G. Breskal is a fine, friendly shop and the eyes of the girl who takes your money are black like thunder-clouds and full of the promise of a cataclysmic storm.

If you prefer the fey, then perhaps Sid Ki-Ki Ltd. of Shepherd's Bush Road would be more to your taste. If you are of a religious inclination, then there's always the nearby G. Neighbour.

But the Harrods of Betting Shops, the Tiffany's, the Mecca and (more appropriately perhaps) the Jerusalem, is to be found in the Whitechapel Road opposite a sign which reads: 'This Week's Thought: *Smiles* are *Contagious*, Let's start AN EPIDEMIC!'. Here then is Morry Israel, modestly self-styled 'The finest betting shop in the world'.

This is indeed an emporium, a complex, a factory of fancies and fantasies with a host of cheeky East End talent to take your gelt and a petrified forest of punters exhorted by an insistent notice: 'Don't be Sorry—Bet with Morry'.

More to the point perhaps is the assurance that they pay fourth place in handicaps of fourteen or over, which concession includes doubles and trebles and accumulators. This is a concession which used to be more frequently found, but is now confined to the truly competitive.

Among betting shops which cannot be recommended for their terms are L. A. Bellamy of the King's Cross Road, which is opposite Freddie the Butcher's, and the Terry Downes branches which are inclined—as they are entitled—to limit your total winnings. Jack Pearce of the Finchley Road advertises a comprehensive list of eleven limitations, bless his heart.

But these are lessons which you must learn for yourselves and, if you are wise and you feel you must bet and your credit is good and your name's in Debrett and you study the 'form' (that's a horse-racing term), then start an account with a bookmaking firm.

And if you genuinely want to win—not many gamblers do—then that can be arranged too. But it is necessary to approach the business in a logical way. And the only logic about horse-racing is to learn from the bookmaker, whose business it is to win.

The wise bookmaker will refuse to take any each-way accumulating bet which (wait for it, this is a historic moment, six months later four thousand bookmakers jumped *en masse* off the dome of St. Paul's while the remaining few laid odds on which would reach the bottom first) includes a high proportion of fancied horses in two-year-old non-handicap races.

So, the wise punter will find a foolish bookmaker or betting shop which will take such bets.

But, perhaps the wisest punter of all is the one who doesn't. For then he can never lose.

Night Clubs

Unlike a gentleman's club, anybody can become a member of any night club. All it takes is money.

A selection of the nicest possible ways to night club. And afterwards, if you've any money left, how to find a stimulating experience, plus a warm inviting bed to slip into when it's all over . . . (But please check first. Clubs come and go. Especially go.)

A London night club can be anything from a tarted-up cellar under the rotting cabbages of Covent Garden (and smell like it) to a plush, perfumed, thick-carpeted mansion in Belgravia where the orchestra's repertoire still includes 'That's Why The Lady is a Tramp'.

What they must have in common, however, says the Greater London Council which licenses the city's clubs, are two lavatories: 'One for each sex.'

(This stipulation shows how sweetly innocent our civil servants are on the subject of clubland's clientele. Any night club regular could tell them that the clients of most London night clubs come in three sexes. Some even boast a fourth.)

Night clubs must also have a certificate from the Fire Brigade showing that the place won't go up in flames if a drunk misses the ash-tray in the dark.

Judging by many of the people who run clubs in London, it would appear that anyone who can meet those two requirements and swear with his tongue in his cheek that he won't engage in sidelines, like running a brothel upstairs, can set up in business.

The West End's night clubs are variously described as 'dens of iniquity, stinking sewers, haunts of the famous, havens of rest, clip joints, places to rendezvous with the little lady, and licensed whore shops'.

It all depends on whose clichés you believe—*The Stage*, *What's On*, the publicity men's blurbs, *The War Cry* or the Holy Joes' billboards.

But be sure of one thing: London at night has more to offer the pleasure-seeker than any other city in the world.

Paris is over-rated, New York can be a yawn and Berlin a bore. Americans, who fondly imagine themselves to be the fathers and mothers of gay fun-lovers, readily admit that London has the swingingest clubs around.

Occasionally, some swing too high and get closed, like the old Keyhole Club in St. James's. The place was a great embarrassment to the area as soon as it opened its doors. For it was right in the heart of the leather-bound daylight clubland of the Blimps.

The night before it was closed by the police, they had a plump naked lady climbing the flagpole of a raft. She was apparently trying to grasp a seaman's sweater, which was supposed to be a distress signal, panting heavily and sweating profusely under a property department sun. The audience was loving every tortuous move the lady made.

'It's all very symbolic, see,' whispered a pimply-faced press agent.

Eventually, when the plump lady got her hands on the sweater the lights went out and nobody ever did find out why she wanted the sweater. Perhaps she was merely seeking protection against sunburn.

Anyway, it was more than the cops could take and the place was closed the next night.

London night club customers are known as clients. They include royalty, movie stars, diplomats, gangsters, alcoholics, debs, philosophers, lawyers, queers, churchmen and prostitutes. But most of all, the client without whose cheque-book they could not exist— the flush, lush, my-wife-doesn't-understand-me, tired British businessman.

They also include *young* fashion models, bright *young* stage designers and photographers, *young* TV and screen writers and the best-heeled members of the community, the *young* pop stars.

From the small back rooms, where the old-style club owners count the takings, there are envious looks being cast in the direction of the young impresarios who are opening up the discotheques—a kind of kindergarten clubland.

While the 'traditional' clubs still paper their walls with synthetic appliqué velvet and won't let in a girl wearing trousers, the discotheques go in for synthetic fur-lined walls and girls with jeans and bare midriffs. They go like a bomb and the music from the hi-fi amplifiers is just as loud.

Thirdly, of course, there are the clubs whose main attraction are girls who wear nothing, from their ankles up to their false eyelashes —the strip clubs.

Opening time at a London strip club (lunchtime in some places) produces one of the strangest rituals in the great metropolis.

Businessmen hang about on the pavement outside, trying to

look as they are waiting for a bus or about to hail a taxi.

The doors open and there is a surreptitious shuffle into the club's bar. There are muttered: 'Oh, er, hello old man. Just thought I'd look in for a lunchtime drink. As good a place as any, don't you think?'

Then the lights are dimmed and the bar becomes suddenly empty. Half-finished pink gins lie on the counters. In the darkened auditorium bowler hats are pulled down over the eyes in an effort at greater anonymity.

But not too far down to spoil the view of the stage where variously assorted young and middle-aged women go through their acts.

Kathy Keeton, said to be 'the highest-paid stripper in the West End', wears little black dresses that come up to her Adam's apple and she drinks iced coke. She could pass for a school teacher—when she is not on duty. She once danced with the Royal Ballet for £8 a week.

She's a stripper, 'because if one is *artistic*, as I am, one makes so much more money'. Miss Keeton gets £125 a week.

'And one meets such interesting people in this business, er, profession.' She says that one admirer, a 'Prince Bobo' (anonymity is everything in the strip club business) once gave her a white E-type Jaguar.

But whatever pleasures you seek in the night spots of London they do not come cheaply.

It will take £10 to cover two people on a night out, although club owners deny this. They chew on their fat cigars and throw up their chubby hands in horror and cry: 'You can get out of my place for less than a fiver.' So you can—if you're on a diet, drink Perrier water and can put up with the impudent stares of waiters who want you to make room for the sugar daddy and his thirsty entourage coming through the door.

Some night clubs also have hostesses. Many pleasure-seekers think that the least said about these ladies the better. But no objective guide to night life can omit them. For they have given lonely men a shoulder to cry on on lonely nights—and have also been the cause of some of the biggest punch-ups and marriage mix-ups.

Hostesses are paid according to the amount of booze they can get the customer to consume and usually start the conversation by suggesting a bottle of good champagne at £6 which ends up as a bottle of bad champagne at £8. Some of them also like you to buy them teddy bears, cuddly toys and posies which go straight back into stock after you have gone home.

Hostesses, unless you are the most melancholy man in town and want to quadruple your bill, must be avoided.

When you come to picking your night spot don't be influenced by the name in neon above the door. If you go to Churchill's do not expect turtle soup, saddle of lamb and Napoleon brandy. Churchill's is a place that takes its drinking seriously and its eating light-heartedly.

Drinking is the main hobby of the night club classes. The fashion in drinks changes every few months. Gin has been 'out' and vodka and Scotch 'in' these last few years, but boozers are as fickle as a pop idol's following, and gin will be back in again any minute.

But crazy mixed up drinks, however, have always been 'in'. The man in charge of refuelling the clients at The Society finds the following concoction popular but potent: one measure of vodka, one measure of pernod and a jolt of grenadine. He calls it 'Asylum' for reasons that become obvious after you have had one.

One night club press agent says that the old Bloody Mary (vodka and tomato juice) has had its day and on its way in is the bloodiest mary of them all—vodka, gin, Scotch and tomato juice laced with a champagne and pepper sauce.

Among the young discotheque set, who have more money than good taste, the 'pop' drink is Scotch and Coke.

Having whetted or soured the appetite of the gay, the fun-loving, the licentious and the just plain curious, here is a brief guide to the night clubs of London.

LET'S LET OUR HAIR DOWN AND GET SLOSHED, DARLING-TYPE CLUB

STORK ROOM, Swallow Street: Run by Mr. Al Burnett, also known as the Knave of Clubs and the ham comedian who hasn't been cured.

Every morning at 12.30 he leaves the supervision of his other West End interests (the Society and the Pigalle) to his partner and leaps on to the stage here to spin the same jokes he has been telling for 25 years. The club has a loyal clientele, many of whom were night-clubbing in Burnett's places when the jokes were almost new.

Burnett explains to new members: 'I'd be double-crossing my clients if I told new jokes. The gimmick here is that the clients can bawl out the tag lines before I do. It makes them feel real sharp at three o'clock in the morning.' Heckling is encouraged. You can get sozzled here and no one throws you out. No one minds if you break a glass, so long as you don't attempt to do anyone an injury with the broken bits. Burnett simply puts the accident down on the bill as breakages. He says: 'A party of exuberant Greeks came in one night and threw down their goblets after every toast. They added £50 to their bill that way.'

If you must eat, try the steak sandwiches.

Sunday and Monday mornings are when this club's at its most uninhibited. Theatreland's hell-raisers look in then.

LET'S HAVE A SING-SONG-TYPE CLUB

ASTOR, Berkeley Street: Gregarious, raucous, it has a good band that plays everything from the Top Ten to the 'Marine Hymn' as a quick-step. The cabaret is usually three brash acts and The Astor Girls. It is essentially a place to drink. You can get a meal but few people remember the last time anybody asked for one. Nobody bothers much how you dress or if you smoke a pipe. The manager and 'genial mine host' is Verdi (top hat, carnation, cigar) who leads the brethren in song.

LET'S PUT ON THE SAVILE ROW AND PLAY IT COOL-TYPE CLUB

THE SADDLE ROOM, Hamilton Place: Sophisticated and inclined to be a bit debby. Young male escorts are not exactly chinless wonders, but neither are they Twickenham types with chin lines like the Cornish coast. Run by the Queen of Clubs (Helene Cordet) and a horse-riding enthusiast called Peter Davies.

Among Miss Cordet's claims to fame is the doubtful one of bringing the Twist to London's West End.

The sprinkling of hall-marked names would make this place very okay with Aunt Agatha if she demanded to see where you got to at night.

The book at the door includes names like King Hussein, and Lords Derby, Blandford, and Milford Haven. And they still talk about the night in 1960 when a tall Texan called Lyndon Johnson looked in at one of Cordet's other clubs and insisted on doing the Limbo with the boss.

LET'S SEE WHAT THE WILD ONES ARE UP TO-TYPE CLUB

FLAMINGO, Wardour Street: Get here around ten on a Saturday night and catch the free Pantomime of the Pavements. Out of town girls walk up and down the street looking for men with the price of admission. Coloured men walk behind them clinking the coins in their pockets. Middle-aged men in faded raincoats hang around seeking the fringe benefits. The police take in the scene from nearby cafés.

Inside, you can cut the atmosphere of beat, smoke and Coke with a chiv! The West Indian half of the clientele keep the jazz music standards high. There are two sessions at week-ends when you can dance from 7.30 until 11.30 for 5s. a head and from midnight until 6 a.m. for 10s. On a busy night you could be one of 800 on the floor. Doormen greet female clients with a cry of: 'Check your handbags, ladies. If you don't check your handbags keep them in your hands.'

LET'S GO TO THE LATEST (AT LEAST IT WAS YESTERDAY MORNING)—TYPE CLUB

SIBYLLA'S, Swallow Street: This is the latest mecca of the swinging set. Its motto should be 'Nothing succeeds like excess'. It has the most ear-splitting and expensive amplifying system, the strongest drinks, the biggest helpings, the hardest seats, the shortest skirts, and the most exhibitionistic members. Its much-heralded decor by David Mlinaric is completely invisible in the near darkness and the vast blue lamps on the walls give one a feeling of being on the set of Dixon of Dock Green. The appeal of Sibylla's lies in its membership list. This is the place to see and be seen. All the stars of London's discothequocracy, aristocracy and plutocracy constellate here.

LET'S SEE IF THE PLACE IS JUST AS DADDY DESCRIBED IT-TYPE CLUB

QUAGLINO'S and ALLEGRO, Bury Street: Yes, dear, it's much the same as Daddy left it. Hutch (Leslie Hutchinson) who has been around these parts off and on for close on 30 years, still keeps coming back like a song to send pleasant little shivers up and down the spines of his (now) matronly following.

If you are to believe the proprietors of most ancient inns in England, Queen Elizabeth I slept around quite a bit. But the royal tales are true at Quaglino's when they tell you that you are sitting at the very table the Duke and Duchess of Windsor (or Princess Margaret, or the Duchess of Kent or Lady Mountbatten) dined at. Posh, but friendly. You can eat reasonably or expensively.

LET'S TRY OUT THOSE TARTAN TREWS YOU BOUGHT IN THE BRITISH HOME STORES-TYPE CLUB

SCOTCH of ST. JAMES'S, Mason's Yard: It looks like a Scottish roadhouse that has been decorated by a Sassenach set designer. There are oak beams on the ceiling. The upholstery is tartan. So are some of the walls and carpets. The bar has been built out of hundreds of (empty) Scotch whisky bottles. But don't try to be funny and make with a phoney Scots accent, for no one will understand you. The drinks come in little sealed bottles so that you know no one has been watering it down.

It used to be a good place for whispering sweet nothings in a lady's ear. But it became 'in' with the pop groups and the music went up a million decibels. If you have anything to say to the lady, semaphore is the only communication system that will get it across to her, until the pop boys go elsewhere.

LET'S SEE THE DANCE OF THE SEVEN VEILS-TYPE CLUB
MURRAY'S CABARET CLUB, Beak Street: The place where the late Stephen Ward took Christine Keeler. They try to get too many half-naked showgirls on to the small dance floor with the result that you are apt to get a buttock or something in the eye if you are dining at a ringside table. Eastern gentlemen are among the regulars. They sit with inscrutable smiles on their dark faces, as if they were supermarket-shopping for a few more wives.

LET'S GO AND SEE MY OLD REGIMENT CHUMS, DARLING-TYPE CLUB
BLUE ANGEL, Berkeley Street: When Marlene Dietrich is in town she is frequently to be seen, elegant legs crossed, perched on a bar stool gazing at a larger-than-life picture of the said legs above the bar.

La Dietrich first became a close friend of the late Max Setty when he ran the old Orchid Room. When he opened the Blue Angel he dedicated it to his chum by calling it after her old movie. A favourite refuelling stop for guardees and their debs. It serves drinks at pub prices until 11 p.m. and is about the only nightspot where you can get a pint of draught beer. The cabaret is usually made up of middle-of-the-bill (but good) performers.

LET'S GET WITH IT WITH THE GAY YOUNG THINGS-AND THEIR DADDIES TOO-TYPE CLUB
THE AD LIB AT THE 400, Leicester Square. This is now a straight-forward discotheque. As The 400, it used to be one of the most snobbish and old-fashioned night clubs in London. But its snobbest box (for Royals only) has gone. It's now a bar. Now almost anything goes, from the Bertie Woosters to the mini-skirters.

Showman and public relations man John Kennedy, who has a hand in running the place, says: 'Where else can you find Lord Plunkett, Lord Blandford, Diana Dors, James Ormsby-Gore, a pool of typists, fashion models and fashion photographers and the occasional highly paid young docker all dancing together?'

Sartorially, anything goes from white sharkskin dinner jackets to jeans. Usually there is a Beatle or two sitting quietly in a corner or a group of Rolling Stones noisily drinking whisky and Coke. The atmosphere is heavy with Gauloise smoke.

CROMWELLIAN, Cromwell Road: The Beatles have also given this one their blessing. Popular with the young pop idols and their fans who like the noise and the fact that you never know who's going to get up and sing next. It also caters for those who think Dusty Springfield is a neglected rifle by having three bars and a gambling room. Rule of the house: no autographs. Three hundred gay fun-lovers can crowd in at at one time. The six directors take it in turn to shepherd the flock. Five of them are professional wrestlers and between them they weigh 80 stones. So don't go looking for a punch-up.

LET'S SEE A DRAG SHOW–TYPE CLUB
DANNY LA RUE's, Hanover Square: There's a story going the rounds that a drunk once staggered in here, weaved his way to the stage, kissed Danny La Rue on both cheeks and proposed marriage to him. This is strenuously denied by Mr. La Rue, a female imperso-nator who says: 'Everyone out front knows there's a fellow under-neath the gowns and the wigs. That's the giggle. Everyone knows I am a fellow impersonating a bird. I am also a chap letting birds know that he has caught on to them.'

His cabaret offers what he calls 'subdued satire to sophisticated audiences'. A good place to go if you think you've seen it all before. It is one of the few places in the late-late supper beat where the food is really good. Lady Lewisham (probably the fussiest woman in London about food), Vivien Leigh and Judy Garland have been here.

IS THERE A STRIP CLUB YOU CAN TAKE ME TO, DARLING?– TYPE CLUB
RAYMOND'S REVUEBAR, Brewer Street: The most imaginative strip club in town—it also has girls who wear clothes *all* the time. Mickey Spillane went there and reported that it had 'the sexiest girls

I've seen'. Its girls have names like Peki and Boo and it offers improbable attractions like Nudes on Real Ice, The Girl in the Golden Fish Tank, The Golden Nude and nude films in sin-erama. The bars are comfortable, the restaurant expensive and the hostesses a little too persistent.

I'M GETTING A LITTLE SHORT OF CASH, DARLING-TYPE CLUB

PIGALLE, Piccadilly: For people who like to see what they are eating and also what's going on at the other tables. It is a big, well-lit room. No one will stop you spending a tenner, but they'll settle for a 30s. minimum per person. For this you can also dance and see two floor shows. Tell the head man that you are enjoying yourself on a limited budget and he will see that you are not worried by predatory waiters.

LET'S AVOID THE PLACE LIKE THE PLAGUE-TYPE CLUB

Any room that advertises itself as being 'the haunt of stars of stage, screen, radio and television'. It's 100 to 1 that the nearest you will get to ogling a member of the show business profession will be a quick look at the doorman from a neighbouring theatre in for a quick one.

BUT WHAT THE HELL WILL I DO WITH THE CAR?-TYPE CLUB

L'HIRONDELLE, Swallow Street: Joseph Mourat who started in the club business when he was twelve (he ran a café in a Cyprus village barber's shop) sees that the doorman parks your car while you eat his special dishes and drink his Turkish liquor. Two girlie floor shows at night and one for the lunch-time crowd. Food can be pricey, but it's the best you will find in the West End clubs. If the food takes its time getting to the table it is because every main dish is cooked to order.

If the pleasure-seeker has done his club-crawl too conscientiously it is more than likely that he will be faced with the following poser: 'It is four a.m. How the hell do I get home to Bexley, have a sleep and get up in time for the ten a.m. board meeting without a hangover?'

The answer to that one, as any dusk till dawn reveller will tell him, is that he doesn't. He seeks out William Morrison, who is the superintendent of the Turkish bath in Jermyn Street. Mr. Morrison is a dab hand at dealing with a hangover before it actually happens. 'We have been here since the turn of the century,' he says of the establishment, 'so we are not without experience in dealing with this age-old problem. We have handled some of the most sophisticated potential hangovers in the West End.'

Mr. Morrison, a soft-spoken Scot, will remove all his client's clothes and give him a little chequered loin-cloth in return. He will also take his client's watch and his wallet, if there is enough money left in it to classify it as a valuable, lock them away and hand him to a Mr. Jack Raymond, who says: 'The Romans and the Colonel Blimps, who knew how to acquire a hangover, had the right idea— the therapeutic luxury of the Turkish bath.'

Mr. Raymond then puts him in a steam room for ten minutes. The client next finds himself in a drying-off chamber marked 150-170 Fahrenheit in which he is incarcerated until he cries 'Help!' Wrapped in hot towels, he is put to bed, given hot coffee and told to sleep it off. Nine times out of ten it works and the client makes his ten o'clock appointment.

Cost of the cure: 30s.

Visit the Serpentine at 7 a.m. and see High Court Judges and others bathing.

Gentlemen's Clubs

Once inside one, so they used to say, a gentleman was safe from his wife, his creditors and the world outside.

Now, the world has caught up with the clubs. They all need credit, if not money itself, however vulgar. And some, why, they even allow women inside.

But gentlemen's clubs are still one of London's unique attractions. The question is, which gentlemen for which clubs?

Gay young clubmen, it is said, used sometimes, in jollier days, to play the London Golf Match, teeing off from the steps of the United Service Club and holing out through the door of the Berkeley. This very English jape would have taken them along a dog-leg of two uniquely English streets, Pall Mall and St. James's. In that quarter-mile stand fourteen of the most famous clubs in the world. Other countries have imitated them; the Jockey Club in Paris, the Century and the Knickerbocker in New York, seem almost more English than their originals. They pay tribute by their existence to London, the mother city of clubs.

The golfer's first drive whistled past the Athenaeum and between the massive grey fronts of the nineteenth-century clubs which proliferated in the expansive years following the defeat of Napoleon.

The second shot must have been played near where the rebuilding of the Army and Navy and of the Junior Carlton now indicates the shape of things to come.

But the real heart of clubland is round the corner and up the hill. The approach shot would have passed Brooks's on the left and Boodle's and White's on the right; those beautiful Regency fronts and bow-windows behind which the London club first emerged, butterfly-like, from the chrysalis of the coffee shop.

Nowhere on this enchanted fairway would you find the Drones Club, which P. G. Wodehouse is said to have based remotely on the now defunct Bachelors. Nor will you find Blade's, which, in the course of James Bond's adventures, was imperceptibly transformed from a sort of raffish Almack's to a version of Boodle's. Ian Fleming himself usually lunched at Boodle's because, he said, he 'liked dull clubs' and at White's the members 'gassed too much'. But the

Drones and Blade's will always be Platonic ideas in some celestial clubland.

Fiction has, however, affected reality, colouring not only the outsider's image of clubland but, to some extent, the clubman's own notion of how he ought to behave.

In Buchan, Sapper, Dornford Yates and Francis Beeding, the Club is a 'totem', the place 'where all good fellows meet', the jumping-off point and the haven of adventurers. The passer-by may hope to glimpse through the window lean bronzed men, grouped round a roaring fire, swapping stories of their latest adventures in the Hindu Kush or the hinterland of Brazil; or possibly an armament king and a politician plotting a war; or the head of the secret service briefing his newest agent.

If the passer-by in fact sees nothing but a few old gentlemen asleep or reading newspapers, this scene too conjures up some famous anecdotes—like the Peer whose demise was only noticed because *The Times* covering his face was yesterday's edition. Or the two elderly members, who hadn't spoken to one another for twenty years, sitting together in the bow window of their club. One, having glanced through the obituary column of *The Times*, lowered his paper and said: 'I see that you've just buried your wife.'

'Yes,' replied the other. 'Had to. Dead, you know.'

Clubland is rich in anecdotes; of young bucks and venerable eccentrics, of Bishops in the Athenaeum and peppery Generals in the 'Senior', as the United Service Club is known, because there used to be a Junior United Service.

A Bishop saw on the notice board that the 'Senior' would be billeted at the Athenaeum during August. 'Oh dear, oh dear,' he wailed, 'all those brutal faces.'

Conversely, a member of the Guards Club was asked what it had been like giving hospitality to the Savile. 'They were quite decent little fellows,' he said. 'No trouble. Make their own trousers, of course.'

If the passer-by, nourished on such legends, were to go in through the swing-doors, he might find the reality disappointing. Club life is not what it used to be. In the evenings, many clubs are almost deserted, positive mausoleums, or, as was said of Brooks's, 'like a Duke's house—with the Duke lying dead upstairs.' The members have been sucked into domesticity or suburbia.

But there is still a core of members for whom the Club is a very important part of life. If they live in London, they go there every day. If they live in the country, the Club is their base when they visit London. Most of them probably belong to more than one club.

Max Beerbohm said that clubs were his form of economy, because he could entertain more cheaply there. Since the average subscription now approaches forty guineas, clubmanship is not a cheap form of economy, though by historical and international standards London clubs are a bargain. The house dinner at White's cost 12s. without wine in 1797. It costs only a shilling or so more today. Subscriptions and the price of meals have been rising lately, but not *pari passu* with inflation.

What does the clubman get for his money? He gets an elegant and spacious house with old-fashioned servants to welcome him; deep peace; a safe retreat from the modern world; a warm vantage point, from which (as an aristocratic member of Boodle's once put it, gazing loftily through the window at St. James's Street) to 'watch the damned people getting wet'.

On the material level, he gets tolerable meals in civilised circumstances. It is much pleasanter to lunch at one's club than in a noisy restaurant; pleasanter, at least, for anybody who has learned the lesson of Oxford and Cambridge—'to prefer a silver salt cellar which doesn't pour rather than a plastic one which does'.

The food at its best is apt to be of a nursery or prep school kind: steak and kidney pie, rice pudding, Boodle's Cake, bananas and cream. The wine is usually very good indeed, and substantially cheaper than a restaurant could offer.

What he gets in the way of company rather depends on the particular club. There is a sharp division between talking clubs, such as the Garrick and the Savile and *par excellence* the Beefsteak, and non-talking clubs, such as the Travellers' and the Oxford and Cambridge and the R.A.C. (The R.A.C., with a membership of 15,000, is more like a hotel than a club; its facilities are superb, its atmosphere is nil.)

Most clubs have card rooms, and some, notably Boodle's and the St. James's, still play backgammon. But the revival in London of genuine gambling clubs, such as Crockford's and the Clermont, has syphoned off many of the keenest players. 'Candle-money' at White's—fines of £2 an hour for keeping the club open after 1.30 a.m.—dropped from £4,828 in 1952 to a mere £400 ten years later.

The average age of clubmen is high. Not so very long ago one elderly gentleman, standing in front of the fireplace at the Junior

Carlton, was overheard to ask another, 'Do you ever read thrillers?' 'Oh, yes,' replied the other. 'I read *The Woman in White* by that feller Wilkie Collins.'

The Athenaeum, it's slanderously rumoured, elects members as old as possible, in order to get the biggest turnover of entrance fees.

Most clubs, however, are so anxious to recruit young members that they offer reduced subscriptions to anyone under thirty. Even so they are not conspicuously successful. The most desirable form of recruiting is for fathers to propose their sons. At Brook's there are sixth, seventh, and even eighth generation members. But in club-land, as in Oxford and Cambridge colleges, though for slightly different reasons, such traditions are in danger of being broken. Too often, the younger generation cannot afford, or may not even want, to follow the old ways.

White's has currently an eight-year waiting list. Pratt's is in the same enviable position. At Brook's and Boodle's the waiting list is about eighteen months. Very few other clubs have any waiting list at all, and some periodically send out a discreet circular urging members to propose suitable candidates. At the best clubs candidates need the support of perhaps a dozen signatures: at others a single proposer and seconder will do.

In more robust days, blackballing—sometimes malicious recipro-cal blackballing—was a real terror and could become a threat to a club's continuance.

Most clubs have now delegated the power of election, and there-fore, in effect, of blackballing, to a committee. Candidates are scrutinised, and their names posted, shortly before election days. But any unsuitable ones have been quietly eliminated long before. A letter to the committee, a word in the proposer's ear, and the offending name is ruled through in the Candidates' Book with the courteous explanation 'Withdrawn at candidate's own request'. The stories, told both of Brooks's and of Boodle's, about some venerable club servant slipping an extra black ball into the ballot-box because he feared the election of a notoriously unsuitable candidate, belong unmistakably to the past.

Which is not wholly a good thing. Blackballing was undoubtedly abused, but, as a member of the Garrick wrote in the 1870s, 'it would be better that ten unobjectionable men should be excluded than that one terrible bore should be admitted'; a bore can very easily drive people out of a club. And there are other legitimate grounds for exclusion. Indeed, if any considerable group of members object to a candidate for any reason, no matter how arbitrary or frivolous, their objections must carry weight: for to let the candidate in will provoke dissention and schism and bad feeling, which are fatal to the atmosphere of a club.

The admission of active socialists, particularly members of a Labour Government, is just such a cause of dissention. At political clubs, such as the Carlton and the Constitutional, the difficulty does not arise: and the Reform (where candidates are obliged to say that they support the Reform Act of 1842) perhaps deserves to have Dr. Kaldor and Dr. Balogh among its members. Lord Longford, however, was blackballed for the City of London Club by certain members who said they weren't going to let a man in who was dedicated to destroying the whole system on which the City and the Club depended. Lord Longford treated his rejection as a joke, while his proposers were embarrassed and indignant: but the blackballers' argument seems not unreasonable.

Socialists can, nevertheless, be found throughout clubland, though not in great numbers because not very many have wished to join. Sir Jock Campbell is a member of White's, Roy Jenkins of Brook's: Hugh Gaitskell joined the Garrick and Harold Wilson is a member —*ex officio* rather than because he wanted to be or because anybody particularly wanted him—of the Athenaeum. All sorts of people who would have been contemptuously rejected in the high days of clubland, because they lacked breeding or were in trade, are now welcomed. Charles Clore was recently accepted by the Carlton.

Just as there are 'good' regiments and 'good' schools, and everybody knows which they are, so too there are 'good' clubs; clubs which retain a certain quality and bestow a certain prestige. White's, Boodle's and Brook's are the premier three, accompanied by the two dining clubs, Pratt's and the Beefsteak. Even these aristocratic clubs have not altogether escaped the erosions and alterations of time. To get into the Beefsteak, someone once said, you have to be 'related to God—and a damned close relation at that.' No such exclusiveness applies today. To get into even the best clubs now you need only be a reasonably acceptable sort of person, familiar with the proper use of a knife and fork, capable of speaking the Queen's English, and acquainted with half a dozen of the members: and, in the case of White's and Pratt's, prepared to wait rather a long while.

Brooks's, house of the Whig Grandees, once the most famous political club in England, is political no longer; most of the members are conventionally Conservative, though there remains a small Liberal residue. At Boodle's in the old days, if a visitor asked for 'Sir John', half the members were said to turn round; there is still a solid core of country squires, but there are plenty of businessmen too.

Buck's, though more than 200 years younger than White's, comes quite close in social *cachet*, and can claim two notable distinctions: that it is owned by the man who started it, Captain Herbert Buckmaster, and that it has given its name to 'Buck's Fizz', the delicious combination of champagne and orange juice. The Turf, too, has an aristocratic membership, including, at the last count, no fewer than sixteen Dukes; but it is by no means as prestigious an institution as the Jockey Club in Paris, with which it has reciprocal arrangements.

The Athenaeum has intellectual, rather than social, prestige; it is large and not cosy, but it does contain a great many academically distinguished people. The Garrick, with its carefully maintained balance of actors, lawyers and journalists, is perhaps more universally praised than any other club. Everybody, however loyal to his own, would like to belong to the Garrick as well.

Then comes the mass of decent, but less romantic, clubs. The St. James's and the Travellers' (referred to in the Foreign Office as 'the office canteen') specialise in diplomatists. Candidates for the Travellers' must have journeyed 500 miles in a straight line from London. Time has devalued this qualification, just as a change in the type of undergraduates has devalued the qualification for entry to the Oxford and Cambridge or the United University: but in practice the committees do demand a little more.

Of the political clubs, the Carlton is unquestionably the best—almost every Conservative MP with any social pretensions belongs to it: and the Junior Carlton is the most political, holding regular discussion groups and dinners, and, at election time, raising a special fund and sending teams into the constituencies. The Constitutional used to be known as 'the lava-Tory', but now enjoys the more salubrious premises of the deceased Union Club. The National Liberal has little, either architecturally or socially, to recommend it.

Of the Service clubs, the 'Senior' is indeed the senior, the solidest and the most famous. The Army and Navy Club (known for doubtful reasons as 'the Rag') has a shiny new building, which does seem to be attracting some younger members; an enterprise in which it has to compete with the Naval and Military Club (known, from the words on its gateposts, as 'the In and Out'). The Guards Club and the Cavalry Club are more select and more prosperous, more youthful and jollier, because membership is almost *de rigeur* for officers in the Brigade and in cavalry regiments.

The Savile has been described as 'a pullman car version of the

Savage'. Both are made up of writers, publishers, artists, entertainers and kindred spirits. Conversation is plentiful and gossip prevalent. They are not 'Establishment' clubs.

Membership of the Bath, the Devonshire, the East India and Sports, the Public Schools or the R.A.C., is no doubt convenient and agreeable but bestows little distinction: nor does membership of such 'cock and hen' clubs as the Lansdowne or the Overseas League.

Around the constellation of 'good' clubs lies a whole Milky Way of lesser establishments, from the Arts Theatre to the United Hunts, from Hurlingham to the Farmers' Club, from the Caledonian to the Number Ten (which belongs to the Institute of Directors and provides directorial-sized lumps of sugar and ballpoint pens disguised as quills).

About the very few women's clubs, such as the Forum, the less said the better. They are an anomaly. Women are not clubbable, and they resent spending money on a hearty lunch or on wine, which are the essence of club life.

With the notable exception of White's and Brooks's, however, both of which have perhaps been inhibited rather by architectural limitations than by any theoretical objection, most clubs now either have a Ladies' Annexe or else allow women guests to dine, on at least certain nights of the week, in a carefully segregated part of the Coffee Room.

In some, the Ladies' Annexe has become almost a separate entity. Not only can wives and daughters of club members use the Annexe unaccompanied, but they can become 'Associate Members' and even (for example, at the Oxford and Cambridge) propose and second other women who may have no connection with any male member of the club at all.

The latest Ladies' Annexe to be built is at Boodle's, a benefit reaped by the club from the neighbouring redevelopment scheme. Considering with what care Boodle's itself has preserved the atmosphere and solid comfort of a beautiful country house, one might have expected something of unusual elegance. Surprisingly and unfortunately, the result looks more like a ship's bar than a drawing-room.

One of the newest club buildings, that of the Army and Navy, has no Ladies' Annexe, for the simple reason that women are allowed through the main entrance and in all the best rooms; it is the misogynistic males who must be content with rather gloomy purdah.

In the grand days of clubland even male guests were allowed, if they were allowed at all, only grudgingly and in special rooms. Now the entertainment of guests of both sexes has become an important source of revenue. Young men in particular are said, when deciding on a club, to want one where they can entertain girls. 'Nonsense,' reply the managers of Brooks's. 'There's Prunier's just down the road, and the Berkeley at the top.' It is certainly true that in most Ladies' Annexes there seem to be more elderly wives and juvenile daughters than girl friends.

As costs, especially rates and wages, continue to soar, the search for new sources of revenue becomes increasingly urgent. The generally accepted view is that subscriptions should be kept down as far as possible and money made from the sale of drinks and food. Not so long ago the very idea of a bar was considered rather vulgar: now it is a vital part of every club's economy. (Not quite every club, as a matter of fact; the Athenaeum still disdains to have a bar.)

The trouble is that in most clubs, except at lunch time, the mood is scarcely jovial enough to encourage heavy drinking. There is a distinct lack of the cheerful bread-throwing which guests at the Drones Club were warned to expect. White's is the most successful. It has a touch of raffishness still, and the bar makes a big profit. At Brooks's, Boodle's and the Carlton, the dining-room may be almost full in mid-week while Parliament is sitting, but at other times business would be considered brisk if the candles were lit at more than two or three tables.

Bridge dinners, annual club dinners, private dinners sponsored by individual members, even cocktail parties, provide useful additions to revenue at the cost of some slight inconvenience to other members.

More ambitious celebrations are rarely expected to do more than pay for themselves. Such celebrations are infrequent, elaborate and rather splendid. The Pall Mall clubs, when they hold a dance or a big party, light the gas flares which line their parapets, projecting a splendid Victorian glow against the night sky or into the autumn mist. In St. James's they make do with the glitter of tiaras.

Both Boodle's and Brooks's recently celebrated their two hundredth anniversaries with a 'Rout' and a dance. Routs are less bacchanalian than they sound. Old gentlemen do not fling half-naked girls across their immaculately tail-coated shoulders and run, chuckling, upstairs to the bedrooms. A rout is merely an evening party: but how many evening parties are there in modern Britain at which everybody is properly dressed and good champagne flows freely?

Modern Britain is not helpful to clubland (smoke-control regulations even make it difficult to have a decent fire), nor congenial to clubmen; indeed, one of the chief functions of a club is to be a fortress against modernity and the outside world. It should be cosy and protective. Once inside, a man should be safe from his wife and his creditors and from the pestering and jostling and raucousness of vulgar persons. It must, therefore, be reasonably exclusive. You could no more let everybody into White's and expect it still to be White's than you could fill Eton with children from broken homes and scholarship boys from council schools and expect it still to be Eton.

The death-rate among clubs has been high. Almack's and Arthur's are long gone. The Marlborough, Wyndham's, the Bachelors, the Junior United Service, the Thatched House, the Union, are one with Nineveh and Tyre. But there may still be too many clubs for the present-day population of clubmen. There will probably be more amalgamations, more deaths.

For death (and a distribution of the assets, which generally come to about £300 a member) is preferable to too much compromise. If clubs are to be no different from hotels, if the standard of service—and it is the servants as much as the members who make a good club—is to decline and become as surly as in the outside world, if the old traditions are to be discarded, outsiders let in and the whole enterprise commercialised, what is the point in belonging to a club at all?

The essence of a good club is that members should treat it as their own house. (Old-fashioned clubmen therefore believe that no member should buy a drink for another member; a tradition which revenue-hungry committees are glad to see forgotten.) A member of White's once said that a club ought to have only two rules:

(1) That every member should pay his subscription.
(2) That he should behave like a gentleman.

Alas, even in clubland things are not as simple as that. With the influx of the middle classes at the beginning of this century, much of the easy *camaraderie*, not to say bloody-mindedness and eccentricity, was lost, and the rules multiplied.

Bad behaviour and memorable insults are now as rare as black-balling. The last *cause célèbre* was the occasion when John Fox-Strangways kicked Aneurin Bevan on the steps of White's. Fox-Strangways was obliged to resign, but part of the guilt must lie with Sir John Slessor, who brought Bevan into the club; an act as foolish and inconsiderate as parading a fox in a kennel of hounds.

Though much is taken, much remains. To those without the

instincts of a clubman, London clubs may seem musty and boring. But to the true clubman, the dog-leg of Pall Mall and St. James's is Mecca still.

Every city, every nation, every stratum of society, has its own clubs. Communist Party clubs, chess clubs, jazz clubs, clubs for all sorts and conditions of men. But the glory of a London club, its unique quality, is that it was built by, is organised for, and still contains, that peculiar and dwindling species, the English gentleman.

If you like the English gentleman and feel at home with him, you will like London clubs. Even if you don't, it is still one of the last places to see him in captivity, sitting in a deep leather armchair in front of a blazing fire, with old oil-paintings on the wall, an old port at his elbow, taking refuge from the vile and vulgar world outside.

Gentlemen's Clubs

The First Eleven
Not just gentlemanly, positively aristocratic. All socially and architecturally attractive, with great prestige.

The top five usually have a long waiting list. But they are not as completely exclusive as they once were.

WHITE'S, ST. JAMES'S, S.W.I
Probably most prestige of all. Certainly the best gossip in London. Up to eight year waiting list.

Reciprocal arrangements: None.

BOODLES, 28 ST. JAMES'S STREET, S.W.I
Ask for Sir John and half the members will turn round, at least that is what they used to say. Still lots of titles, but many more stock-brokers.

Reciprocal arrangements:
The Somerset Club – Boston, U.S.A.
The Travellers' – Paris
The Union Club – Sydney, Australia
The Kildare Street Club – Dublin
The Melbourne Club – Australia
Nouveau Cercle – Paris

BROOKS'S, ST. JAMES' STREET, S.W.I
Formerly the most famous political club of all, full of Whig grandees, now mildly Conservative.
    Reciprocal arrangement:
        The Knickerbocker – New York

PRATT'S, 14 PARK PLACE, S.W.I
Essentially a dining club. Long waiting list.

BEEFSTEAK, 19 IRVING STREET, W.C.2
Also essentially a dining club, but excellent talk as well.
    Reciprocal arrangements:
        The Traveller's – Paris
        Beefsteak – Melbourne

BUCK'S, 18 CLIFFORD STREET, W.I
Founded and owned by Captain Herbert Buckmaster who invented 'Buck's Fizz' a cocktail of orange juice and champagne.

TURF, 5 CARLTON HOUSE TERRACE, S.W.I
Owners, not bookies. Very aristocratic—sixteen Dukes at last count. Not as prestigious as Jockey Club of Paris.
    Reciprocal arrangements:
        Jockey Club – Paris
        Caccia Club – Rome

ATHENAEUM, PALL MALL, S.W.I
Intellectually exclusive—full of academics and Bishops.

GARRICK, GARRICK STREET, W.C.2
Easier to get into, and nicer atmosphere than Athenaeum. Top actors, journalists, writers.
    Reciprocal arrangements:
        Players Club – New York
        Lotos Club – New York
        Century Association – New York
        Travellers' Club – Paris

TRAVELLERS, 106 PALL MALL, S.W.I
Full of diplomats, sometimes known as 'Foreign Office canteen'.

ST. JAMES'S, 106 PICCADILLY, W.I
Diplomatic; has a 'younger' set of Old Etonians and high bridge and backgammon games.

The Rest

Good, solid and gentlemanly, but not in the same Establishment league as the top eleven. They tend to be rather dull, especially the first four.

OXFORD AND CAMBRIDGE UNITED UNIVERSITY, 71 PALL MALL, S.W.I
Now that anyone can get into Oxbridge—such as all those Grammar School lads—not much prestige left.

SAVILE, 69 BROOK STREET, W.I
Actors, journalists, writers. Good talk.

SAVAGE, 37 KING STREET, W.C.2
Tourist class version of Savile.

R.A.C., PALL MALL, S.W.I
Has to be mentioned as it has 15,000 members. Excellent facilities, but as much atmosphere as Butlins.

Political Clubs

CARLTON, 69 ST. JAMES'S STREET, S.W.I
Traditionally THE Conservative Club.

JUNIOR CARLTON, PALL MALL, S.W.I
Conservative, but mainly businessmen, not politicians, but much political activity.

CONSTITUTIONAL, 86 ST. JAMES'S STREET, S.W.I
Conservative, but dull.

NATIONAL LIBERAL, WHITEHALL PLACE, S.W.I
Liberal, but dull.

REFORM, PALL MALL, S.W.I
Candidates obliged to subscribe to principles of the 1832 Reform Act, but Club is no longer political. Excellent building.

Service Clubs

UNITED SERVICES, 116 PALL MALL, S.W.I
'The Senior'.

ARMY AND NAVY, PALL MALL, S.W.I
'The Rag'.

NAVAL AND MILITARY, 94 PICCADILLY, W.I
'The In and Out'.

THE CAVALRY CLUB, 127 PICCADILLY, W.I
No nickname, but jollier, younger membership.

A Guide to the London Jazz Clubs

Cafe des Artistes, corner of Redcliffe Gardens/Fulham Road, FLA 6200
Dark, labyrinthine cellars for subterranean pleasures of Chelsea set;
juke-box and honkers nightly for twisting till 3 a.m.

Eel Pie Island, Twickenham
Boasts a magnificent bar, blaring R & B and pop trad. for multi-
farious youthful disaffiliates, who turn most sessions into a wild
party, especially at week-ends.

Flamingo & Allnighter Clubs, 33-7 Wardour Street, GER 1549
Of all the city's cellars the most favoured by coloured population,
which means wailing audience participation and a ball for the best
bands—Ronnie Jones's and Georgie Fame's; more R & B than
serious modern jazz; Thursday—Sunday, with sessions from
midnight to dawn Fridays and Saturdays.

100 Club, 100 Oxford Street, GER 0337
New Orleans (Mike Daniels), Mainstream (Alex Welsh), electric
R & B (Graham Bond), and meaty representation of all the jazz
styles in between; every evening of the week.

Ken Colyer Club, Studio 51, 10 Great Newport Street
Back to the delta, with heartfelt revivalist fervour—for afficionados
only.

Marquee, 90 Wardour Street, GER 8923
Atmosphere a cross between lush swimming-pool and young
people's night-club; crowded out on week-nights for some of the
best rhythm-&-bluesniks (Manfred Mann, Long John Baldry), as
well as some of the worst; less acclaim at week-ends for top
mainstream and modern groups (Lyttelton, Brown/Fairweather,
Don Rendell, Joe Harriott), but transformed into a throbbing
whirl of authentic jazz feeling when visited—about once a month,
by transatlantic giants (Red Allen, Memphis Slim, Stan Getz).

Ronnie Scott's, 47 Frith Street, GER 4752
Most enterprising, and most dedicated to present the best new jazz
from anywhere—from the most formidable Americans to obscure
Poles, Belgians and Italians, and otherwise untapped local talent
(Stan Tracey, Bobby Wellins, Dick Morrissey); capacity only 160,
so it's advisable to reserve tables in advance; only club licensed for
real food and drink open till 3 a.m. nightly.

Tiles, 79 Oxford Street, GER 2977
Not jazz, but the latest teenage pop scene (at least till the next one
comes along).

The Scene, Ham Yard, Great Windmill Street
For teenagers, sociologists and passing fad-fanciers of beat music;
till dawn at week-ends.

Jazz has become an international language which speaks to all, and
by means of which all may meet, speak openly and enjoy themselves. The substrata through which its origins have been diffused
are well represented by the distinctions between the main London
centres.

Most fans tend to stick to one club, which they may visit more
than once a week. Ask the regulars why they go to a particular spot
on a particular night, and you'll get a learned critique of the finer
points of the resident band and its musical genre.

Enthusiasts from all over the world are welcomed by most
managements and clienteles, and a common interest in the music—
be it traditional, folk, mainstream, modern, rhythm-&-blues or
beat, can lead to lively friendships. A newcomer to the scene should,
however, tread softly until he's sure the clubs of his choice have
something in store to please his tastes.

One of the most open houses—socially and musically—is the
Marquee, where a great deal of trouble has been taken to create an
atmosphere of luxurious comfort, with ample space to dance or just
be cool in, and diverse jazz messages sounded each night.

Another melting-pot is the *100 Club*, where sweating dervishes
in jeans and thick jerseys lump about lustily alongside neat but
unprotesting shopgirls, clerks and students. If you want to avoid
seeing anyone, or being seen, this is the place—even the stand is often
in semi-darkness.

At both of these clubs high-spirited adolescents dig in amiably
enough with surviving first-generation jazz-club types, e.g. the
sharp besuited ex-Teds with their chicks in the latest continental
fashions, the intellectual/bohemian/beatnik fringe, and the woman-
chasing, beer-swilling hearties who spend half the evening in pubs
round the corner, college scarves rampant—dubbed Hooray
Henries by the musicians. Sample chat in this ambience: 'Is this the
Jazz Club? Where's Humph? I don't see any darkies . . . We want
"the Saints"!'—'Seen anything of Gwen lately?—No—She's got a
new boy-friend, I hear—art student. They go out to *Eel Pie*—Oh
yea. Where they dance in their slips—An' wear beards instead of
shoes—Still, the music's all right—You bet—If you like that sort of
thing—Better than the old records . . .'

191

The trouble is, of course, that it isn't. As the clubs are completely at the mercy of public demand, a genealogy of the popularisation of jazz will be in order.

The Southern U.S. environment of negro immigrants begat the blues and traditional jazz. Chicago-style and Dixieland were the result of this new negro music's impact on white American musicians, and British 'mainstream' is our translation of what grew out of this—the multi-coloured amalgam of variations on Basie's '4 beats to the bar an' no messin' ', Kansas City and swing styles.

The inventive 'bebop' or modern jazz of the early '40s was the revolt of geniuses such as Charlie Parker, Dizzy Gillespie and Thelonius Monk against the narrow harmonies and technical limitations of traditional jazz and the stereotyped big-bands of the day, pioneered in Britain by George Shearing, and then men like Kenny Graham and the prodigies Victor Feldman and Tubby Hayes —at the same time as Humphrey Lyttelton and Chris Barber were disseminating the New Orleans Revival.

Out of this, and the renewal of researches into American music from that of plantation slaves onward, emanated the 'skiffle' of Lonnie Donegan, and the more conscionable transposition of 'race' records and folk-song at places like the *Round-House* in Wardour Street (consecrated to Folk by Cyril Davis and Alexis Korner circa '54, and still one of its most eloquent mouthpieces in town).

The crazes for trad, and subsequently R & B or beat music, are peculiarly British phenomena, dependent for their popularity on adulteration of their genuine sources with rock 'n' roll and concomitant (usually white American) corruptions.

Louis Armstrong held that 'rock 'n' roll is only cold soup warmed up', and in the cheapest British menus it's the same recipe many more times over-boiled, with little to recommend it except the hunger of its new young public and its often newer, younger chefs.

The exuberant yet self-possessed audience for these latest excesses has all but taken over several clubs, and the management of *Tiles* has gone so far as to discourage over-25s in order to cater for it ('No ogling the teens').

At the other end of the scale, the solid prices for solid fare at *Ronnie Scott's*—and its lack of a dance-floor, rule it out for any but the most sophisticated absolute beginners, really hip to music it's worth listening to intently.

The Flamingo and Allnighter Clubs, too, are peopled by an older, more mature, if no less 'crazy' set of devotees, drawn largely from the ranks of coloured American servicemen—whose finger-snapping, jungly jive and uninhibited delight in the music constitutes a direct reflection to it, in the archetypal strain of call-&-response, rather than an 'audience reaction'.

The only authentic traditional jazz haven that still extends the revival in New Orleans terms, apart from outposts in Wood Green and Wembley, is the *Ken Colyer Club*, at which the purist leader and his peers warm their constituents with sustained ensemble improvisations as to the Storyville manner born. Unlike younger, slicker musicians who exploited the trad boom of the last five years (though it's nearly all over now), Colyer was inspired to learn and play with masters like Bunk Johnson and George Lewis in the crescent city itself. If you like ragtime and the blues, you can expect to be moved by really sympathetic playing at this club, and let your hair down unselfconsciously with fellow-patrons responding to it. But, be warned—there's not much room for a cat to swing in.

Studio 51 is one of the smallest metropolitan dives and, as it fills up, the heat becomes stifling, and it's difficult to dance or even listen in comfort. When the herd thins out for the intervals there's generally a boogie pianist worth hearing.

The most satisfactory clubs from any point of view have always been those run by the musicians themselves—but things aren't what they used to be. If today's beat-clubbers are going to frequent the Golden Mile at all in a decade or two, they'll as likely as not be consigned to the clip strip, sick with neon, that's turned a cosmopolitan village of melody and joy into a tarted-up Bowery of unfulfilled desires. In the early '50s *Club 11* was a co-op enterprise.

Cy Laurie produced a stirring carbon of Hot Five music but retired to a Tibetan monastery with the incipient gimmickry of trad, leaving his Piccadilly caves to gravitate into *The Scene*, for 'ravers'—energetic, fun-loving extroverts, 'weirdies'—introspective and often beautiful eccentrics of indeterminate sex, smooth urban sprites and blocked mods. At intervals some of these elements also flock to boites de juke or semi-speakeasies, viz. *The Roaring '20s*, Carnaby Street and the *Discotheque*, Wardour Street; and the more earnest, woollen-stockinged-type archivists to the spate of week-end pubs featuring well-met harmonica/guitar and sing-song folk sessions. Johnny Dankworth's club lasted only a few months, and the attempted big-band revival has been virtually swamped by the teenage premiums—probably the same reason Lyttelton surrendered his base at 100 Oxford Street.

The more genuine trad bands get a more appreciative hearing in the provinces and abroad, and many polished modern musicians unwilling to be drowned by the plethora of over-amplified organs, guitars and imitative vocalists, and unable to live on the odd broadcast or gig at Ronnie's, swell the palais orchestras and studio sessions—which hardly afford them much musical consolation.

Pretty alcoholic at the best of times, the life-blood of London jazz has been substantially transfused to assorted pubs—of which a selection is appended, and it's their stock alone—(not 'bread')—which keeps the most dedicated jazzmen going. It's quintessentially a performer's music, and the dearth of strongholds for live improvisation augurs ill for its future in Britain.

Ronnie Scott's, which has recently celebrated its sixth birthday, is the doyen of modern British jazz clubs, and the only one to eschew entirely the compromises which keep others from closing. It presents nothing that is not of the best new-wave jazz every night of the year—something not even the big American clubs bother to afford. Its smart night-clubby aura is instinct with the implications of modernism, to enhance the strictly musical integrity and social prestige of jazz—but the musicians aren't encouraged to hide behind their horns (as modernists feel obliged to do elsewhere). The informal high jinks that might be expected of a jazz workshop are sublimated with in-group wit—nonetheless witty, as indicated by the titles with which the genial host sends up his originals—'Some of my best friends are blues', or 'Through the night roared the overland express with a broken bridge ahead and a madman at the throttle' . . . Scott and his William Bendix-like partner, ex-saxophonist Pete King, working from an office-cum-bandroom which wouldn't earn a licence from the GPO as a telephone-booth, are constantly refining the club's possibilities in décor, comfort, acoustics and instrumental experimentation. The cream of British jazz talent blows and listens here every night, and doesn't always suffer by comparison with the American greats—Zoot Sims, Roland Kirk, Jimmy Witherspoon, Ben Webster, Sonny Stitt, J. J. Johnson, Sonny Rollins—imported periodically to make the place viable at all.

As soon as they touch down for concert-tours, visiting bands make a beeline for Ronnie's, and jostle with native zealots, bearing out his conviction that 'I thought that it was time there was an adult sort of club . . . a place where you could get a civilised drink and a

meal and jazz, not the usual modified teenage jiving hall.'
London jazz-clubbers are with him all the way in hoping he'll be as
successful in his new premises. Perhaps he'll now change the tune
he's called 'I'm sick and tired of waking up tired and sick'.

Jazz in London Pubs

Klooks Kleek, The Railway Hotel, West Hampstead. Good R & B
and some modern jazz; Monday—Wednesday.

Thames Hotel, Hampton Court. Best N.O. at week-ends.

Six Bells, King's Road. Austere rectangular jazz room vivified by
excellent jumping jazz in all styles, from Wally Fawkes & Bruce
Turner, etc., at week-ends; predominantly student clientele.

The Crown, Twickenham. Trad and mainstream, week-nights.

Palm Court Hotel, Richmond. Soulful blowing sessions at week-ends.

The Plough, Stockwell. Antique pub with dizzy atmosphere, all
kinds muck-in nightly, with Kathy Stobart resident week-ends.

Lilliput Hall, Jamaica Road, Bermondsey. Dockland mock-Tudor;
extrovert modern jazz, guests jam with resident boy-wonder
pianist Roy Budd.

Tally-Ho, Kentish Town Road. Mainstream/mod week-nights inc.
the excellent Alan Littlejohn Quintet; trad Thursday; Sunday
middays and evening traditionally fierce, free-for-all big swing band
session with spirited nucleus of veteran gassers.

King's Head, Old Kent Road. Professional ballads and standards in
soft blue light; homely singers and alternating bands nightly.

Thomas à Becket, Old Kent Road. Boxer's pub; Diz Disley leads
belting, R & B scene—hottest at week-ends.

Bull's Head, Barnes Bridge. Lovely riverside-setting, Buck Clayton
and the like.

Not the tube, the criminals. Although they also go around in circles, overlapping and touching at certain points.

But in crime circles you don't have tube maps. The law of libel, for a start, wouldn't allow it.

So, as we can't name the villains, here at least is how they are organised, how they operate, how they think, plus a tip for the successor to the Great Train Robbery.

The underworld is a mirror of life, but not quite contemporary life.

Like the respectable life of the provinces, it tends to reflect the picture of what was *avant-garde* a year or two ago but now has become old hat.

It is a tight, intimate community, though a large one. Within it, there are the same class distinctions as elsewhere. It has its 'prestige' castes and families, its bourgeoisie and its untouchables. It permeates polite society and it has its own haunts. There is no guide to it, because it is everywhere. But it is recognisable, if you know where to look and what to observe.

The British underworld is traditional throughout. Every country, every city, it seems, gets the underworld that it deserves. Everything about the British underworld has the same respect for age and tradition as has the law-abiding clerk in his suburban home.

There are 'Grand Old Men' of the shadows, just as there are elder statesmen. The young crook, cocky and full of his own importance will yet seek the help of the legendary figure who, forty years ago, invented the celluloid method of opening Yale locks, though the student will be anxious to disclaim such help.

These old boys are to be found everywhere. They keep pubs, they live 'retired' (but unable to resist an occasional flutter). They are the backbone of many a betting-shop. They never miss a race-meeting. They are often the telephone-exchanges of the underworld. They know the form and they keep the records.

Sometimes, regrettably, they get soft and run with law. Then there is a deal of head shaking and regret, seldom any overt ill-feeling. 'Gone senile' is the sad verdict, in the same way that a respectable family might regard a weakness for shop-lifting in a favourite aunt, or for mild indecency in a respected uncle.

It is a close world and a closed one. Based on fear and mistrust, where the normal world has its foundations on confidence and trust (however often misplaced), the families of the shadows keep together. They intermarry. They take their pleasures together. They feel themselves to be part of an entity—it is always 'we' when talking of themselves.

The interknowledge is startling. The structure of this world is not concentric, it is more like an infinite number of interlapping circles, placed in a pyramid, whose points of contact can be indicated, roughly, something like this.

At the top, there is the circle of the élite. This will be the ruling class of the moment, the gangs who are pulling off the big and the successful jobs. At the time of writing, there is, for once, no clear circle here. The break-up of the South-Western gang, who organised the Great Train Robbery, has left the underworld without one. The enforced exile of its financially successful leader, Bruce Reynolds, has also deprived them of its hero.

Reynolds was a really top criminal. He had all the attributes of the successful dictator—the charm, the brains, the ruthlessness and the ability to inspire devotion. He had the good general's concern for his men.

Watching the efforts of lesser, more brutal fry to make the grade, one is forced to remember the words of Hilaire Belloc: 'Be sure to keep tight hold of Nurse, for fear of meeting something worse.' But Reynolds was exceptional. Normally, another élite would have stepped quickly into place, the circle would be there and would continue until another circle swung up into its place, by right of deeds. It doubtless soon will.

Below the pinnacle come a varying number of circles overlapping a little. These will comprise the backbone of the working community who live outside society. From their ranks, the recruits will be drawn to do the big jobs. Occasionally they will be the 'fall guys', as, for instance, when one gets picked up stealing a car for the use of his superiors.

One of the continuing developments of crime is that it is increasingly broken down into small, specialised and scattered jobs, making detection much more difficult. Thus any safe-breaker ('peter-man' in the vernacular) who is picked up with 'jelly' (gelignite) on him may now and again be speaking the truth when he alleges that it is a police 'plant'. 'It's a liberty' said one recently. 'They know as well as I do that one of us always has it on the joint at least ten days before, but why should I be carrying it when it was somebody else's job?' The indignation was real indeed.

When a big operation is planned by the *élite*, the donkey work will, in all probability, be done by men selected from these lower ranks. Men—not women. One of the traditions in British crime is the general tendency to decry female ability. There is at least one remarkable exception. But, in every sense of the phrase, this is a *rara avis* indeed. Some of the older hands, who have Continental links, speak with scorn of the French habit of using women.

The personnel of these lower circles will all be known to 'somebody'. They will be cousins, nephews, in-laws, even school friends.

A remarkable piece of tradition is that the same areas of London remain predominantly breeding grounds of crime. The poverty which Victorian optimists considered to be the root cause of illegal sin has gone. The sin lingers and flourishes with the welfare state.

Prosperous blocks of flats rise on the same sites—the back of Waterloo, Fulham, the East End, Croydon and wherever the routes used to open out for the mail coaches with their chances for easy plunder. The environs of canals, where once the thieves unloaded from the loaded long boats now breed a race of lorry hi-jackers.

Television aerials sprout from the roofs of many a far-from-humble criminal home. Within the well-furnished flats, the cocktail bars, so much criticised by design-conscious journalists (who see them mainly at the Furniture Exhibition), groan beneath a varied assortment of drinks, which will, in the last resort, actually have been bought, sooner than not keep up with the criminal Jones's. 'The thieves' kitchen,' said an eminent Counsel recently, 'ought nowadays to be called the thieves' cocktail bar!'

The ecologist may know why crime keeps to the same areas. Anyway, it does. The top boys will use all the best places up West. But they will still go back to their old pubs, very often the same ones which once welcomed and laid traps for the highwaymen, two centuries ago.

Below, again, will be the increasingly petty criminals. These will not be closely connected. Their circles will contain some who will never make the grade. Some who, because they depart from 'respectable' crime will remain outside the 'best' society (of this more hereafter). And some, probably juvenile delinquents, whose progress will be watched. Their spurs are yet to be won.

This, roughly, makes up the hierarchy of the orthodox underworld. It is not, of course, the whole. But it is the part that lives by the rules, or at least likes to think that it does. Outside, live the bad men, the unmentionables. They have their uses, as will be seen. But there is no social mixing between them, though they will be aware of each other's names and occupation; and dignity will stoop, on occasion, to use them.

These shunned members of the underworld belong to several main groups. Amongst themselves, the 'protection boys', who often embrace the lowest moral factor of the race-gangs (always marginal socially) rank top. Blackmail is disliked by the professional criminal, as is more than minimal violence. Sometimes this is regarded as hitting below the belt, the position of which is always variable.

'Villainy', by comparison, has become almost an affectionate term for approved crime. It is psychologically interesting that police who have incurred criticism are usually referred to with this adjective, but in a different tone of voice. (The protection gangs are known as 'bad men'.)

There is also disapproval of some sexual offenders and killers— unnecessary killers, that is. Anyone could have an accident.

Real 'badness' is never forgiven. There is at the moment one man whom the moralists might like to hold up as an example of reform- ing and making the grade. The respectable world accepts him. Not the underworld. 'That bad man!' they shout. They cannot refuse to know him, but he is treated with a chilliness that would freeze out most sensitive people.

He has an enemy who is almost more disliked than himself—as a person. But he might 'get' the reformed bad man. If he did, no one would give him away.

The remaining outcasts are such lepers as dope-pedlars. No one has any use for them. Their only connection with the true under- world is geographical. The aristocrat, in a word, is the skilful, artistic thief and that sort of success is the youngster's dream.

No one understood the London underworld better than John Gay, author of *The Beggars' Opera*. If he returned to the London scene today, he would have only one adjustment to make—that of prosperity, for crime today often pays handsomely.

Where would he find his characters? How would he recognise them? In his day, they frequented the gaming houses and loaded their women with drink and stolen clothes. So it is today, only the gaming houses are in the West End and the stolen clothes are likely to be mink and re-set jewellery.

The best restaurants and clubs know them. The innocent who wears her best jewellery to the expensive charity-ball has little idea that a coolly appraising eye in a partner may mean something else than disinterested admiration.

The modern criminals look like, they behave like, they *are* like other people. Yet they are not. They themselves recognise this, band together, keep to their own rules—often model husbands (if sometimes absent ones). They are almost invariably loving fathers—when gambling, which runs right through criminal life and is at the very root of crime itself, has not got them in its grip to the exclusion of everything else.

One of the major crimes of our time was planned largely in the Astor Club and the Pheasantry. There, across the room, used to sit some of the unrecognisables, the bad men. When the unwritten law was broken and someone close to the top gang had 'grassed', the code allowed the aristo to cross the room to talk to the bad men. They were then hired to execute gangster vengeance on the traitor, and the aristo thereby did not lose face.

If you want to be among the underworld, go to the 'best', i.e. the most expensive places. Unless you have an expert with you, do not expect to recognise the stars. But, if you fancy yourself as a psychologist, what would you—and Gay—look for?

The big tip. Money. Everyone throwing round money in a smart club is not a crook—at least not necessarily an illegal one. But the crooks are always amongst them. It is the symbol of their 'security'. Money talks. Money buys.

One does not have to be much of a psychologist to recognise the longing for security, almost pathetic, which sets some of the young off on the trail of crime. One can still see it in the hardened offender, when his greed has become so offensive that pity is stifled.

Greedy, show-off, touchy, violent, mistrustful, lying, callous—caricatures, exaggerations of all that is below the surface in the 'respectable' world. The huge tip to the waiter. The throwing-away of betting money that would make an ordinary citizen blench. The excellent clothes, just too expensive, the purple and fine linen just too evident. These are the signs and signals of the West End crook. The club manager knows them. He knows the show-off customers. He will also know the speed with which they cover up a mistake in their favour; for even twopence won illicitly is a small feather in the cap. The flash-living might read like a cliché—but they all do it, all live flash the minute they make a killing.

The cap and scarf burglar, unshaven, jemmy protruding from his pocket, is no more. The man who robs a flat of jewellery today lives, as likely as not, round the corner and enters the block with a polite salute to the porter, who takes him for a visitor. The affluent society has spread to the underworld, where the wife of a successful robber was recently described as 'dining out' on a story connected with her husband.

Living standards are high—very high. Crime, increasingly professional, is paying. There are even signs that it may be attracting a higher class of operator. For, despite the money, the luxury and the luck, the bulk of the criminal classes come from well down in the social scale. Fortunately for law and order, most crooks are also still well down in the intelligence scales.

A full strength, more imaginative police force could do a deal more to catch them as yet. But if the profits rise, things may indeed become bad. It is no longer ridiculous to see that crime could have a certain appeal for a certain sort of intellectual. The slips made in the Great Train Robbery—and its lack of sustained intelligence—suggested many careers for intellectuals *manqués*.

This rise in the social status of criminals is reflected in underworld slang. There is still the old form of speech, the rhyming slang and the quick repartee which it is hoped will get past the young policeman.

The prison service still complain that the slang is always moving with fashion and gets past their comprehension. But some things are always current—'nick', both for prison and arrest, 'gone on his toes' for a flight, 'stir' or porridge' for a prison sentence. But on the whole, underworld language is losing a lot of its piquancy.

The old superstitions remain. There are many who will not use the word 'rat', though you may refer to the quadruped by many another name, such as 'gentleman with a long tail'. To call him by name is unlucky. Amulets abound. (But so they do in other circles.) There is a general belief in following your luck: an enterprise that starts well will prosper: one that does not, will go wrong. Perhaps it's because a lot of old gipsy blood still yeasts away in the underworld.

On the whole, however, foreigners—even gipsies—are no more welcome than are their counterparts on the right side of the law. The English are xenophobic: so is their underworld.

But many a villain's heart beat hard with patriotism during the war. Some members of the fraternity rendered excellent service in the cause of King and country. It did not of course prevent the successful burgling of friendly embassies and their subsequent double-crossing on occasion. To the question 'Do you love your country?' (once put by a keen prison worker), the answer has been an unqualified 'Yes'. To the subsequent 'How do you vote?' it seems that a virtually 100% reply gave 'Tory, of course.' Capitalists, believers in private enterprise to a man, naturally enough.

That is where Bruce Reynolds is different. Unlike the majority of his colleagues, he belongs to the Left. (This, no doubt, is the reason for the wildest stories of Bruce The Communist Ally, which circulated at one stage). Once the foreign element in the underworld ran the brothels and what there was of protection. That time is past. Yet, strangely, the shadow of Sax Rohmer still walks! There exists today at least one good criminal from the Far East.

The toleration—unwilling but now present—of what was regarded as disreputable crime is something new. It is partly accounted for by the general fall in morals, but most of all by the incredible speed with which the money has been picked up in such things as protection in a place like Soho.

Soho is not the real underworld, but you can glimpse the training grounds of crime. Many a young apprentice has won his spurs in the Soho clip-joints and sleazy strip-tease clubs.

When the Street Offences Act became law in 1959, one unforeseen result was the speed with which clubs—enclosed and made legal within the sanctity of private premises—became big money.

It was too much to expect that English insularity would stand out against such easy pickings. So the protection game, which had hitherto existed as something which was done by 'nasty foreigners', often Maltese and Cypriots, became an English institution. (It is still regarded as faintly disreputable, though it is wonderful what money and power will do to make people respectable.)

With so much money around, some police corruption was inevitable. It is an unfortunate truth that one bad policeman does more harm than can be corrected by two hundred good ones. Police corruption is nothing like as bad as the public now suspects. It remains true, however, that it exists in sufficient spots (and strategic ones at that) to do great harm to public morality.

Naturally, the underworld, opportunists to a man, seized upon this fact of life with alacrity and glee. One old crook remarked that there was no need to bribe prison officers or police, once you had persuaded them into one misdeed. 'After that,' he said with relish, 'it's easy. They just have to go along with you.'

'Blackmail?' he was asked. 'I suppose you could call it that,' was the reply. 'I prefer to call it co-operation.'

London Society

Or The Enclave. *Or the Establishment. Any term is misleading, because you can't define it.*

You can't devise a passport either. You can't even name names, although the gossip columns try. It's all an attitude of mind.

These attitudes are subtle and devious. They're not particularly attractive, but they do attract. They are not worthwhile, but they are worth studying.

There is no nation so receptive to etiquette books as the British. Even the Americans, who are supposed to be so absorbed in the niceties of behaviour and status, rely on only one. And the author of that, Mrs. Emily Post, was English—beginning her career, it is sometimes believed, on the boards in Streatham which may account for the doily-ridden refinement of American manners.

It might be supposed that the British concern with etiquette books, their absorption with titles and their universal aping of what they imagine to be the manners of the aristocracy, stemmed from an overweening snobbery but, more probably, they are the result of the virtual impregnability of society as it has been termed. (Though nowadays what used to be society has thrown away the term, like men on a sled in the steppes might throw their fur caps to the pursuing wolves).

For our purposes we shall have to employ a new term. For want of a better, let us call it the enclave. There are so many new books of etiquette, published by journalists, foreign countesses, governesses, ambassadresses, simply because the aspirant, to be a member of Britain's social summit, finds that all their advice cannot provide the key. He buys the book and reads and learns—but no doors open. He feels there must be a key, so he buys another book. He rapidly succumbs to the nymphomania of the unsatisfied, not, as we had all imagined the nymphophilea of the addict. He is not a snob because he enjoys the intimacy of the enclave; he is a snob because he finds that intimacy unattainable.

The truth is that there is no key, no set of rules to be abided by, which will automatically confer upon the seeker membership of the enclave. Perhaps the word impenetrability is not altogether accurate, because the whole secret of the survival of the aristocracy in this country lies in the exceptional mobility of the classes. It is, and has always been, possible to sweep almost at one stroke into the enclave, but what that stroke is it is almost impossible to divine. To most it is not given. No single characteristic or even set of characteristics is enough. To be rich, to have a title, to hold high office, to marry a member of the enclave are not any of them passports to the inner-most sanctums. Even all of them combined will ensure nothing but the reasonable certainty that you will be asked to enclave parties.

The empirical evidence from examining those who do succeed in joining the enclave is almost always contradictory. Any question of manners must be jettisoned at once. The late Mr. John Fox-Strangways, who booted Aneurin Bevan down the steps of Whites, was surely an example of the atrocious rudeness which in no way interferes with membership. Mr. Randolph Churchill is hardly noted for easy-going beneficence. At the other end of the scale Sir Alec Douglas-Home and Mr. Michael Tree are exquisitely courteous.

If a criterion applies at all in this field, it is the old one of arrogance. On the whole the enclave are particularly polite or particularly rude. Both characteristics stem from arrogance; the good manners from noblesse oblige and the bad from noblesse doesn't give a damn.

The first clue to success might lie, then, in confidence—not brash-ness but absolute, impervious confidence—not a characteristic readily detectable in aspirants. Few can learn that delicate inflection by which 'thank you very much' becomes a pretty acknowledge-ment of tribute.

Money means little. In the first place the enclave carry on, when they are millionaires, either as if they had little money at all, like the Duke of Buccleuch, or as if the stuff went rotten if not spent, preferably in occasional gambling most discreetly conducted—vide: Lord Derby, Mr. William Sterling and Mr. Henry Vyner.

When they are poor they carry on in much the same way, spending money freely or scraping in an embarrassing fashion which the middle-classes would not tolerate. Money probably used to be a significant factor but in the post-first-war era the not-so-rich were accepted and you now find Mr. Alistair Forbes, many McEwans and a variety of intellectuals who are admitted to full membership of the enclave.

Money alone cannot buy even the semblance of entry. It may buy a little food in the shape of a dinner or two and plenty of lunches and cocktails; but not acceptance. The enclave are quite happy to take advantage of the eagerness-to-please of aspirants.

Not long ago Mr. Charles Clore plunged into the London social scene. With the aid of one of the Duchesses of Westminster he gave a party. They came in force to batten upon the innocence of his generosity. They drank and took presents. And they laughed at the vulgarity, as they termed it, of their host. Yet at the same time they gathered Mr. Miki Sekers to their bosoms. What has a Hungarian cloth merchant got that an English property whizz lacks? Something which wins the Hungarian a knighthood while the home-made magnate remains a commoner.

But culture or even intelligence has small importance. A sort of lip service is paid to the arts, as witness the dutiful trudge to Glyndebourne, the spasmodic glitter at Covent Garden, the ready sale of coffee-table books, the patronage of Heywood Hill's bookshop, the invitation lists at the art galleries, the inevitability of having known Berenson.

Nevertheless the enclave is largely philistine. A certain facility comes to many of them with their upbringing. You can hardly live with two Rembrandts, four Canalettos, a Titian, five Gainsboroughs a spattering of Cuyps and Stubbses; a Wynkyn de Worde and a Caxton; a bundle of Chippendale and Hepplewhite; ten Aubussons and some Grinling Gibbons in a house on which Adam, Kent and Repton have all left their mark without some faint imprint being made on the most obdurately unseeing eye.

Then again it seems pointless to know the leading politicians, the most talked about writers, the two fashionable dancers, the selected musicians and not to be able to communicate with them at all. So a superficial knowledge of affairs and of the arts and the skill which a public school imparts, to deploy scant information to the maximum advantage is all that is required.

We can dismiss money and intelligence, then, as passports. The enclave likes both because they bring power and power, preferably the power to manipulate rather than overt power, is the one quality which the enclave respects. They believe it is their prerogative to be able to divert the course of things to their immediate and selfish purposes rather than alter the democratic business of the country entirely. They do not object to laws for others, provided there are evasions which they can arrange for themselves.

Perhaps in this characteristic lies a clue to the qualifications for membership. A deep and genuine concern for matters of principle is a considerable hindrance to success with the enclave. It is possible to be eccentrically philanthropic but a serious humanity is a great obstacle. This is not to say that to be a member you must be cruel or greedy, vicious or even evil. It means more that your loyalty must lie, emotionally at any rate with the enclave rather than with an ideal or a party or a cause or anything else whatever. It is hard to explicate this fundamental truth as, of necessity, they go to some considerable length to conceal it. Roughly speaking it can be equated with someone who feels a colour prejudice. It is inexpressible; it would be damaging to give voice to it but it underlies all thinking.

They do not, for instance, really dislike Sir Oswald Mosley. Some of the bolder spirits—Sir Roy Harrod, Mr. John Betjeman to name a couple—will happily dine with him. Mosley was an enclave man. Nothing can ever eradicate this. Provided not too much public odium descends upon them, they really do not care what a person stands for, what he has done, what he may do. They might draw the line at a murderer, but a sex criminal means nothing to them. Among paedophiliacs they prefer pederasts to girl molesters, but it wouldn't occur to them to report either to the police. They chat merrily about the perversions of their friends and are a little put off by financial dishonesty.

Of course, they appear to subscribe to moral views, to sympathetic political opinions, to humane ideals, but behind the façade lurks a completely different set of values. It is this lack of basic importance which attaches to their expressed views which enables them to embrace left-wing parties and people. Politics are to them a game. They can entertain a Mosley or a Weidenfeld, a Thorpe or a Wyatt with equal insouciance because they do not believe that a man's politics interferes with his enclave potential. It is noticeable how rapidly those whose beliefs are more staunchly held to the exclusion of enclavism are speedily dropped or derided like Lord Longford and Lady Violet Bonham-Carter, Michael Foot, the gentlest of men, is dismissed as an unbalanced firebrand.

Certainly everyday morality is of no importance. A glance through the list of Dukes reveals people with morals and attitudes which in any other society, indeed even any other branch of society in this country, would provoke instant ostracism. Some have treated their first wife in a fashion which would have incurred odium among the more primitive Kikuyu tribes. Yet both are received, as the etiquette books would put it.

But let no one suppose that a title on its own is anything like enough to ensure acceptance. There are Dukes whom virtually no one has heard of. The Dukes of Manchester and Somerset are regarded by the enclave as positively commoners. Leinster, poor soul, is beyond the pale, particularly since his television appearance. St. Albans would never be thought of were it not for the un-scholastic inclinations of his progeny. This question of common-ness is very hard to pin down. Before the war, even the Royal Family were regarded as being too middle-class really to bother with And it is not for nothing that, when the enclave had a game in which they allotted new Christian names to people, they chose for the Queen and Prince Philip the names Brenda and Brian.

It would seem to depend largely on whether the person in question is possessed of any of the more stolid virtues. The two great adjectives of the enclave are 'boring and' 'amusing'. We can all understand that worthiness, honesty, kindness are in themselves boring attributes. They do little to enliven a party or a long week-end. Whereas instability, bitchery, perversion, infidelity, are all good subjects for gossip and provide diversion. They are amusing.

Virtues, then, of the kind normally associated with the respectable elements of our society, are not welcomed or highly thought of by the enclave. Of course it should be added that the obverse of this theory should not be carried too far. The enclave does not like too much light let in upon its activities. Prosecution, for instance, should be avoided or, at any rate, bought off by aspirers.

There are various minor attributes which may be regarded as impediments to membership of the enclave, though none is totally insuperable. To be Jewish is a great disadvantage. The Rothschilds are the one family said to be accepted, but it is the foreign branches who are more welcome than the indigenous variety and there are many enclave members who would prefer their daughters not to marry them. Other Jews may be partially accepted but must be prepared for sly digs if they slip up in any way. Various professions are a grievous obstacle. Anything much to do with industry is not liked, unless it is a financially rewarding directorship acquired as a result of being an M.P. The food trade is particularly contemptible in all its ramifications from hotelier to grocer, but anything to do with drink is perfectly all right.

The enclave on the other hand is quite clear about entertaining people who might be useful to them. Various solicitors, for instance, are invited to enclave houses although they would never be finally admitted to intimacy. Their visits are explained away on the grounds that they are good shots or may be persuaded to spill the beans about some member's affairs. Doctors are totally unacceptable and so are most scientists. (The enclave seems to recognise that all progress is inimical to its interests.)

In order to become a member of the enclave, we now see there are various qualifications. The first is a supreme, overriding arrogance. There must be in the aspirant's mind no doubt that he is better; not cleverer, richer, better looking (vide Lord Astor), wittier or talented—just better than the common run of common people. The second is an ability to subjugate all emotions to loyalty to the enclave. No matters of principle must be allowed to overcome faith in the rightness of the enclave. The third is the abandonment of average virtues to the ultimate criterion of whether or not something diverts or entertains—is amusing.

Given these three achievements, preferably unencumbered with Jewish ancestry, the wrong profession, too terrible an accent or a police record, anyone is qualified to attempt to climb to the summits of elegant British society. But the question which London Spy will not attempt to answer is, given all that, would any decent person want to?

London Prostitutes

Prostitutes exist. Because the demand is there, so is the supply.

You may think this sad and bad, or good and proper, or even unimportant. But they are still there.

This is a report of the present state of the market. How it's organised, how it works, what the language is. It's not meant to condemn or condone. Just a report.

Never call a London prostitute a prostitute. Not even a whore or harlot, nor even by that meaningless phrase, a good time girl.

It may seem surprising, but the personal pride of such girls can be easily upset. London's professional ladies are a very touchy group of females.

Most of them have feelings and tempers as well. Ask a girl if she is a 'pro' and even the most obvious of them is likely to reply with a good old-fashioned verbal slap around the face. Unlike the girls of Paris or Hamburg, they don't as a general rule glorify in their chosen profession.

Just how many there are in London no one really knows. The total fluctuates from day to day, almost from hour to hour. But a conservative estimate has put it at never less than 10,000.

This works out at one to every 500 men in Greater London at any one time. Take away children, the impotent, homosexuals, those who are scared of VD and the downright faithful, and the ratio becomes frighteningly small, or attractively small, whichever way you look at it.

The total cash which changes hands is really an unknown quantity, but a figure once attributed to a Home Office official a few years ago was probably not very far out. He put it then at around £10,000,000 a year. Add a million or so to cover the increased cost of living, and you have a fairly good figure for Britain as a whole, with at least two-thirds of it going into the hands of the girls in London.

Only a minor part of that vast sum goes, however, on plain ungarnished sexual intercourse. For any girl the real money these days is in the 'extras', and there are very few of them who are not anxious for every additional fiver which 'extras' can coax out of a client's pocket. The result is that there are girls in London to satisfy every known taste and fad in sex and it wouldn't be difficult either to find some who would even be prepared, for the right money, to try to find something still new to the oldest profession in the world.

Whatever is asked for, somewhere in London there is a girl who will quote a price.

To the man for whom sex has so far meant common or garden intercourse, the variations which London can provide may seem repulsive, even horrifying. They can also be downright dangerous.

But it is very easy to get the girls. Lavish payments for the beating of middle-aged and elderly men with ropes, whips, riding crops and even walking sticks, according to their whims, is often preferable to 'hustling' along the Bayswater Road for clients at £3 a time.

Following close in popularity to beatings are the perversions in which various forms of rubber wear are used. In these activities, the client takes off all of his clothes and then dresses completely in tight fitting rubber trousers and jerkin. The feel of the rubber against the bare skin soon produces the desired sexual climax.

Usually the dressing up in rubber wear is accompanied by an 'exhibition' by the girl.

For the client who doesn't like rubber next to his skin, London provides opportunities galore for dressing up in prostitutes' clothing, including every stitch of a girl's underwear, and for prancing about a flat in high heels. This service usually ends up with a session of so-called 'french' love.

For the more normal of the men with tastes for perversions, there are hundreds of girls who specialise in 'bondage and correction'. This means being firmly bound with a rope followed by a good thrashing with a cane swished by the girl concerned with as heavy a hand as she can manage.

This can go on till her client is sexually exhausted, or the man pleads for intercourse and this is then graciously allowed.

Men who want the beatings to be the other around find it a great deal harder to pick up a girl ready to be whacked. A few years ago, there were many girls who, for an additional few pounds, were prepared to take a beating with a whip or a cane. Times change and the girls have found that now they don't have to 'work' so dangerously. But there are still a few around who will.

Although these girls don't like to admit it, they are mainly the old hands. Their looks have gone after years in the business, their chances of making anything but a poor living at ordinary prostitution gone as well. There is one girl—she is actually 48—notorious in Notting Hill and Paddington, who will take up to 50 strokes from a client. The cost is, however, a little disturbing. Her rate is £1 a stroke and one of her sales talk claims is that she is the cheapest in town in that line of the business.

She is one of the real old-timers in London prostitution, although by no means the oldest. There is one girl still at it in Soho who remembers business in the first world war. She is one of the few who describes herself as a whore.

The younger girls, especially those in their teens, are not likely to be as honest as that. Few of them will face the fact that they are prostitutes and cling to some remote outline of respectability.

Some of the girls will go to great lengths to put a façade over their professional lives. One of the favourite descriptions of themselves is 'business girl'. Many more cling to the 'model' description. A few venture as far as 'call girl'.

But be they 'business girls', or 'models' or 'call girls', they are not too hard to find.

In 1959, a new Act of Parliament became law. It was aimed at clearing prostitutes from the streets of the West End and several other points in London.

It had been said that the sight of girls touting for clients offended decent men as well as decent women, especially those from abroad.

It obviously did offend many, but most stayed to watch the girls haggling over prices with the actual would-be clients. There were often more watchers than clients and girls put together.

However, the Street Offences Act came into being and the police got busy and very soon the girls had almost vanished off the streets.

The supporters of the new Act put their heads in the sand and said: 'What a wonderfully cleaned up and moral city London has become.'

Facts are a little different. Any moral welfare worker knows that there are now more girls on the game than there ever were before the Street Offences Act became law.

It is just that the girls now try to steer clear of the law.

They do this in five different ways. The clubs. The 'coded' advertisement boards. The 'madams'. The few girls who risk prosecution and Holloway and still walk the streets. And the country lane beats.

The No. 1 method, the clubs, attracts most of all the man from out of town. Chatting up a girl by a club bar doesn't seem to be so sordid, even if the drink she keeps ordering is coloured water yet costs more than honest whisky.

By no means all club hostesses take men back to their own flats after the club or drinking dive where they supposedly work has closed. But there are not many who will still say, 'No,' if the offered payment is high enough.

Any doubts about whether a girl does or does not can usually be settled in a night club with a £1 slipped to a waiter or in a lesser establishment with a drink for the barman. Their knowledge and advice is always correct. That is because usually they get a cut back from the girl—10%.

But the girls in some expensive night spots are not for the kinky brigade. For them it always has to be straightforward sex only. Girls who can ask, and certainly get, £20 for one act of intercourse will very seldom agree to take part in any perversions.

The genuine hostess doing part time on the game usually doesn't cheat. She offers nothing that she will not provide and tells the client she doesn't get off from the club till 3 a.m. or even 4 a.m. and that he'll have to be around till then. Naturally she expects him to pay for the taxi to her flat, probably in the Ladbroke Grove area or in Earls Court.

She is likely to offer coffee or a drink when she and her client reach her fairly well furnished—probably on the never-never—home. Intercourse comes between clean sheets on a well sprung bed and provided the client is gone by about 7 a.m. he can stay as long as he likes.

In the London prostitution market that is real value for money. The place to find the right sort of clubs: Mayfair and as far east as Charing Cross Road and south as far as Pall Mall. Taxi drivers are the best bet for the clubs with the best girls.

But the preliminaries in the clubs are usually more expensive than most would-be clients can stand. They frighten off many men long before they get around to discussing the girl's £20 or more 'present'.

This would be only part of the total cost. To get as far as discussing terms will cost a small fortune. Most girls in night clubs, even in the smallest, demand a hostess fee of £5 before they will condescend to talk to a man. With fees like that they can pull the wool over the eyes of the club owner about their real business if he happens to be one of the few who honestly believes that all of his girls are good girls.

The drinking habits of these hostesses can also be rather shattering.

Champagne by the gallon, quite literally, is common. Of course, they don't actually drink it, but as fast as one bottle is opened and a couple of glasses poured from it, a hovering waiter whisks it away 'empty' and obligingly returns with another, no doubt an 'empty' from another table topped up from an 'empty' from yet a third table. A bill for a twosome encounter full only of promise can easily reach £40.

On top of that, the £20 or so required for the privilege of actually having the girl concerned in her own bed can be a disastrous blow to the sexual urges of many men. Very often the girl goes home to a cold bed alone and the man returns to a lonely hotel room to lick his financial wounds.

The clients in the know, looking for real value, choose the small drinking clubs. It is in these that girls new to the game, not too hard, happy to agree to £5 and ready to give in return a personal service because they like it, can often be found. To find one, don't ask a policeman, hop in a cab. Most taximen will know the very spot. It is likely to be in Notting Hill, Paddington, Bayswater, Earls Court, Hampstead or Streatham, in that order.

Girls in this type of club have another attraction. They get out earlier. The club almost certainly closes a couple of hours earlier than the night clubs do. Two hours less drinking to be paid for and two hours less waiting for what is to come.

This sort of girl is also more likely to be the type who doesn't mind sneaking into an hotel bedroom. The chances are she knows of a 'helpful' hotel proprietor anyway.

The No. 2 Method is a study of the notice boards outside the sort of shops where not too many awkward questions are asked about the real meanings of the words on postcard advertisements.

There is an elaborate unofficial code used for these.

The whole business of this 'code' is supposedly to deceive the shopkeeper into thinking that the postcards he accepts for his advertisement boards have nothing to do with sex.

Presumably some are deceived. But not many. They just like the certainty of income which postcards at 5s. a week can provide. A score or more postcards at that price can add a fair sum to the week's shop takings.

The police aren't deceived. Not that they seem to worry. This is because four years ago they prosecuted a shopkeeper in Bayswater for living partly on immoral earnings. Their case was that the money used to pay for the postcards must have come from the previous sexual earnings of the girls and that the shopkeeper must have realised that.

The police got a conviction at the Old Bailey, but the shopkeeper appealed and won.

Since then, the boards have flourished, although still with the ridiculous respectability of the 'code'.

What makes this even more ridiculous is the fact that at least half of the sex advertised on the boards is kinky sex. The boards have become the recognised medium for the girls who want to advertise anything other than ordinary intercourse.

A few boards can be found in Soho and some in Earls Court, but most of them are in the Paddington and Bayswater districts with Westbourne Park Road, Westbourne Grove and Queensway competing with each other for top ranking.

Ask for it, no matter what it is, and it is an odds-on that there is a postcard advertising it:

'Rubber and rainwear made to measure, phone Miss Rodd at Riverside . . .'—she goes in for all the kinky stuff with the tight fitting rubber clothing and high heeled boots.

'Lovely fireside rugs made to order, Fulham . . .'—Here is a girl who specialises in intercourse on the floor with all the forms of perversions thrown in for good measure.

'Riding boots always for sale, Park . . .'—Riding crops used for beatings.

'Young lady gives Swedish lessons, Shepherds Bush . . .'—Sexual massages for men who don't want intercourse for fear of catching VD.

'Accommodation for bachelors, Freemantle . . .'—Straightforward intercourse with no 'extras' and out of the girl's 'gaff' again all within five minutes.

'Dusky dolls for sale, Park . . .'—Coloured girls working together and both available for any man who thinks he can take on two at a time.

'Ex-governess seeks part-time work, Park . . .'—Sticks and whips available, also ropes, maybe even the cross.

'Young kitten for sale, Park . . .'—Normal intercourse.

'Madam has vacancies for a few pupils, Knightsbridge . . .'—Another provided with anything kinky.

Whatever is wanted, if it comes under the general heading of sex, then the chances are it is advertised somewhere on a board and certainly in Bayswater.

The charges—£5 for intercourse, possibly a pound or two cheaper if the client haggles, with the girl stripped off completely. With most of her clothes still on, £3 at the most. Costs for the more 'sophisticated' services offered on the boards start at a tenner.

The No. 3 method of finding the girls is through the 'madams'. There are three big time 'madams' in London and several with lesser collections of girls available. Most 'madams' do very well indeed and take their holidays in the Bahamas or South America. They can afford to.

They strive to keep their business on a high plain. They form the background of the genuine call-girl system. It is as expensive and as extensive in London as in any other capital city and the 'madams' claim that by providing a 'high-class' service of prostitutes for visiting businessmen from abroad they are playing an important part in Britain's export drive.

They are always equally concerned about the British businessman visiting London. He provides the bulk of their business and they mainly become known through their names and phone numbers being passed around at the big London exhibitions such as the Motor Show.

The three leading 'madams' claim that once a man has used their services, he goes back to them year after year. One of them boasts: 'Exhibitions are held in London only so that my best and wealthiest clients can come up to town to meet my girls.'

They guard their girls as if they were debutantes. Some of these are respectable housewives living in the suburbs, who pop up to town one or two afternoons a week, unknown to husband, to earn an extra few pounds for clothes. One well-known girl on the lists, until quite recently, of all three of the leading 'madams' was the wife of a serving Royal Air Force officer.

Others among these girls who are the stars of London's professional ladies are genuine models, who don't mind an afternoon in bed. There are still others, usually nymphomaniacs, whose wealthy Mamas would have heart attacks if they knew what their daughters did on spare afternoons.

They are available, however, only to the very best clients and for the more ordinary man who gets an introduction to the circles of the leading 'madams' there is usually something rather less refined. She will still be a lot better quality than the girl picked up in the drinking club and often also better than any girl out of a top ranking night club.

Introductions are, however, hard to get. Apart from hearing the 'madam's' phone number from a friend at an exhibition, the only real chance most men have is through an obliging hotel porter. If he is one of the comparative few trusted by the 'madams', the tip he will expect will be at least a fiver. Even then there is no guarantee. If the 'madam' doesn't like the sound of a would-be client on the phone, the introduction gets no further. Their security standards would be a credit to M.I.5.

This is because the success of the circles run by the 'madams' depends on there never being any trouble and that could arise if the wrong man spoke the wrong words in the wrong places.

The top 'madams' all run two systems—they have a central point, usually their own flats, where men and girls can meet, and sleep, by appointment. The flats are also used as clearing houses for the arrangements of assignations elsewhere. In either case, the 'madam' would be a sitting duck for the police, either for running a brothel or for living on immoral earnings, if they could once infiltrate. Hence the security.

The No. 4 method is picking up the girls who are walking the streets—and risking the 1959 Act of Parliament and arrest by zealous young police constables.

They fall into two very definite groups—the old hands, with faces lined by years of hard work and language to make any old-style sergeant-major sound like a clergyman. And the very new, who have gone on the streets to earn enough to keep themselves from starving. Frequently they are the not very intelligent girls who have found that a dull factory job in London doesn't pay enough to cover the rent and also provide for eating. The 'game' is the sad but easy answer.

Soon this second type get scooped up by a ponce. After midnight, the Bayswater Road has as many, and even more, ponces on the look-out for new girls as it has would-be clients.

These are the girls for whom prostitution can be a tough life. It can also be rather rough for their clients.

Very few of these girls have flats to which they can take a man and their usual offering is a very short time in the back of the client's car, parked in the darkness of a nearby mews.

The commons and the adjoining roads at Clapham and Wandsworth and also Shepherds Market in Mayfair—not to be confused with Shepherds Bush—have a few girls, but the best beats, and therefore the best girls in Method No. 4 are in Bayswater Road itself and Chepstow Road and Talbot Road in Notting Hill.

The girls are always very anxious to get back on the beat within a few minutes. This means that for the usual £3 fee, the time allowed is enough only for intercourse at its quickest. It also means that the spot in a mews which the girl claims is 'safe' from Peeping Toms, may be in full view of a couple of passing policemen just itching to make a couple of 'kiss in car' arrests.

The number of such cases in a year which come before the London courts is not high, about 100. In most cases the man pleads guilty to get it over with quickly in the hope that there will be no newspaper publicity and there seldom is. The girl, of course, pleads guilty. To her it's just like paying income tax—distasteful but essential.

Method No. 5 for finding sex for cash is the country lane beat. It is becoming more and more popular. Some of the girls, it seems, like to get away from the smells of the city and breathe in the country air.

For the man with time on his hands, it seems also to have its share of attractions. It offers all that No. 4 method does and it is all done with much less chance of an inquisitive policeman breaking it all up just at the wrong moment.

The country beat first came into its own about six years ago. Girls started to appear among the bushes along the main A40 road to Oxford, near Denham, in Buckinghamshire. Their customers were mainly lorry drivers.

The girls are still sometimes to be seen there, but now their clients are men who arrive in Jaguars and Mercedes.

Two other country spots are more popular with the girls and far less conspicuous. To get to both a car is a must. There are no buses in the lanes which the girls have made their own in Essex and in Surrey.

The best of these spots for business is a series of quiet lanes winding among cornfields between Lambourne End and Ongar in Essex, yet only around 20 miles from the West End. The second is the top of Box Hill, the Surrey National Trust beauty spot.

Both have very pleasant countryside and a fair selection of girls, provided that the client doesn't mind the worst of the old-timers or the bottom of the barrel scrapings from among the 'scrubbers' of the Cable Street area of the East End. The consolation is the price—£2 a time, either in the corn or in the car.

There is one big drawback for the clients on the country lane beat. It closes down very early. It is strictly an afternoon market and round about 6 p.m. the girls all vanish.

The old-timers and the scrubbers all rush off to their night-time beats. Most of them then operate where the casual seeker after sex for cash can risk running into trouble, the London Docklands and in Soho.

Sex in Dockland is strictly for the seamen. The girls who use Cable Street as their main market at night might seem almost pleasant during their afternoons in the Essex lanes. At night their interest is only in the cash in the pockets of seamen. They act strictly under the orders of their ponces, most of them Maltese, who don't want ordinary visiting 'mugs'. The seamen offer such better prospects for 'rolling'—the art of knocking a man unconscious while he is in the middle of intercourse and then relieving him of all his money.

Soho is for the real 'mugs'. In some windows red lights burn brightly. The 'girls' are likely to be ancient and their personal glow will certainly not match the light in the window which advertises their availability.

They will all use the title, 'young model'. But most will remember better days in Soho of 20 and even 30 years ago. The description 'young model' applies in Soho to the age of 60 at least.

Easier to find there are the 'professional virgins'. It would be extremely hard to miss them.

These are the clip joint girls who haunt the pavements outside near-beer clubs, promising the delights of intercourse and a lot more too if only the 'mug' will spend all his money on alleged fruit juice drinks in a dimly lit and usually dirty cellar.

The attraction is the fact that so many of these girls are in their 'teens, the 'fairies', the newcomers, running away from home, who have been picked up at the main railway stations by eagle-eyed ponces.

Soon, most of them will be fully 'on the game'. But while they work as 'professional virgins'—that is the police name for them—only about one client in 100 is ever likely to enjoy their sexual abilities.

But they are still the first reserves for the real ranks of the girls selling sex and there is a never-ending supply.

Most of London's prostitution comes from the provinces, or from Scotland or Ireland.

And the Emerald Isle provides more than its fair share. Every third girl 'on the game' in Bayswater and Notting Hill seems to be Irish, but the Scots are well represented.

In almost every case of a Scottish or Irish girl becoming a prostitute, whether to work in the streets or to mix it with hostessing at some club, there is an illegitimate baby as the reason.

This can be a good thing for the client. If the girl has a baby to keep, the chances are she isn't keeping a ponce as well and she will treat her client well. The money from future visits which his interest promises will more than likely ensure she does her best to please.

If the girl does have a ponce, he will probably be out working as well. The 'blue films' business is always booming and that is his line.

Some of the club girls, from the night spots and the drinkers, can fix up a film show for those who like to see others demonstrating how it should all be done.

For real live demonstrations, lesbians together or a man and a girl, the girls who advertise on the postcard boards are the most likely for introductions. Any girl whose advertisement indicates that she goes in for 'extras' will usually be able to arrange an exhibition if given an hour or two's notice.

Such exhibitions are, however, costly affairs and the participants and the girls who do the arranging will usually want to know from past acquaintance whether the clients can afford their charges. A show will cost at least £20.

But 'blue films' can be available at a much lower charge and it is with these that Soho regains some of its old 'glory'.

Stand on a street corner in Old Compton Street or Wardour Street for more than a few minutes and the chances are a proposition will come along. Blue films are the real thing for the thugs in Soho who a few years ago would have been content merely to ponce on a girl.

Their charge—£5 a time and the client pays the cost of a taxi from the Soho spot where he is approached to the scruffy back room where the show takes place.

For a higher price—usually at least twice as high—the doormen at some West End clubs can arrange an introduction. It is just the same show, though, in just the same place, with even the same girls around if their services should be required as well.

The films will be mostly old, some pre-war, scratched and faded, an indication in themselves that the world of sex for sale doesn't really change—except in one respect: the merging as a ponce class of the tough, mannish, 'butch' type lesbian.

Their influence in London's prostitution is growing. In many cases the butches are the ponces who drive the girls the hardest and many of the younger prostitutes who walk the streets of Paddington and Notting Hill are under their control.

The partnership arrangement made by a 'butch' is always the

same. The 'butch' has a regular job—petrol pump attendant is one of the favourites. She works all day while the girl 'on the game' sleeps off the ravages of the previous night's sexual work and also the demands made on her body by her 'butch'.

In the evening, the 'butch' becomes the prostitute's maid and a well built 'butch' can be rather a menace for a client with his trousers down who doesn't behave.

A great deal of the 'rolling' is done by 'butch' lesbians, who are usually safe in the knowledge that even the client who would complain to the police about being robbed in a prostitute's bedroom by a man would never risk the publicity of a case with a 'butch' lesbian involved.

'Rolling', with or without the physical attack, can be a very profitable way of thieving for some of the girls and even those from the top class night clubs may have ponces waiting to pick the pockets of wealthy clients. The girl, of course, would always claim that no one else could possibly get into her flat and that the client's claim to have been robbed was really just a way of getting out of paying her the money he had promised.

These are the rules for avoiding a situation like that:

Avoid like the plague the bedroom with two doors, or the room with a wardrobe large enough to conceal a ponce waiting to nip out and grab the wallet the moment the trousers are laid aside.

Avoid the flat where you pass a man on the stairs. He may be just off out for a drink while the girl does her stuff. He may be going round to the fire escape which leads to the bedroom and so again to the trousers and the wallet.

Avoid also the girl who has in her handbag an official looking card. If you catch a glimpse of such a card, green, red, blue, any colour, forget her quick. It's probably her hospital card for VD treatment.

The chance of catching VD from most prostitutes, except the real scrubbers, are probably a great deal less than are the chances of catching it from an enthusiastic amateur. But even if there were no risk, and there is, whether sex with a London 'pro' is really worth all the trouble is rather doubtful.

As any girl on the game with a touch of honesty in her make-up will admit, nine times out of ten the man ends up feeling that he has been cheated, hurried too much, and sometimes actually sexually unsatisfied.

Homosexual London

The law is almost as mixed up as many of the homosexuals themselves, which makes things even more difficult, dangerous and degrading.

It affects writing about the subject as well. But although some place-names can't be named, this is a factual and informed guide to the present position in London.

This is what happens, how and when. Not to incite or encourage. (In fact, because the law has helped to make it more pathetic and sordid than it is, it will probably have the reverse effect.) It is just a report.

It is estimated that there are over a million active homosexuals in Britain. Yet, despite the recommendations of the Wolfenden Committee six years ago, we are, as a nation, only moving slowly towards the recognition that homosexual relationships between consenting adults are not criminal acts but moral decisions best left to the individual. The law being what it is (and it precludes giving any precise directions as to where a queer may find a companion of similar proclivities) the homosexual in Britain must still find his contacts where he may, and in so doing often runs the risk of embarrassment, humiliation and downright danger from the police, the crazed and the really criminal.

The situation however, is not so black as it might at first seem to be, and certainly there is a great deal more tolerance and understanding than there was, say, even ten years ago when the very word 'homosexual' was still socially taboo. Now it is considered a perfectly acceptable subject for books, films, plays, journalism and general conversation. Members of all political parties in both the Commons and the Lords, senior members of the Judiciary and heads of the established Church have all publicly proclaimed their support for Wolfenden's findings, while a very active Homosexual Reform Society constantly lobbies for the reformation of the law.

This easing of sociological tension over the subject has not, of itself, done much to increase the number of rendezvous for queers. It would more likely be true to say that this has come about by a few people with business acumen realising that a cellar room, sparsely furnished but equipped with a juke-box and fruit machine, and serving coffee and coke will be a lucrative means of attracting quite a lot of queers who want to continue the hunt after the bars have closed.

It is somewhat ironic that, although legislation has not yet been passed to free the queer from criminal stigma, the newly enacted laws regarding gambling and licensed premises have considerably widened the scope of his activities.

For various reasons, many of them self-evident, London is the magnet which attracts queers in Britain. While each major provincial city (probably each village) has its little coteries and one or two discreet bars, London offers not only almost unlimited scope for finding partners but also the often necessary anonymity for such associations.

The pattern of homosexual life has changed considerably during the last twenty years. For some time after the war many men remained in the forces, or were still being conscripted. Apart from the all-male society in which they found themselves, most un-married (and many married!) servicemen gravitated naturally to London while on leave, and what with poor pay and the expense of taking a girl out for the evening—without, perhaps, achieving the ultimate relief of their sexual frustration—it was easier for them to make friends with a queer in one of the West End bars.

This often resulted in their being invited back for a drink and the casual friendship more often than not ended up in bed—indeed, the accepting of the drink was a tacit acceptance of a lot more. Both parties were satisfied; the queer with his easy-going masculine companion, the soldier or sailor (the navy has a long tradition of homosexual relationships, with its own vocabulary) with his weekend's lodging and, perhaps, entertainment. In addition he would probably be given a pound or two for pocket money and his fare back to his unit.

Such men would not think of themselves as queer, and certainly not as male prostitutes; it was a convenient arrangement which suited both parties and often led to genuine friendships quite apart from the sexual relationship.

In Bloomsbury, Piccadilly and Chelsea there were several pubs where such pick-ups could be found, along with a Bohemian element of actors, writers, poets and painters, and other hangers-on of the artistic fringe.

With demobilisation and the end of conscription this 'natural source' of basically heterosexual servicemen gradually dried up. Some of the well-known pubs changed hands or were rebuilt and the new managements tended to encourage a more normal type of clientele. London, the queers said, was not what it was.

Yet the ending of the serviceman era coincided with the several social revolutions which followed the war. These included: a considerable breaking down of the class structure; an ever-increasing recognition of sex in all its forms and the freedom to express it; and the growing importance of the teenager within society. All this with a gradual rise in national prosperity and, among the many manifestations of the new patterns of living, the establishment of coffee bars and clubs on the social scene.

For these reasons young people grew up with a much more sophisticated awareness of sexual deviation, and, for those who recognised the urge within themselves, it was not only easier than it had been for earlier generations to come to terms with the discovery but the opportunities to indulge their needs were correspondingly greater.

Looking at the homosexual scene in London now it is possible to see the two patterns sometimes superimposed, almost archaeologically, like a new city built upon the remains of the old one: the old haunts, lingering here and there, and the new ones extending the opportunities in both space and time.

The queer pubs of London are spread over a wide area, from the dockside pubs in the East End to the tourist pubs in the West End; from the smart pubs of Chelsea and Belgravia to the bed-sitter areas of Earls Court and Fulham.

The pubs in the East End of London are by far the liveliest and most amusing. Several of them have music, either professional groups or local talent. Some, near the docks, attract the shipboard homosexuals and their tolerant sailor boyfriends. Twenty years ago they would almost all have been full of rough, tough, friendly East-Enders, indifferently dressed except for the odd 'wide boy' of the period in his American draped suit. Now, worthy of a full sociological study to themselves, the local boys—still tough, still friendly—are elegantly dressed in silk and mohair suits, expensive shoes, shirts and ties; all very sharp, very sophisticated. Their birds are equally smart, well groomed with elaborate hair-dos. These burly, worldly dockers are the natural bait for the itinerant homosexuals who make their forays from further west and amuse the locals with their jokes and mannerisms. Some of the pubs have gained real social distinction and it is not an uncommon sight to see Jaguars, Lancias and Mercedes jostling in the car parks with the less exotic machinery of the locals.

The queer West End pubs are nothing like so lively or friendly, but because they are right there in the middle of London's sight-seeing and entertainment area they are usually busy right through the week instead of only at the week-ends as are the East End pubs.

Piccadilly, naturally, is a focal point of homosexual activity, but apart from the tourist customers, or the provincial queer out to explore the exciting possibilities that he has heard London has to offer, these pubs attract a large proportion of rough rent. These, too, are often from the provinces, young layabouts and semi-delinquents attracted by different prey and who have heard, in their turn, of the potential offered by the metropolis . . . a case of the hunters hunted. It is an area that queers have learnt to patrol with caution. There are one or two pleasant pubs in the locality, however. These have either some historical associations, or a nicely restored Edwardian or Victorian décor or, because of their proximity to Theatreland, are the haunts of actors and artists connected with the stage or films. For all these reasons they are pubs which appeal to the sensibilities of the queer.

To the south-west lies Chelsea, the arty quarter of London and, one would think, the natural habitat of the homosexual. This is no doubt very true but, curiously enough, it is not very well served with pubs offering themselves as a suitable rendezvous. There are, of course, one or two, but they are somewhat seedy and attract an odd assembly. One or two have music, mostly played on a piano but their popularity fluctuates and, again, it is only at the week-ends that they become really busy.

Belgravia offers one or two elegant little pubs in odd mews but these too only come to life at the week-ends; one, in fact, is limited almost entirely to Sunday lunchtime as a venue for homo-sexuals to meet. On these occasions it is usually more for them to compare notes and exchange anecdotes and information concerning the previous Saturday night . . .

Not far away, in Knightsbridge, there are one or two pubs which have traditionally been the meeting place for homosexuals. This is because of their proximity to the Barracks. Her Majesty's Horse Guards and Household Cavalry have, equally traditionally, pro-vided military escorts for the queers who possessed both the money and the inclination for breeches and breastplates. Even though, during the rebuilding of the barracks, the mounted guards are quartered at Wellington barracks, the Knightsbridge pubs continue to serve their function.

Wellington and Chelsea barracks, homes of the foot guards, are served by the pubs of Victoria but, apart from being a little more diffuse, the whole set-up is less arranged, less organised—though not much less commercial. It is more of a catch-as-catch-can, far less focussed.

Across the river, there are one or two other pubs with their tough but tolerant Londoners who welcome the clientele of queers for the gaiety they bring to the proceedings.

Back on the north side of the Thames, there are two pubs which attract queers with rather more esoteric interests. It has been a feature of all sexual activities in recent years that there has been a considerable rise in the practice of sado-masochism. This is true of homosexuals, only probably more so. Closely linked with these interests is the leather, plastic and rubber cult, and also homosexual motor-cyclist enthusiasts. They don't all actually *have* motor-cycles, of course, but dress as if they do. Sometimes identification of interests is made easier by having the letters S/M worked in studs on the leather jackets.

So much for the pubs. The homosexual clubs of London fall into two distinct categories: the chi-chi places—mostly in the West End, and the newer, starker establishments in Chelsea and Victoria. The chi-chi places have nearly all been established for several years— some dating back to war-time. The décor is usually regency stripes, red velvet and candelabra, or has some irrelevant and overdone motif, like the cabin of a ship. Clientele are often the discreet businessman type looking for a young man to set up in a *pied à terre* or perhaps to help run a men's boutique; at any rate the image they create is one of elegance and sophistication—albeit rather passé.

The clubs of Victoria and Chelsea are more aware of what is currently fashionable in interior design, pop art and pine, with a much greater mixture of customers—students, artisans, actors, shop-assistants and waiters. The atmosphere ranges from the way-out and with-it to cosy suburban; the choice of partner is correspondingly more varied. Entertainment ranges from a languid pianist through a pop group to the ubiquitous juke-box; in one or two instances there is a roulette table complete with croupier, but gambling is more usually limited to a fruit machine. New clubs open quite frequently then close after a few months as fickle fashions change. They offer a small extension to the licensing laws and a sense, perhaps, of belonging to an exclusive minority rather than a persecuted one. At any rate there is no doubt that for some homosexuals, the clubs provide not only a meeting place but a sense of safety and belonging —of being somewhere where the law is less liable to penetrate and where the mask can be dropped and inhibitions banished.

Catering to a rougher, tougher and younger element are the coffee bar clubs. Entrance to these often does not demand even a nominal membership; it is just a matter of paying a half-a-crown entrance fee and then something over the odds for each cup of espresso coffee or bottle of coke.

They are mostly situated in or near the lower ends of the Kings Road in Chelsea and the Fulham Road, and nearly all in dimly-lit cellars. There is always a juke-box blaring incessantly and dancing is not discouraged. In fact, on busy Saturday nights it becomes more like a rugger scrum and has even been known to approach the orgiastic . . .

The crowd is very mixed: mods, rockers, beatniks, layabouts, hustlers, simpering young hairdressers, crew-cut truck-drivers, students and tourists, blue jeans and leather gear. At week-ends the scene survives into the small hours. This sort of club is very much a product of the 'sixties and has done a lot to enliven the homosexuals' milieu.

In London, as the world over, another sure-fire set-up for homosexuals may be one of the turkish baths. Because it is possible to stay all night in these places they obviously provide quite a lot of cover for homosexual activities. The staff mostly turn a blind eye to much of the midnight prowling or conveniently ignore the more or less obvious fact that a cubicle designed for one is occupied by two; at least they do if the activity is not too blatant. Periodically the management carries out a purge or, following a complaint, maintains a stricter watch which seems to lapse a little after a week or two.

The West End baths are naturally more expensive and the amenities more elaborate although, in truth, the furnishings are faded and threadbare. Neither can offer anything as ornate and exciting as Paris, Hamburg, Amsterdam or Vienna but they might possibly please gerontophiles or collectors of Edwardiana.

To the East of London, and also south of the river there are several turkish baths run by local councils. These vary a lot in comfort and cleanliness but they are all comparatively cheap and the customers are generally a lot younger—many of them the local dockers and factory workers who genuinely go to the baths in order to avail themselves of the facilities—but are not averse to enjoying the other activities . . . These baths are never open all night—they mostly close at about 8 p.m.—but the opportunities they present for a liaison are probably more concentrated because of it.

The darkness of a cinema has always been an obvious place for furtive fumbling no less for homosexuals than for heterosexuals.

Some of the most notorious London cinemas have recently been pulled down or are scheduled for demolition but others remain. These are mostly in the vicinity of Piccadilly Circus and the West End, but there are others. The older and smaller the cinema the greater the activity seems to be—in fact the less the customers will be attracted by the programme the more they can be expected to go for each other.

News cinemas are an obvious lure because the programme of news and 'shorts' need not be taken seriously and in any case starts to repeat itself in an hour so that anything missed through amorous dalliance can soon be seen again. It is a common practice for queer customers to get up frequently and go to the lavatory; they then return to a different seat where something more attractive—or more responsive—can be found.

Apart from the cinemas in central London there are many others in the surrounding districts and suburbs where local queers concentrate some of their activities. Again, the scruffier the location the more likely is it to yield something of interest to the exploratory homosexual.

Even more extensive than the cinemas in both possibilities and location are the public lavatories, and it is true to say that wherever they are there will be a couple of queers also.

Naturally, there are some areas that are very well known and where, despite police activities and watchful attendants queers will always foregather to 'cruise the cottages'. Many homosexuals find such places extremely distasteful, but even more are lured by the element of danger, or even prefer the swift, anonymous contacts such places afford. For a stranger it may be, after all, the only immediate way of discovering the way in to more general homosexual activity in the city.

The most obvious places are the lavatories which serve the main areas of the West End—and of course they are the most dangerous too, as they are regularly watched by both uniformed police and plain-clothes officers. Even so they are always thronged with queers obviously importuning—many of them visitors and tourists. There is also a high proportion of young male prostitutes drifting in and out—especially in the vicinity of Piccadilly—but these people can usually be identified by their unkempt appearance although this is by no means an infallible guide; a young man who is, perhaps, more than usually well dressed might be looked upon with equal suspicion!

The main railway stations are another source of prospective

encounters for lavatory-lovers, although, for some obscure reason, the main termini on the Southern Region are by far the most popular. Again, these locales are extremely dangerous, with watchful attendants and occasional visits from the police.

The men's cloakrooms of West End hotels where there is a constant traffic of men in and out are another easy means of contact, especially where they are situated not far from a public lavatory and it is therefore possible to promenade between the two without occasioning too much notice. In one or two hotels very close to the heart of the West End it is a commonplace for the ground-floor cloakroom to be used for making an initial contact while the quieter lavatories on the upper floors provide cover for—to use a legal phrase—indecent acts. Of course, it is also quite common for a homosexual visitor to stay at one of these large hotels and then prowl the foyer and cloakrooms in search of a partner; he then has accommodation to hand.

It is possible to extend the lavatory locales almost indefinitely as every suburban area has its pissoir serving the local queers. Some become so notorious that they are the frequent object of a special pilgrimage by queers living on the other side of London.

Apart from the main-line stations, many stations on London's underground are equipped with lavatories which are the regular haunt of queers who like to make their contacts in this way. On the District and Circle line in particular it was once a well known 'progress' for queers to make, and for the price of the cheapest ticket it was possible to ride backwards and forwards for hours on a journey of discovery. Many of the lavatories on this line have been closed, but some still remain very much in operation.

Nearly all parks and recreation grounds (and there are literally scores in the greater London area) have 'cottages' where the odd queer may be found cruising. In addition many pubs have outside lavatories which, during drinking hours—and often all hours—are well known for their homosexual possibilities.

Department stores all over London have men's lavatories where occasional activity takes place; in fact the possibilities are limitless in this field if the itinerant queer is ready to run the not inconsiderable risks attached to this form of hunting; obviously, in circumstances like these the homosexual is at his most vulnerable.

Possibly the most sure-fire means of contact in London is to be found in the several recognised open-air rendezvous which in scale and scope are possibly unique in the world. London has always been famous for its many and beautiful parks; just what those parks are famous for is not necessarily limited to the flower-beds and landscaping . . .

The mysterious opportunities that they offer to the queer who considers this type of activity are almost limitless, for the parks and commons and fields are the haunt of every type of homosexual. Of course, as always, there are certain dangers to be reckoned with but, on the whole, raids by the police and rolling by roughs is not so prevalent as to make visits unwise. Certainly they present nothing like the dangers of Central Park in New York or the Zappeon Gardens in Athens. In any case, the sort of queer who gets his kicks from this kind of activity often claims to have some form of prescience or extra-sensory perception enabling him to anticipate danger. In fact it is surprising to find the number of otherwise timid men who run what normal men would consider hair-raising risks.

Because many of London's parks and common grounds are so extensive it is not always so easy for a queer to discover the particular area in which the homosexual activity takes place, but as it is usually (but by no means entirely) at night almost any person walking late at night along the paths and through the wooded areas is more than likely to be interested in something other than the nocturnal habits of the local fauna.

On Wimbledon Common the homosexual activities take place around the perimeter of a small lake, known, appropriately enough, as Queen's Mere. It is quite a romantic setting, the lakeside bordered by fine old trees and thick shrubbery. From dusk onwards individuals begin to arrive and stroll around the lake and the immediate paths. Contacts are of all types, old and young, butch and bitch, with quite a large proportion of leather and motor-cycle fans. The police make occasional sporadic visits but their arrival is usually heralded by flashing torches and a noisy approach through the undergrowth. There has also been the occasional unpleasant beating-up of individuals by gangs, but this is infrequent.

A particular part of Hampstead Heath offers similar activities, not far from the famous Bull and Bush pub. After dark, from April to October, the paths are quite busy with promenading queers; even on a January night with snow falling a few hardy habituees can be seen searching for al fresco partners.

Day-time activities, though obviously more restricted, take place at two or three localities. Foremost among these are the fields bordering the towpath at Richmond. These fields are used by queers for nude sunbathing so that the venue is essentially a summer-time one. A little way back from the towpath the grasses grow long and clumps of bushes afford cover for amorous associations.

Highgate Ponds in North London offer an official enclosure where nude sunbathing is possible. Naturally this affords easy opportunities for queers to solicit one another. The enclosure is small, approximately 20 feet by 70 feet, and primitive. A natural segregation takes place between the queers at one end and the muscle-men from the adjoining gym and swimming club at the other. Outside the enclosure, on the grass, more circumspect sunbathing takes place and while, unlike Richmond, no actual sexual activity takes place, many queers find it, on a summer's day, a pleasant place to contact each other.

The Hyde Park Lido is another summer-time rendezvous for queers which has the advantage of being right in the heart of London. Once again the homos and the heteros divide themselves up fairly obviously, and, as at Highgate, the picking-up process is confined to the casual exchange of a glance or a word.

Perhaps, in a year or two, the archaic laws of the country will be changed so that the homosexual in Great Britain in general and London in particular will not be driven to these desperate and dangerous measures.

Nobody may consume more than a half-bottle of spirits while travelling on the London Underground.

Lesbian London

No one knows how many there are. Homosexual males are now accepted, but homosexual females are still a hidden minority.

In public, they can expect to be derided. Even in private, there are scarcely any places they can meet together as themselves.

Here is one of London's few lesbian clubs. And who, why, when and how its members meet there.

It is Friday night. Down the Kings Road, past Chelsea Town Hall where the hip young things are already ascending and descending their own private Jacob's ladder to the lighted church windows of the ballroom.

Past His Clothes and Glebe Place, where the P.E.N. Club is raising decorous martinis to a visiting Russian writer whose works have never appeared in English.

Then behind a dull green door and down the cellar steps where the girls are gathering to inaugurate the week-end. This is the famous Gateways Club.

It has been in existence since the 'thirties and acquired its present exclusive flavour during the war. A war which affected a class-revolution in lesbianism, as it did in so many other fields of English social life. The equality of uniform khaki or blue lowered the barriers, letting in the other ranks who refused to return to anonymity when the war was over. They wanted to dance; they were willing to spend. The juke-box ousted the piano and afternoon tea.

The older members regret it, remembering the panache of white flannels and blazers, with nostalgia for the days when to be different was to be doubly different. 'They knew how to spend too,' one of them said. 'All shorts and none of this lasting out half of bitter all evening. I've seen money flow like water. Now it's just teddy-boys and typists.'

Admission is strictly controlled, for members and guests only, and madame scrutinises you as you enter. No guests are admitted after ten o'clock to discourage people from trying to get in after they've spent their money elsewhere. Rowdies or trouble-makers are barred immediately, even when their errors arise from misery at the end of an affair rather than drunken brawling.

To be barred is not only embarrassing, it is also extremely inconvenient. The nearest place which has two or three comparable clubs is Brighton. This makes social life more expensive than most people can afford, even with a car or scooter which most of them try to have, to avoid public transport where they may be open to stares and comments.

Any offenders at the club, therefore, usually try to make their peace with the management as soon as tempers have cooled. They are received back with a caution. Their friends try to see that they keep out of trouble until someone else comes along to fill their loneliness.

It is half-past-eight. There are already between twenty and thirty people sitting on the padded benches along the walls, usually talking gossip about friends not yet arrived or detailed accounts of the progress of the current affair, stretching out their hands to the glasses on the small round tables, waiting.

The juke-box is kept constantly fed but hardly anyone is ready to dance yet. The two fruit machines swallow their quota of sixpences. Each new arrival peers round defensively for her group though there are a few walkers by themselves who stand on the edge of the dance-floor, coolly appraising. Soon the numbers will grow to fifty and then a hundred and the serious enjoyment of the evening will begin.

The room is low-ceilinged with a long bar at the back. The walls are covered with frescos showing the life and characters of the club.

Until the recent repainting many of the war-time originals still surveyed the floor under peaked caps or wearing baggy trousered suits. Portraits of the proprietors smile down paternally through the subdued lighting and heavy smoke pall.

By now the floor is rocking under the dancers' feet. The tunes are those popular in the charts at the moment but there is a distinct preference for songs to and about girls. Some catch on because they can be very equivocally interpreted.

Lovers dance locked together to the slower records but the beat numbers are the most popular because of the opportunities for display like the dancing of cranes and for sheer physical response to rhythm. Neither partner is committed except to the music.

The floor becomes so crowded that it is impossible to do anything more than gyrate on the spot and by half-past-ten nearly two hundred people will be packed between the bulging walls. Eyes smart and water in the smoke and a trip to the bar and back is an obstacle race with the prize a full glass.

There are few men and they are likely to be homosexual themselves. Mostly they simply stand and talk but sometimes they will dance with one of the girls, often a young butch in fly-front trousers and button-up shirt whose gestures are more obviously masculine than her partner's. At the other extreme are the femmes (pronounced as the first syllable in feminine), in their tight-skirted cocktail dresses, while in between lie infinite variations and degrees of masculinity.

Sometimes a bi-sexual woman will find her way here on the rebound from a male lover and there are many who have tried and failed to adjust to marriage and the requirements of conventional society. Most are looking for a permanent relationship and many will find it, but there are also dozens of affairs which begin promisingly and founder after a couple of years, the danger point for heterosexual affairs too, when physical attraction has lost its novelty and something must be found to replace or rekindle it.

As couples set up home together they drift away from the club. The reasons for this are fairly clear. If you are lonely and looking for a partner you will go where the other lonely searchers are likely to be found. Young married couples do not as a rule go to the pub or the palais two or three nights a week. They are too busy getting, and keeping, a home together and the same is true of homosexuals. The club population is a shifting, seeking one with groups forming and reforming as couples drop out and newcomers take their place.

The newcomer may find it difficult to get herself accepted into a group until she has been seen there two or three times and found people with similar interests or jobs. They will want to know if she is a scrounger or mixed up with the criminal world in which case she will probably drift away to one of the seedier little clubs in Notting Hill.

There is less mixing of the levels of society among female than among male homosexuals: teachers talk to other teachers, factory workers and petrol pump attendants clan together with lower-paid office workers and bus conductresses.

Jobs where slacks can be worn are popular because these as a rule involve less deception. Many girls work unsuspected in offices but, like their male counterparts, they must be careful to keep the two halves of their double life apart.

A lot of lesbians are professional women struggling against anti-feminist discrimination and they are unlikely to visit the club, very often because their own difficulties make them intolerant of people whose intelligence does not match up to their own. Select dinner parties, evenings at the theatre are their social outlet. They do not want to be regarded as second-class citizens themselves and so avoid contact with people who are obviously this. For the same reason they avoid extremes of dress. They are closer to social acceptance; the others realise that they can never have it without a radical change in the whole attitude of society to women, particularly as semi-skilled workers, as well as the more obvious acceptance of minority groups.

Most people come to the Gateways because they are looking for forms of amusement and chances of meeting partners equivalent to those they would find in the heterosexual world that their ex-school friends and neighbours now inhabit.

Dance halls are out since although women do dance together in public they do not do so exclusively or affectionately. Pubs are still often risky places for unaccompanied women, youth clubs are impossible. Dining out with the girlfriend is an expensive business and few women earn as much as men. Restaurants often bar women in slacks but a great number of homosexual women feel uncomfortable in anything else.

From time to time girls are beaten up but they don't as a rule complain to the police. They know that in a sense they are guilty of provocation simply by being themselves and they don't expect anyone else to sympathise.

At the clubs they can dance together and dress as they like with no need to pretend to like someone if they don't and no fear of difficult or ugly situations beyond their control.

Most of their friends will be homosexual so that they are spared embarrassing questions about marriage and boyfriends. Families pose a problem. Some people manage to tell their parents and remain on good terms with them but others either lead a double life, dressing up when they go home to visit and fending off questions as they arise, or drift away from their families altogether.

They come to London from the provinces and from all over the world. The Commonwealth provides a generous quota, principally of Australians and South Africans, who are looking for freedom from a basically pioneering culture where men are still men and women stay home and rock the cradle.

Like other young people who come to this country they are drawn to Bayswater, Notting Hill and South Kensington, because of the chances for flat-sharing and reducing expenses and because of the shifting cosmopolitan population which doesn't care what you are or how you dress as long as you add to the atmosphere of freedom and excitement.

There are Indians and Africans, girls from America and Italy, and there is a constant to and fro between the clubs of London and Paris. Holidays abroad are extremely popular, and many girls give up their jobs to travel au pair or to go hitch-hiking. Jobs are either taken very seriously as careers or picked up and dropped as a means of getting from day to day with enough for a room and the week-end's entertainment. Faces which have been missing for months suddenly reappear suntanned from Israel or Tangiers with hair-raising tales to tell which are always good for a free drink.

New Year's Eve is the big night of the year when hundreds of members look in during the long evening and as many as possible jam the floor at midnight to see in the new year with its promise of new affairs that must surely last longer than the old, resolutions to drink less and work more, nostalgia for past failures. The end of an affair does not necessarily mean the end of a friendship. After the first bitterness is over people continue to see each other, and under the bursting balloons and thrown streamers old relationships are renewed on the level of affection.

The Gateways has thousands of members—membership is cheap at ten shillings a head—but fortunately they don't all try to get in at once. Many live outside London and rarely come up, but like to know it's there if they want it. The hard core live in London but all have their favourite nights. Friday and Sunday are usually full house with Saturday an unbelievable crush. Thursday and Wednesday have their following and a few people drop in at lunchtime for a quiet drink and talk.

The Gateways' only serious rival has been a club which recently moved to new premises in Westbourne Park. The clientele is slightly different: there are more tourists and more of the extreme trans-vestites, many of them from the women's barracks. There are also one or two after-hours drinking and coffee clubs in this district, mostly patronised by prostitutes and their girl-friends, who live on the fringes of the criminal world and are therefore more likely to be involved in fights and drug-taking.

One of the saddest offshoots of the lack of facilities in London is the number of small clubs which mushroom and shrivel almost overnight, illegal because they are selling drinks without a licence and often pathetic because they are in private houses. The living-rooms are thrown open, the carpet is rolled back and a few couples dance unenthusiastically among the souvenirs of private lives, the photographs and holiday mementos.

The motive behind these attempts is a combination of the desire to provide somewhere else for people to go with the urge to make a little money: although there is no entrance fee, the drinks cost rather more than average.

It is our English licensing laws which make the setting up of clubs particularly difficult. Our phlegmatic natures seem to need well lubricating before we can let ourselves go and by that time the sacred hour of eleven is on us. For those who feel the night is just starting there is the problem of where to go. An impromptu party is the usual answer. Bottles are crammed into pockets, car doors slam, scooters are revved for the long run out to the edge of Essex or deep into Middlesex where someone has a large flat with accommodating neighbours. These are like any other parties with the one difference: men dance with men and women with women.

Many of the girls have one or two friends among male homo-sexuals and they often make up groups to visit the boys' clubs or pubs. Two of the most popular where there is often a good sprink-ling of the girls are one in Battersea, a mainly working-class pub with two-piece band and soloists from the audience, and one in Notting Hill which caters for the more sophisticated. These relationships are of mutual benefit. They borrow each other's partners when they want to impress the outside world at the firm's dinner and dance or at a family wedding or birthday party, and they also provide a link with the opposite sex in however modified a form.

Language is another common factor. The terms 'gay' and 'queer' for themselves are used by both male and female as is 'butch' for a masculine type of either sex. The rest of the world are 'normals' or 'heteros', sometimes but not often 'straight'. 'Drag' for clothes of the opposite sex is used by both and also 'camp' for anyone whose behaviour or appearance is obviously homosexual in an effeminate way. No parallels exist however for 'trade' and 'rent' since there is no prostitution among the girls themselves. 'Who pays for what they can get for free?' as one put it. Sometimes they imitate the boys' gestures and accents in fun but it is laughing with them, not against them.

Recent expressions from the American Beats have become current via the drug and pop world. 'Scene' is probably the most popular but 'hooked' and 'hung up' to describe a relationship are coming up fast. The term 'lesbian' itself is universally detested and hardly ever used except when quoting an outsider. They themselves prefer to be known in formal terms as female homosexuals or colloquially as 'the girls' or 'gay girls'.

There are however many to whom all this mixing in a minority group, with its tenuous links with the world of drugs and prostitutes, is psychologically and even physically repellent. They are shocked and disgusted by even the well-ordered and carefully supervised gaiety of the Gateways. Not having fully come to terms with their own condition they still want to keep it in some way separate from themselves. 'Just because I'm like this it doesn't mean I have to mix with a lot of layabouts I've nothing in common with.' Standards of middle-class behaviour are upheld and this often leaves a residue of guilt and shame.

In mitigation it should be pointed out that many belong to an older generation and have been brought up in circumstances where secrecy seemed the only course if all kinds of unpleasantness were to be avoided. These women are often intensely lonely and may feel that they are the only homosexuals in the world, therefore an aberration, a freak of society if not of nature. For them the Minorities Research Group founded two years ago may be the only social outlet.

Until recently the group held meetings in the back room of a pub in Clapham but these have been discontinued as unsuccessful, presumably because most people were not very clear whether they were there to talk or to dance and because of the difficulty many of them find in making a satisfactory social adjustment even among people with whom they have most in common.

Activities are now split into various more serious hobby groups, literary, indoor sports, rambling, outdoor sports. The society also publishes a magazine called *Arena Three* which provides in its correspondence column the only social outlet the more timorous may ever have.

A peripheral and more eclectic pleasure female homosexuals may indulge in, if they have their public image at heart, is to take part in an intensive piece of research being painstakingly conducted by a sociologist from Cambridge. They can enjoy three-and-a-half hours of assorted intelligence and personality tests just off Bond Street on wintry Sunday afternoons.

But for those who like their pleasures rather stronger, the Gateways is still the best answer.

You will need a member to sign you in, a few shillings for a couple of drinks, a fashionable rig, preferably from John Michaels or one of the men's boutiques in the King's Road, and then you are ready to dance the evening through or mark the variations in dress and character from the dark-suited butch in the corner to Little Lord Fauntleroy in velveteen jacket and ruffles.

The public are much more knowledgeable about lesbianism than they used to be, as anyone knows who has listened to an audience at the National Film Theatre howling its way through an oldie. But acceptance is a long way away. Two women together, particularly if they are young and one has a masculine air or style of dress, are quickly recognized and remarked upon.

So a club like the Gateways is not only the best place. For most people, there is nowhere else to go.

This is the true down and out, the tramp, the vagrant, the destitute. Not the temporary down and out, who is just waiting to bounce back.

The down and out who mentally, socially and emotionally can't change his ways. How does he live, how does he eat and sleep? How would we make out if we had to do the same?

In London he doesn't beg or bare his soul in public, as in other cities, so he can be easily ignored. There are probably 200,000 in Britain as a whole. They concern us all.

A real down and out is someone who is really down and out. There are no simple causes and explanations and reasons. That's just how he is.

But until more is known about the true determinants of man's social behaviour, there will always be the generally accepted belief that the individual is responsible for his actions, and his predicament. It is thought the down and out must deserve to be down and out through his own fault and should be suitably ashamed.

The individual is in fact quite wonderfully helpless. For the greatest social injustice is his lack of choice in the milieu of his birth.

However, the Welfare State, while not entirely agreeing with the fact that the vagrant is indeed as helpless as the tycoon in his choice of life, pragmatically assumes that it is just to help him. Which is something. But it is really only geared to those who come out of the cold and ask for help.

The first and obvious place to go to if one is down and out is the local National Assistance Board office. But in practice help varies in different offices. Some will insist on the applicant having an address before assistance is given, and others will not. The emergency assistance may vary between a few shillings and a pound or vouchers. One 'address' accepted is a bombed cemetery in the East End, the 'home' of a group of meths. drinkers.

There is only one Reception Centre in London where, of course, accommodation is initially free. But the resident is expected to apply for work. The address of the Reception Centre, which he must give to the prospective employer, being hardly a recommendation. As success in this enterprise takes him out of our category, we can leave him there. But since the turnover in the 'rescued' by these means is small, we can meet him again in the next paragraph. In any case he will have tended to be of the elite in vagrancy, a wise selector of his parenthood, deserving of our congratulations.

Meeting him again, we note that he has (properly) lost self-respect, a rather essential commodity. But before he reaches the bottom he will have learned how to imitate this—an earnest, sincere look, humble, yet proud.

If more proud than humble he can use various outdoor facilities in more clement weather.

Regents Park, for example, has little areas of thick shrubbery suitable for rest and sleep. In one of them (near the Zoo entrance) there is still a useable sleeping bag and the top half of a book by Lowry for bedside reading.

All the parks are suitable, but some less than others, depending on the amount of shrubbery.

In the very cold weather, something better is recommended—for example, Waterloo Station. After the wiser citizens have finished going home, late at night, the benches may be seen well-occupied by the 'skippers'. Sleep here is liable to be interrupted by calls of nature—often the final call of all. It is not unknown for some occupants to die in the night, which is disturbing. An average attendance might be about sixty persons.

Failing this, there are bombed houses, bomb sites. The Salvation Army is not easy to get into without money. Having no money presumably shows a complete lack of self-respect. But in extra-ordinary circumstances it is overlooked.

If one is reduced to sleeping 'rough', one may break one's slumbers to get tea and a bun from 'The Silver Lady' on the Embankment. She arrives three nights a week for this old-established dispensation. 'She' being the daughter of the first 'Silver Lady'.

Nevertheless, this is a very hard life. If one is totally destitute and hasn't enough initiative either for legal or illegal private enterprise, consolation is needed. As alcohol is expensive, methylated or surgical spirits (about 2s. for a medicine bottle) substitutes for a shortened, but relatively unconscious life. A few weeks of this will make one thoroughly undesirable, and what then?

Fortunately there are a few private charitable bodies whose aesthetic and 'moral' principles are as nothing compared with their curious desire to help these unfortunates.

Outstanding among these, if only for the scope of its activities and the total permissiveness of its attitudes, is the Simon Community movement, directed by Anton Wallich-Clifford, an ex-Bow Street

Probation Officer. Wallich-Clifford estimates a figure of 200,000 'misfits' in Britain.

Until recently something like twelve hostels in and out of London were under their administration. A recent schism has altered this, but Wallich-Clifford is again expanding his activities.

If by any chance the destitute has committed a crime and served his sentence, the Golborne Centre (24 Percival Road, S.W.14, PRO 7485) will probably accommodate him if it can. This also is a permissive refuge for the undesirable, administered by the Rev. Bertram E. Peake.

'Permissiveness' is indeed a spreading concept, as punishment becomes more obviously ineffectual. It has affected attitudes of officials in Reception Centres, for example. There is no longer the bullying and moralising attitude so long associated with the work-houses which they have replaced. But they are limited by what they *can* do.

The really hard case, the man totally allergic to employment (not necessarily to work), is beyond them. Many of them will not venture even into these, such is their terror of anything approaching authority, of Them over Us: a hiatus with, probably, still a long future.

But *if* the destitute man rigidly refuses to avail himself of any help—as many do—the prospect of an early death is a likely one.

Alcohol, barbitone addiction (a rising scourge—the drug is easily available) all lead to death on the instalment plan, as Céline called the life of poverty.

Round Camden Town Tube Station, for example, will be found a small group of outcasts shivering in all weathers. Some of them dive into the lavatories when they open. If things are 'good', they take a bottle of cider and one of a certain 'British Wine' which, mixed, make the mind fly to happier regions.

The really hard cases of 'jake' drinkers inhabit empty houses and building sites all over London, staying for a few days or weeks until they're discovered.

There are also the arches under certain bridges which afford temporary refuge. 'Communities' of 'jake' drinkers abound, and the feeling is, socially speaking, rather good. There is complete acceptance of course, exchange of news about accessible houses and missions, sharing out of booze, cigarettes and money, and the essential fire. There are *known* to be between 200 and 400 of these 'jake' drinkers wandering abroad in London. Those drinking the stuff more privately must be many more. The effects are, of course, terrible. Even alcoholics' hospitals refuse them as does the Salvation Army (which costs about 7s. 6d. a night) and other hostels. The last place in London which did take them in was Simonlight in Cable Street, now under a new dispensation which has changed its policy. The 'jake' boys may also be met near Charing Cross Tube station, round a brazier near an accommodating coffee-stall proprietor.

Clean hostels are not rare but neither are they cheap to the destitute. One Rowton House has been turned into Mount Pleasant Hotel at around £1 a night.

The Society of Vincent de Paul runs a very clean and pleasant hostel under The Rev. Austen Williams known as St Martin le Tours. The charge here with breakfast is 11s. 6d. a night, and is used by working men as well as a few non-working men. St. Martin works in close touch with the local N.A.B. office. Unemployed residents draw their National Assistance to stay there. Some totally destitute are allowed in, on the general understanding that rehabilitation—a job—is the aim. But there are a few there who cannot work.

Bruce House (by Covent Garden) is clean and comfortable—cubicles, like St. Martin—and costs around 7s. 6d. a night, as do most hostels and lodging houses.

For the really hungry, vegetables of quite good quality can be found and picked up in Covent Garden, which some nuns and the Simon Group do regularly. The porters are very pleasant about this, and it's become a recognized practice. There are, of course, dustbins. And gutters. London's pavements and gutters are not badly stocked nowadays.

But unless one is indeed a very hard case there is no real difficulty in getting some National Assistance because, though a fixed address is always demanded, the N.A.B. have the right to waive this requirement. On the whole the officials are understanding and helpful.

But of course getting work becomes progressively more difficult as one descends the grades in destitution, and having to give a hostel address is no help for non-manual work. The cruel point that emerges is that the greater the need of the destitute, the less the help available.

The majority of meths. drinkers obviously need hospital attention, and they don't get it. It is a spectacle indeed to see them on the stations, where the police sometimes, but not always, move them on. Waterloo at 2.30 a.m. is the critical time. It is an astonishing spectacle to see in a civilized country.

Being down and out is, like everything else, a vocation, a matter of temperament. Some do not dislike it. But we must be suspicious of what 'liking it' means. Any addiction wears the appearance of a preference. The pit pony isn't happy in daylight after a life-time below; nevertheless his sufferings there were real enough.

What appears to go with the vagrant and destitute life is a monastic temperament, acquired or pre-dispositioned. Hostel life suits this. Indeed if an enlightened tycoon were to build all over London 'lay monasteries' with provision for solitude or community life, clean, rather spartan and well-run by an unobtrusive and competent staff, he would make even more money.

With the few amenities for good health, no more relaxing experience exists than that of temporarily retiring from society. Destitute people have immense tact and good manners with each other. Little in the way of personal information is asked, though much is offered. There is a strangely pioneering spirit and atmosphere in the milieu. London begins to resemble an urban Wild West, dotted with kips and benefactions, places to keep warm, places to avoid. Characters abound—Manchester Fred, Stepney Fred, Canada, etc. Their comings and goings are noted and discussed, like a living newspaper.

Stepney Fred, for example, is totally unexpected. By day he engages in activities of, perhaps, a devious kind. By night he acts as liaison officer between skippers and available shelters. He does this for nothing and on his own, and looks forward to having a van to extend his uses. He is an ex-skipper himself. His belief is that 'you've got to trust people. If you don't, they don't. And you've got to do this for nothing. If you get paid, it's a job, and then you think of a better job and off you go.'

Nowhere is there such easy communality, profound consideration of an unstudied kind and tolerance above all, as in hostels for the bad cases. The tone is far in advance, in the community sense, of most of the respectable world. Lack of initiative is a general characteristic—not lack of intelligence, though the life does eventually dull the mind. But the lack of initiative makes for good company and friendship. In 'St. Joe's', for example, in Malden Road, a group of misfits engage in a kind of pragmatic training in helping their own kind. Only their own kind can be effective. The poorest destitute are suspicious of authority, even down to the hygiene associated with it in the cleaner hostels. This is why Wallich-Clifford in Cable Street refused to clean the place, because he knew his 'customers' would avoid it because of this pure but rooted association. The stink was phenomenal. But the alternative was quite simply not getting the people he wanted to help.

The great danger of prolonged destitution, apart from the obvious physical ones, is a mental breakdown—very often it is finally brought about by meths drinking.

This is induced, of course, by the feeling of being totally un-wanted, and the bitter experience of walking the streets among the prosperous with no offer of help. The isolation that this induces may easily drive a man crazy.

It can also be caused by 'moving on', which becomes as com-pulsive as a tic. When he rests, the environment, kept at bay by perpetual movement, encroaches on him in retaliation. People have the same effect on him: paranoiac symptoms appear.

To add to the mental casualties, there are large numbers of self-

discharged voluntary patients who enter London from mental hospitals without supervision and take to meths and barbiturates.

The sad thing is that help is most available to the least destitute, which is to say to the least needy. It is the most denied to the most needy, especially those who end up as meths-drinkers in the 'meths pits'.

By law, for example, people found wandering abroad without a minimum amount of money are committing an offence and could be arrested. Two shillings is looked upon as minimum—it wouldn't even get you into a hostel. Yet which of those 60-odd people on Waterloo Station have that sum on them? Which are asked if they have?

The truth is that the police don't want them fouling the cells.

They regard them as incurable nuisances. Many of them would be only too glad to spend the night in a cell. This attitude to vagrants prevails all over the country. Very few are arrested.

London's destitute differ in one important respect from the Paris *clochards*. As visitors know only too well, the militancy with which the beggars descend upon everyone for money, around 11.00-12.00 p.m., can be alarming.

London vagrants are very nervous beggars, when they beg at all. It is not too much to say that they are, when not under the influence of their tipple, ashamed of themselves. In being ashamed they are senselessly colluding with the still widespread 'belief'—and what a convenient one it is—that they are responsible for their plight. We are all responsible.

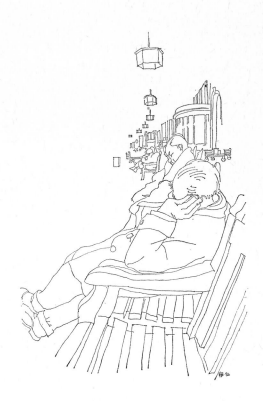

FOREIGN

LONDON

Foreign London

London is now one of the most cosmopolitan cities in the world. It is possible for an Irishman, an African or a Pakistani to live, eat, sleep, work and die in London without ever catching sight of a native Englishman. Just think of County Kilburn, British West Hampstead or Belsize Pakistan.

It is invaluable for the foreigner to know where these areas are—and of course their real names. It can also be a pleasure, perhaps a revelation, for the natives to discover them as well.

The six, in order, are Indian, Australian, West Indian, Irish, Polish and Jewish London. There's also English London, perhaps the most foreign of all.

Indian London

Goodness gracious, what a delicious Indian restaurant. After that, what else is there to Indian London?

For a start, there are many sorts of Indian Londons, and many reasons for coming here. They also do many different things when they get here.

But there is only one real way of preparing Indian rice. Yes, that secret is out. And a few others too.

In the heyday of the British Raj, nearly everyone in London had a friend or relative in India. Now, with one of those ironic swings of history, it is the other way round—nearly everyone in India seems to have a friend or relative in London.

Indian restaurants, Indian food, Indian shops, Indian cinemas, Indian concerts, Indian plays, yoga, garus and contemplation are now all so much a part of the London scene that when a grey Bentley drew into a Swiss Cottage petrol station recently and a 6 ft. 6 in. Sikh stepped out wearing a purple turban, green raw silk coat, white jodphurs, gold slippers and an ornamental dagger with a gem-studded hilt, the Irish attendant did not bother to take more than a passing glance.

There have, of course, always been some Indians in London—students, I.C.S. officers, servicemen on courses, the visiting polo-playing Maharajahs—but it was only after Partition that the few became a community.

First ashore were the Anglo-Indians (used here in the sense that it is now used in India, that is, people of mixed English-Indian parentage, not in the sense of Britons born in India), refugees from a country in which they believed that, with the departure of the British, the breadth of their opportunity would rapidly shrink.

Then came a wave of merchant seamen from that part of Bengal that is now East Pakistan. These men, mostly cooks and stewards, took their discharges here and in groups of as many as eight or ten, pooled their savings to open the first of the suburban Indian restaurants soon to blossom like the Indian birth-rate.

Finally, with the Welfare State, the rush of the early 1960's brought the bulk of the Indian immigrants—small merchants from the Sind, farmers from the Punjab, clerks from Bombay ... Muslims, Sikhs, Hindus, Pharsees, Jews and Christians ... representatives of the dozens of communities of the sub-continent of India.

Muslims are the most numerous and Sikhs the second. The Muslims because they were the most poverty-stricken and the Sikhs because they are the most adventurous of Indians and have a tradition of migration in search of better opportunities. They have prospered in London as a glance at the London telephone directory will show—there are 185 Singhs, *the* Sikh name.

You can distinguish an orthodox Sikh by his beard and his hair, both of which he should never cut, and a steel bracelet on his right wrist. He should also neither drink nor smoke. These days, of course, many Sikhs have a taste for whisky and filter-tipped, shave and visit the barber. But the bracelet usually remains.

There are no physical characteristics distinguishing the Muslims and the Hindus. But the Muslims are generally in the restaurant business and their names are a good indication, being of Arabic derivation ... thus Muhammad, Ali, Hussein, Latif, Abdul, Khaliq etc. The Hindus, the largest community in India, are not heavily represented in London, probably because they are not migrants by nature (strict Hindus break one tenet of their belief by travelling abroad). They dislike the London climate, the food, the strange ways of the British and they long all the time for their motherland. Doctors and students stay for some years, but they are not typical. The true Hindu is never really happy outside India.

The Pharsees on the other hand, take to London and the West like a second home. They are a wealthy community in India, fair of skin, well-educated, and with a strong commercial bent. Air India, for example, would have difficulty in running without them. In London they usually find well-paid positions and slip so easily into the local way of life that their neighbours find it difficult to believe that they are Indian.

To the surprise of many Westerners who regard India as a heathen country, Christians make up a large section of London's Indian community. They are perhaps the easiest to identify because they have Western Christian names (Dolly, Cynthia, Sylvia and Sheila are popular for girls, Oscar, Joseph, William and Aubrey for boys) followed by a Portuguese or Spanish surname. The surnames are limited—Mendoza, Fernandes, Menezes, Verdes, da Souza, da Silva, Sanchez, Dias and Lobo cover about the lot.

The story is that the Spanish and Portuguese priests who went to India as missionaries began by giving the first converts different names. But then the rush started, their inventiveness ran out and they were forced to christen whole batches of converts after themselves. The original Father da Souza now has something like a million Indians carrying his surname.

London's Indian Christians have done remarkably well in the arts—Dom Moraes, poet, novelist, and journalist; Abbu Abraham, 'Abu' of *The Observer*, a leading political cartoonist; Francis Souza, an artist of international fame, and Elliott Fernandes, a young painter experimenting with haunting religious themes.

Unlike in India, London's Indians have not grouped together on a communal basis and are sprinkled throughout many suburbs—with Swiss Cottage, Bayswater and Kilburn the more popular. But wherever they settle they all complain that they find it hard to make friends with the British. One of the reasons for this is certainly the different attitudes of the two nationalities to family relationships. The Indians rate family very highly and, although strained under Western influence, the joint family system (the sons bring home their wives to live under the paternal roof) can still be found in London.

The sons hand their wage packets to the mother or father who divide them as they see fit. With the respect that age commands in the Indian culture, revolt against parental rule of this sort is extremely rare.

There is a 45-year-old advertising executive in London who runs an account with a West End restaurant. He has the monthly bill sent to his office to keep it secret from his father because his father would forbid him to spend money in this manner. The son would never dream of questioning his father's right to make a ruling of this sort, or the father's right to live out his days at his son's expense. The idea that a son would consider allowing his aged parents to enter an old peoples' home, however comfortable, is regarded by an Indian as thoroughly barbaric.

Prospective Western wives look upon a domestic situation of this sort with alarm, so an Indian youth's romantic life in London could be a rather sad one. Fortunately, this is not so. For reasons a sociologist would find intriguing, German girls seem to be irresistibly attracted to Indian boys. Call at the North Star public house in Swiss Cottage any Saturday night and you'll see most of North London's au pair community with their Indian boyfriends enjoying some typically British pub life.

The reasons for this attraction seem based on the fact that German girls are less colour-conscious than their English cousins, and that they find the gentle romanticism of the Indian, his shy manner and air of the mysterious East a welcome change from the pragmatic German youth. Not that many of these relationships end in marriage. An Indian boy still marries a girl his parents find or approve, and, sad though this is, this seldom includes a German au pair.

Indian girls find romance in London more difficult. Firstly, because the prettiest of them seem to remain in India, and secondly because of their inordinate shyness. Also, it takes a certain amount of courage for a conservative London youth to escort a girl in a sari, no matter how attractive it may be. Those Englishmen who do go out with Indian girls seem always to come from the upper strata of society. Why? That's just the way it seems to happen. Perhaps they are less self-conscious.

But it is not because of their family or romantic relationships that Indians are the best-known foreigners in London. It is because of their food. In a country where half the population goes to bed hungry every night, eating is one of the greatest pleasures and in India the cultivation of cooking as an art is as finely developed as in China or France.

One of the world's greatest delights is said to be a meal cooked by an Indian chef from Pondicherry . . . a blend of the subtlety of the French cuisine and the aggressive flavour of India.

In London it is not difficult to develop a taste for Indian food. The trouble is to get the authentic stuff. Most Indian restaurants in London aren't strictly Indian at all but Pakistani, and from one small part of Pakistan at that. The cuisine tends to be what the cook imagines would best suit the English palate and although a lot more tasty than say, Brown Windsor Soup, is not the fare that would be served in a middle-class Indian household, or better still, at the wedding feast of a daughter of a wealthy Punjabi merchant.

Another reason why Indian restaurant food in London is second-class is the time it takes to prepare a genuine Indian meal. Indians either have servants or lots of time. Four hours to prepare the main meal of the day is not unusual. The masalas (spices) are bought fresh, hand-ground on a grinding stone, and blended according to each cook's own recipe. At the best in Indian restaurants in London, the spices are in paste form, or at the worst, in the powder form as used in that abomination of pseudo-Indian dishes, the English curry.

If you are prepared to tackle the grinding of the masalas yourself, then you can buy them at some shops so genuine that the assistants will look with surprise at the sight of a pink face. Three of the best are Jamshids, 6 Glendower Place, London S.W.7; Pataks, 91 Westbourne Grove, London W.2; and Asiatic Stores, 71 West-bourne Grove, London, W.2. Asiatic also has a butcher's shop run on Indian lines. Because curries do not demand top grade Scotch fillet, Indian housewives are used to ordering merely half a pound of mutton or beef 'for curry' and find the choice of cuts in the British butcher's shop confusing.

If all this sounds too complicated and you would like to try an authentic Indian dish, there is a short cut even Indian housewives practise. Buy a bottle of Mrs. Fernes curry paste or vindaloo paste and follow the recipe on the label. From her little factory in Poona Mrs. Fernes sends her paste all over the world, giving many an Indian exile the true flavour of home.

So many passable curries fail miserably because of soggy rice, so at the risk of displeasing every Indian cook in London, here is their simple secret. You fry the rice *before* you boil it. Measure your rice carefully, so many cupfuls (one cup makes a feast for two persons). Fry it in a pan, the bottom of which is covered with oil, until the grains begin to pop and the rice turns white. Add $1\frac{1}{2}$ cups of water for each cup of rice. Cook a couple of minutes on a high flame and then on a slow flame until all the water is absorbed. If you have used a good rice—Basmati or Patna—every grain will be separate and firm.

If you prefer to eat out, look for places where Indians themselves eat. The two obvious ones are the India House basement canteen, off Aldwych, W.C.1, and the Pakistani Students' Hostel, 15 Chesham Place, S.W.1. The latter is self-service only but the cuisine is Punjabi and, to many curry addicts, the best in Britain. Outsiders are welcome at both places as long as they don't come with too large a party (four is fine, two ideal) and crowd out the students. Do not expect viceroy service because the prices are in the 3s. 6d.

to 6s. range, but you will eat like a Maharajah. Other good ones are the India Club, 143 The Strand, W.C.2 (wonderful South Indian dishes here), Sri Lanka, 19 Childs Street, S.W.5, and Jamshids, 6 Glendower Place, S.W.7 (Pharsee specialities).

For night out standards there is Veeraswamys, 99 Regent Street, W.1, a restaurant of glamour and long and impeccable standing, and a new Indian restaurant, the Kwality, 145 Whitfield Street, W.1, a London branch of a chain of restaurants which runs across India. Their specialty is tandoori chicken and if you think you have tried every possible way of cooking chicken, then a great surprise awaits you.

A final word of warning. In the Rabelaisian manner of which they are so fond, Indians say that to be really good a curry has to burn twice—tonight and tomorrow! So take it easy.

Australian London

In proportion to their numbers, they are the wildest colonial boys of the lot. Heaven help anyone who gets in the way of the ice-cold Fosters or the rush to the snakes.

Canadians will agree with you if you run down their theatre, their art or their newspapers. One word against anything Australian, and there's a punch-up.

They have a good reason to be proud. Some of their artists and singers, especially the London-bound ones, are world-famous. It's not these professionals who do the punching, but the amateurs, passing through on their Grand Tour. This is an introduction to the two Australian Londons.

Most generalizations have only a grain of truth in them. But the two most general generalizations about Australians are as near the truth as a generalization can ever be.

They are a clannish lot with no time for foreigners, including the English. And they are easily given to violence. If an Australian says, 'I've got a good mind to punch you in the nose,' then watch out, he means it.

With this in mind, if you meet an Australian in London—and it is hard not to when there are 50,000 of them—then it is a good idea to make it very clear early in the evening whose side you are on. Ever since the first real wave of Australians hit the beaches at Southampton some fifteen years ago, there has been an undeclared war going on against the British.

From their field headquarters in Kangaroo Valley (formerly Earls Court) the Australians have ranged out across London like twentieth-century huns-from-down-under after the Englishman's women, jobs and glory. There is hardly a section of modern life that has not winced at the grate of an Australian's accent or flinched at the grasp of his hairy hand. And it is not over yet, man. The cult of Barry McKenzie, *Private Eye's* Australian strip cartoon hero, is obviously making it easier to break down even more barriers.

Now to any Englishman who has ever been to Australia, the sight of these freckled hordes here is bewildering. Why these lucky colonials should ever want to leave their beaches, bounty and long-haired mates to take up residence in this sun-starved land of limited opportunity, is incomprehensible, especially when one million Britons have taken a £10 ticket the other way.

Basically, there are two types of Australians in London—the professionals and the amateurs. When the post-war restrictions on travel were lifted, the professionals were first on the water, the spearhead of the invaders. Names like Peter Finch, Shirley Abicair, Dick Bentley, Bill Kerr, Keith Michell, Leo McKern, Joan Sutherland, Joan Hammond, June Bronhill, Sidney Nolan and Arthur Boyd. Then there are the jockeys, racing car drivers, wrestlers and pop singers. The list is long and impressive . . . Jack Brabham, Frank Ifield, Scobie Breasley, Ron Hutchinson, Eddie Cracknell, the Seekers, Rolf Harris. They even got into Buckingham Palace for a while (Michael Parker) and had a Lord Mayor of London (Sir Leslie Boyce). The last boatload brought the commercial radio people and a boarding party has practically taken over Radio Caroline.

The professionals came here for one reason only—to get into the big time. They had reached the end of the tramway in Australia, and the streets of London were crowded with Bentleys. In fields noted for their toughness and lack of sentimentality, these professional Australians have fought their way into the big money. They are distinguished from the amateurs in that they are now so smoothly integrated into London life that hardly anyone remembers that they *are* Australians. (Who would ever say the Australian, Robert Helpmann?)

If, rarely, they pronounce *Daily Mail* in that peculiarly Australian way, no one would dream of raising an eyebrow. In other words, they have gone over to the enemy and risk lynching if they ever go back to Australia and admit that they have been away.

But the roots, withered though they may be, are still there, and even the oldest professionals can be seen occasionally at a pub off the Strand called the Surrey (more of this later) getting the twinges of nationalism out of their systems, and at the Australian Restaurant and Kangaroo Bar, 37 Gerrard Street, W.1, a nice and unpretentious establishment run by actor Ken Warren.

But normally, they tend to avoid Australians-en-masse like the smallpox. They look down on the amateurs as residents look down on tourists.

The amateurs have come to London as part of the Grand Tour, known in the south lands as 'doing Europe'. The average level of wages in Australia is high enough to enable even manual workers to save enough in their youth to make the journey. They pour off the ships every Spring and stay six to 18 months. They shun hotels and boarding houses and head for furnished flats in Earls Court where they share with anything up to seven other Australians, often of both sexes. (Nothing immoral here; a pure Australian big sister relationship.)

Often, in the large flats, as one Australian arrives, another leaves, until after a while no one can remember in whose name the lease was signed. There is a large maisonette flat off Old Brompton Road where there have been eight girls, but never the same eight for more than six months running, since 1956. One of the original eight, long since married and back in Australia, hopes that the flat will still be there when her daughter leaves for Europe in a few years' time.

It is possible to spend a summer in Earls Court and never meet anyone except Australians resting between European countries. Doing Europe consists of extended trips on the Continent with short periods of work in between to pay for them. The trouble here is that London employers have become fed up with typists who vanish at the first flush of spring and with clerks who have to do Spain in the bullfight season. They are now very chary of employing Australians unless they show some evidence of planning to stay a few years.

Australia, which has produced some of the world's best confidence tricksters, has naturally thrown up a neat counter to this difficulty. The best proof of job stability is a reference which shows that you have already held a job in Britain for a reasonable length of time. So there is a bearded Australian in Palace Gardens Terrace, Notting Hill, who, for a small fee, provides immaculate references for anything you wish to be. He can turn out immediately very passable papers to show that you served with distinction in the

2nd Punjab Regiment as a Captain—'A nice rank for impressing landlords.'

For a further fee he writes job applications, guaranteed to get you, if not the job, then certainly on the short list. 'Two of my boys are now in the B.B.C., several in Fleet Street, and I've just had a nice little success in Local Government.'

So it is no trouble for the visiting Australian, within a short time of his arrival, to get a job and accommodation.

It is only when he begins to look around for ways of spending his leisure hours that he realises how different Britain really is.

The most popular way of spending the weekend in Australia is flat on the belly like a lizard, soaking up sun on the beach. The beaches are free to everyone. On a Sunday afternoon at Bondi it is difficult to tell the financial barons from the butchers. In London it is different. Here money buys you sun, and if you have no money, then you spend your time in the city regretting it.

There are ways over this, of course. Australian dentists who are making a fortune out of the National Health bonanza can either save for a practice back in Australia or spend their loot here. Three who live at Swiss Cottage fly once a month to Agadir in Morocco for a week-end's surfing. Why Agadir? 'It's got the best surf close to London.'

But for those left behind in London, life can be grim. His brief encounters with the English soon convince an Australian that he would rather spend his time with 'the boys off the boat' than go through the labour of trying to make contact with his hosts. The reasons for this lack of communication are complex and emotional.

The English complain that the Australians are blunt, lack finesse, do not understand the British social system, tend to be aggressive and are scornful of tradition—'you oughta rip down all these old buildings and put up some new ones with decent showers in them.' . . . 'Listen, mate, I don't care if yer *have* done it that way since 1837. I still tell yer it'll get yer nowhere. Now back home . . .'

For his part, the Australian complains that all the English are stilted, retiring, devious, class-conscious, poor drinkers, and worst of all, ignorant about Australia—'Is Tasmania part of the Common-wealth?'

Colouring all English-Australian relationships, consciously or not, is the fact that the British started Australia with boatloads of thieves, prostitutes, trade unionists, and Irish rebels—all sent to Botany Bay for the term of their natural—reinforced later by 'get-rich-quick' migrants.

I

It is also worth remembering that all migration to Australia has been assisted (voluntary or involuntary) and has come from the lower income bracket in Britain. Very few people have settled down-under for reasons other than economic necessity.

This gives present generation Australians a conditioned reflex to Britain. The descendants of the Irish have been told the British drove their forefathers out of Ireland. The descendants of the radicals still believe in dark, satanic mills. And the descendants of the 'get-rich-quick' believe that economic necessity forced their fathers to leave the motherland.

So after a few abortive attempts to get on with the locals, the Australian goes back to his own countrymen, fellow exiles all, and passes the time in the traditional Australian fashion—seeing how many ice cold beers he can sink and still remain standing.

As English beer is neither cold enough nor strong enough for the Australian palate, the few pubs and clubs in London which have been astute enough to stock Australian beer or to ice the English variety are now assured of a steady, if noisy, custom. There is the Ifield, Ifield Road, Earls Court; the Zambesi Club, Barkston Gardens, Earls Court, and best-known of all, the Surrey, Surrey Street, London W.C.2, walking distance from Australian House.

Here, on a Friday night, elbow to elbow, surrounded by boomerangs and familiar accents, London's Australians sip their Fosters (Melbourne) and Swan (Perth), both nearly 11 degrees alcoholic content, and complain about jobs ('lousy bloody seven quid a week'), food ('I haven't had a decent steak since I got here') and the weather ('How can you ever get a tan in this place').

The pace of drinking is, by British standards, express-like, but even so it is unlikely you will see that well-known Australian sight, rare in Britain, the-face-on-the-bar-room-floor. (You can, by the way, pick out the old Australian hand from the newly-arrived. The seasoned man drinks iced *English* beer instead of iced Australian.)

There are often unattached Australian girls in the Surrey and you will find that they appear very feminine and friendly. But a word of warning. The battle of the sexes is waged nowhere more vigorously than in Australia. Anything an Australian male can do, an Australian girl can do as well, if not better. It is highly significant that the first Australian to swim the Channel was a girl.

But if you like what you see at the Surrey, then you should try to get to an Australian party. The best way is to be invited, but if this does not happen, then head for Earls Court on a Saturday night, buy two quarts of light ale, and prowl the streets listening for the unmistakable sounds of Australian voices raised in 'Waltzing Matilda'. (The curious thing about this song is not the strange words but that Australians who never sing it at home are willing, when abroad, to fight anyone who suggests that it is not the greatest folk song ever.)

When you find the party, hand your two bottles to whoever answers the door, say 'How's it going, sport?' and push boldly inside. In most cases the man who took your bottles will be so busy opening them that he will not even notice who came in. If, however, he says, 'Who told you it was on?', just answer 'Harry' and everything should be all right. This might sound improbable, but it works. The story behind this demonstrates one of the better qualities of Australians—their strong sense of loyalty.

It had always been traditional at Australian parties in London to admit *any* Australian who seeks entry as long as he has a bottle for a password. Some years ago an Australian student called Harry, who had fallen on hard times and had been living on sardines for a week, arrived at a party thrown by a better-off compatriot clutching half a bottle of Spanish cooking wine. The better-off Australian greeted him with a surly, 'Oh! Who told you it was on?' His feelings hurt, Harry handed over his bottle and left. When his friends at the party heard what had happened, they not only walked out *en masse*, but arranged it so that for the next six months, whenever the better-off Australian arrived at any party anywhere in London, he was greeted at the door by an unsmiling face saying, 'Oh! Who told you it was on?'

There is not an Australian in London who has not heard this story and to say that Harry sent you has become a password (plus your bottle of course) to any worthwhile party.

Once in you'll have to be able to sing 'Waltzing Matilda' (all the verses), or at the more sophisticated gatherings, 'The Wild Colonial Boy' or any Irish rebel song.

All the girls will be in a group by themselves and will appear unescorted, but keep away from them or someone will invite you outside and punch your nose. Under no circumstances pick up anyone else's glass of beer, even by mistake. Taking another man's beer, is, by Australian *mores*, far worse than taking his girl.

Eating? Well, Australians do eat, but not as a pleasure. They have no national dish (unless you could call steak and eggs a national dish) and consider the preoccupation with food of, say, the French, as decadent. There is only one restaurant in London (The Australian) serving what are called typical Australian dishes—Carpet Bag Steak;

which is rump steak stuffed with oysters; Tom Ugly's Rice; and fruit-salad with passionfruit.

No. It is at drinking, not cooking, that Australians excel. And lest you think that tales of their prowess with beer are exaggerated, ponder on this. A schoolteacher at a mining town on the south coast of New South Wales tendered his resignation saying that the amount of social drinking he was required to do was too much for him. His department enquired what he considered 'too much'.

'Well,' the schoolmaster said, 'The Parents' and Citizens' Association held a gymkhana last Sunday afternoon. There were 70 people there, some of them non-drinkers. Between three o'clock and six o'clock those who did drink polished off *one hundred dozen* cans of beer.'

Never, never cross glasses with an Australian.

Irish London

Drinking and singing and labouring. They're not socially conscious enough to stand up and be counted, for facts to be figured and trends to be traced.

Or sober enough to write neat lists about themselves or their fantasies.

Irish are just Irish. Here are some assorted thoughts and information.

Some Assorted Irish Information

IRISH, HOW TO LIVE CLOSE TO THEM
Rent a room in any of the following localities: Islington, Holloway, Archway, Kentish Town, Camden Town, Paddington, Willesden, North Kensington, Hammersmith, Pimlico or King's Cross. The Irish percentage of the populations of the above areas varies between 10% and $12\frac{1}{2}$%.

Bed and breakfast rates in Camden Town between 15s. and £1 per night. A little higher south of the river. Full board about £6 per week.

IRISH CHURCHES
Good class R.C. Chapel at the French Church, Leicester Square. Democratic one at Order of Passionists, Archway. Many chapels all areas.

IRISH CLUB

Eaton Square. Rates: entrance fee one guinea, six guineas membership. Dinner 12s. upwards. Lunch 7s. 6d. upwards. Bed and breakfast: single room without bath 45s., with bath 52s. 6d.

IRISH NATIONAL ANTHEM, FIRST STANZA
I'll sing you a song a soldier's song with cheering rousing chorus,
As round the blazing fire we throng the starry heavens o'er us,
Impatient for the coming fight and as we await the morning light
Here in the silence of the night we will chant a soldier's song.
(Four stanzas usually. Stand for all of them, at least after the first.)

IRISH BORN PERSONS, OR OF IRISH EXTRACTION, LIKELY
TO BE SEEN ON TV

The Right Honourable George Brown; Right Hon. James
Callaghan; Sir William Carron; Dusty Springfield; Sir Tom
O'Brien; The Beatles; Hugh Delargy, M.P.; The Bachelors; Danny
Blanchflower; Jackie Carey; Gay Byrne; Eamonn Andrews;
Wilfred Brambell (Albert Steptoe); Ronnie Carroll; The Duke of
Leinster; Patrick (Lord Glenavy) Campbell.

IRISHMEN EXPECT TO BE PAID IMMEDIATELY ON STARTING
WORK

On building sites a sub of one day's wages on first day. One week
on Thursday. Writing for TV or radio, half the agreed fee
immediately.

IRISH MEN WORK

on most of London's building sites, British Railways and London
Transport, in most public houses and quite a lot of Lyons Corner
Houses.

Basic rate on building jobs about eleven pounds for a 44-hour
week. Some firms operate incentive and standing bonus schemes so
that wages may in certain cases be as high as fifteen pounds per
week. Twenty pounds very rare. British Railways and London
Transport from nine pounds to about twelve usually.

IRISH SINGING IN LONDON

The Wild Geese Club; Hand and Flower Pub, Hammersmith;
The Duke of Bedford, Balham; The Bedford, Camden Town;
The Mother Redcap, Camden Town; Les Cousines, Greek Street;
The Duke of Devonshire; most pubs in Irish areas.

Some Assorted Irish Thoughts

'An Irishman's home is his coffin,' said James Joyce hopefully.

In the long run, the symmetry of cemetery in the minds of respectors of death is a kind of simony.

On the tube to Camden Town, there was a dead drunk Irishman and an R.C. priest. The Irishman—awakened by the priest's round Irish accent—exclaimed as he grabbed for the hand of the clergyman, 'Ah Jazes! An Irish priest! Let me shake yer lovely hand cos' the only other priests I've met here in London are all bloody Protestants.'

Irish people are religious if well watched. The religion, however, is only skin deep and the moment Rome lets go at all, Paddy is emancipated.

In argument with Mr. Bloom who has described Jesus as a Jew, *The Citizen* cries, 'By Jesus, I'll brain that bloody Jewman for using the Holy Name! By Jesus I'll crucify him, so I will.' Nothing strange intended, nothing paradoxical meant.

Because of his nature, the Catholic Centre was set up in Camden Town to give Paddy a bed for a few bob a week in a place where he could have a drink and meet a few friends other than the organisers of the Connolly Association or the Labour Party.

It used to be said of the Irish worker that he was a nomad. This was a playful derisive term—all remarks dependent for laughter on a man's economic position are derogatory by natural implication. The substance of the statement is true but not of Irish workers alone.

The head of the Coal Board has decided to turn a whole area of mineworkers into tinkers by promising them work somewhere else with travelling time. People working for wages go where the work is, hence transportation, colonisation, emigration. Some of the travelling people settle in houses and are afterwards described as of Norman stock, old family, very respectable.

In the Bedford or The Mother Redcap pubs in Camden Town on a Saturday night for a year you will find a club atmosphere. Everybody knows everybody until the work moves farther out and the membership of the clubs changes.

Language habits and culture peculiar to a people constitute nationality. So the native Englishman is a bit surprised to find that he has suddenly received a thump across the ear during the singing of a fiery song because he didn't notice a bar full of people standing to swaying attention for the Irish National Anthem.

Moving from Camden Town in the north to Brixton south of the Thames you can hear a coal black mass singing 'Mother Machree' or 'Kevin Barry'. Pause awhile and hear them speak like Cork or Kerry men and marvel that because they work with Paddy and learn their English from Paddy they go on for ever more to speak like Paddy.

The coloured migrant won't sing his own National Anthem because it's the same as the English one and he has too often been nearly killed by the same Englishmen in the rush for the cinema exit after the screen credits. Go anywhere in London, the Irishman carries his club on his back as the tortoise his shell.

The Irishman is anti. In economic warfare he is a trades unionist with a tradition of trades unionism. Alun Owen recounts being accosted by a man straight off the Irish Mail at Euston who asked in limited English, 'Could yeh tell me the way to the house of Mr. McAlpine, please?'

The 'Mr.' bit would soon disappear and it wouldn't be long before the same Irishman would sing lustily on a Saturday evening:

> I've worked till sweat has had me beat
> With Russian, Czech and Pole,
> On shuttering jambs on the Hydro dams
> Or down below the Thames in a hole.
> I've grafted hard and got me cards
> And many a ganger's fist across me ears.
> If yeh pride yer life don't join by Christ
> With McAlpine's fusiliers.

Irishmen played a great part in building the Festival of Britain, the Shell-Mex site, the Barbican and of course the M1.

Their civility has the barb of the simpleton Disraeli when they reply to the usual taunt, 'If yeh dahn't like it why the bleedin' 'ell are yer over 'ere?' 'Revenge, me love. Revenge for seven hundred years of English occupation.'

Not all Irishmen work for the building fraternity. Go any evening to 'The Queen's Elm' pub on the Fulham Road and you will find the genial host Sean Treacy surrounded by poets, painters, playwrights, actors and book writers.

Down in Upper St. Martin's Lane another Irishman, Joe Hannigan, may be surrounded by Irish art people with a cheque in one hand and a story in the other. 'I went over to see some friends in Dublin,' says Peter O'Toole, 'and took with me a friend who happened to be black. A decent Irish woman asks of me mate, "Are you an African?" "No," says me man, "I'm an American citizen."

Well, away she goes and has time to realise that she's been gravely indiscreet to say the least. Comes back an *hour* later and says to this coal black man, "Mister, what in the name-a God made me think you was an African?" '

Over in the Irish Club in Eaton Square one usually asks, 'Excuse me, but I came to see Mr. Cyril Cusack.' If he is there, down comes the never-too-tired-to-see-old-friends Cyril, signs his friends in for a drink. A lovely place to be if you like a sort of Churchill's Irish Club and can maybe put up with the endless tales of Mr. Richard Harris burying his endless Marlon Brandos.

In the M.L. Club of Little Portland Street one may enjoy a pleasant drink in the company of the owner, two or three generation removed Owen Geary, who has been host to men as different as W. R. Rodgers and Louis McNeice to Alan Sillitoe and Richard Burton. And in the corner someone is trying to con a B.B.C. producer who waits for furtive escape.

No, they're not all builders.

Bagenal Harvey born in Athlone represents the business interests of Denis Compton, John Surtees, Ted Dexter, Freddie Trueman, Billy Walker, Danny Blanchflower, Jimmy Greaves and Johnny Haynes.

Frank Pakenham is Leader of the House of Lords. Sir Patrick Hennessy is head of Fords while the ones a few generations removed are not starving if yeh can believe what people like Lennon, McCartney, Ringo, and Harrison say, not to forget Steptoe Senior (first gen.) or our second chief naturalised Spike Milligan—the other being John Huston.

Dominic Behan is doing fine with his radio and TV work. When his mother heard he had some work on the B.B.C. Third she said: 'Keep off the drink son, and maybe they'll put you on the first.'

Jewish London

Judaism might have waned a lot, but Jewishness is as strong as ever.

This is an essay-guide on both. On where and how the Jews worship in London—their religion, their beliefs and their synagogues. On how Jewish is Jewish London—the snobberies, the pleasures and the trends.

The London Jew is endlessly fascinated by himself. The non-Londoner, and the non-Jew, will find him equally absorbing.

London has about half of Britain's 500,000 Jews. When the non-Jew thinks about Jews he thinks inevitably of the street traders of Petticoat Lane, or the black garbed, long bearded *Chassidim* of Stamford Hill.

Neither group is typical, numerous, or even significant. But both are colourful, distinctive, warm and, in their different ways intensely Jewish.

The *Chassidim* stand at one end of the spectrum. Today is an irrelevance to them. Their faith is fixed for all time, and any scientific discoveries which may conflict with their creed are treated as passing aberrations. All this can involve them in a great deal of personal and social inconvenience, but anything they may experience on earth is, they believe, a small price to pay against the millenium. Their belief in the Kingdom of Heaven is absolute. It may not be nigh, but they have already waited 3,000 years, so what's the hurry?

They are discernible by their beards, their long side curls, their peculiar garb, any day of the week, but on the Sabbath they acquire a certain swagger in their bearing, as if Jehova Himself has come among them for the day.

If the *Chassid* is dedicated to the next world, the street trader is entirely, almost religiously, of this one. In Petticoat Lane he is somewhat self-consciously folksy, shouting, gesticulating, winking, pulling faces, brandishing chamber-pots and underwear. The patter is continuous and almost unintelligible. The sales pressure is terrific and many who come to look remain to buy. This can make it an expensive experience. Otherwise an outing to the 'Lane' is as good a public entertainment as Speakers Corner. It is open only on Sunday mornings.

Anglo-Jewry divides along religious lines, but it converges along the gastronomic. They may pray apart, but they eat together, and Blooms is one of the meeting points. It is kosher, heimisch, and good, and here the devout may meet with the undevout through a common passion for chopped liver, kreplach and salt beef.

There is a branch of Blooms also in Golders Green, heartland of the great Jewish North-West. It is a place to see and be seen, to hail friends and greet clients. It is packed, noisy and bustling, very different from the Savoy Grill or the Caprice, but a natural resort for the Jew who is solvent, likes the company of his fellows and whose duodenum is yet intact.

Both branches of Blooms are decorated in the same way. A mirror runs along the length of one wall, and facing it, a montage of Petticoat Lane. There is something symbolic in the juxtaposition, the humble, not so distant past, and reflected in the mirror, the glowing, fleshy reality of the present.

One may find among the London families an occasional Mocatta, Mesquita or Mendoza, who settled here about the time of Cromwell, but the vast majority poured in from Eastern Europe in the past 80 years. They came in great waves and settled in and around the East End. From there they filtered along the North-West Passage to Stamford Hill and Golders Green, and indeed, all over London.

The East End still houses the principal Jewish youth clubs—the Brady, the Bernard Baron, the Stepney Jewish—but a good proportion of their members travel in from the surrounding districts. The synagogues are still there, empty or near-empty, marking the recession of the tide—the Agudas Achim in Old Castle Street, the Congregation of Jacob in Commercial Road, the Poltava Synagogue in Heneage Street, and a score of others, their façades cracking, their prayer-books puckered with mildew.

One or two synagogues, such as the Machzike Hadath in Spitalfields, may suddenly come to life at the most improbable time of day, but then only out of reverence for the dead.

Few Jews now live in the East End, but a great many come in for business—gowns, caps, trousers, handbags, buttons, shoulder-pads, chemists' sundries, furniture—and the Machzike Hadath is a handy place for a quick *kadish*.

The Jewish reader will be familiar with the term *kadish* even if he knows nothing else about Jewish life. The goy may require an explanation.

The *kadish* is a propitiatory prayer for the dead said daily by the next of kin (usually the sons) for the first eleven months after the bereavement and on every anniversary thereafter. It is one of the few religious obligations which most Jews treat religiously. Any power which a Jewish parent has over his child is always strengthened by his demise, and many a young man will attend synagogue daily out of respect to his father's memory, though he did not even attend yearly while his father was alive. A father really anxious to correct an erring child need only expire to have his way.

Death, indeed, may be the most important element in Anglo-Jewish life. The English Jew who goes to a synagogue because of a dead parent, will belong to a synagogue because of his prospective dead self. There are no Jewish undertakers. One joins a Jewish burial society through joining a synagogue. Thus a synagogue may have hundreds or even a thousand paid-up members, but only a handful of active worshippers. The rest are not so much sleeping partners, as subscribers to an eternal sleep. Some join a synagogue because it is a subscription to the Jewish race. Some because they believe in all it stands for.

There is evidence that this last group has been growing, but not as rapidly as the boom in synagogue building might indicate. Over a dozen synagogues have been built or redeveloped in the London area since the war. The grandest stands behind a handsome Nash façade in Great Cumberland Place, near Marble Arch. It is richly panelled, thickly carpeted and ornate. It is very handy for travellers if for few others, and might fairly be described as the chapel of the Cumberland Hotel. The Rev. Maurice Unterman, a dapper, well-kempt gentleman, greets visitors with the courtesy of a *maître d'hôtel*, and all in all, the Marble Arch Synagogue is Anglo-Jewry's premier contribution to Britain's tourist trade.

About a mile away, at the back of Oxford Circus, and within a stone's throw of London's garment district, is the Great Portland Street Synagogue, where one can hear the Rev. Simon Hass, the finest cantor in Britain, and rub shoulders with Sir Isaac Wolfson, a former warden of the synagogue, or his son, Mr. Leonard Wolfson, the present warden. The exterior of the building is dignified but the interior has the peach-melba glory of a milk-bar—possibly a reaction to the grey days of post-war London in which it was built.

The most satisfactory post-war synagogue is at the back of Chalk Farm station in Eton Villas. The design is simple, almost austere. There is much aluminium and yellow brick and the initial effect is cold, but one warms to it rapidly. The minister, the Rev. Freddie Broza, is an amiable and dedicated young man. Here is perhaps the most attractive house of worship in London. Unhappily, it is virtually without a congregation.

This is by no means a unique phenomenon. The most charming

synagogue in the country, and the oldest still in use, is the Spanish and Portuguese Synagogue in Bevis Marks, in the no-man's-land between Aldgate and the City. Founded in 1701, its blackened walls witness a constant stream of pilgrims, who come to gaze and admire, but rarely remain to pray.

The ancient families may turn out in goodly number for a state occasion, but the state occasions are becoming fewer and so, indeed, are the ancient families, and today Bevis Marks functions substantially as a museum.

It is difficult to advise a Jew as to which synagogue offers the best pray. One's choice is usually determined by one's religious affiliations. The liberal Jew will go to a liberal synagogue, the orthodox Jew to an orthodox one. Yet if one wants to experience religious warmth and fervour and has fond thoughts of old times, then the best place is undoubtedly the Adath Yisroel, 40 Queen Elizabeth Walk, N.16. But for God's sake (and the expression is used advisedly) don't travel there on the Sabbath. A phone call to the secretary (STA 7087) that you are a stranger in town and wish to be a Yid among Yidden, will yield a deluge of invitations.

If you are trapped in London over Passover any synagogue affiliated to the Union of Orthodox Hebrew Congregations (phone number as above) will find you hospitality not only for the Seder —which is something any Rabbi of any congregation will organise for you—but for the entire festival.

The Union, as its name implies, is the most orthodox wing of Anglo-Jewry. Its thinking—or rather its non-thinking—may be mediaeval, but among the host of Jewish traditions it has kept alive is the important one of hospitality. There is little evidence of it among other synagogue groups in London. Hospitality is among the first casualties of Jewish assimilation.

If you should visit the North-West London Reform Synagogue, 22 Alyth Gardens, N.W.11 (SPE 1676) you may be approached with an offer of hospitality by a member of the ladies' guild or an officer of the synagogue appointed for the purpose. It arises out of a sense of duty rather than as a spontaneous wish to welcome the stranger. Other synagogues do not even display the sense of duty.

Taking the quality of sermon, cantorial rendering, choir and general decorum together, the Hampstead Synagogue in Dennington Park Road offers the most attractive service in London. It can be recommended for nothing else. It is a very English synagogue and nowhere is its Englishness more apparent than in its coldness, aloofness and lack of hospitality. Its congregants do not approach the stranger and they are not easily approached by him either.

Synagogues, like shops, are at their most unwelcoming during their high season—which is to say, Rosh Hashana and Yom Kippur. The exception again is the Union of Orthodox Hebrew Congregations whose synagogues are as full on a normal Sabbath as they are on Yom Kippur, and which therefore have no high season. Approach any of them and you will be well looked after. If you are a bachelor, orthodox and solvent, you may be a little too well looked after.

The United Synagogue, which comprises the main body of London Jewry, has 'overflow services', where one can find a seat with little difficulty, but the serious worshipper is earnestly advised to shun them. These services are generally attended by the most casual of Jews, who are usually ignorant, can't easily find their way about the prayer book, cannot follow the service and spend much of their time in chatting.

In the liberal and reform synagogues, where much of the service is in English, and the prayers are more comprehensible, the decorum is better, but they are often all-ticket affairs, and if you come unprovided a commissionaire at the door may keep you out. If you find that the whole atmosphere is a little akin to that of a gala première at a cinema it is because so many of the overflow services are held in cinemas.

The Jewish student who is new to London should call at Hillel House (1 Endsleigh Street, W.C.1, EUS 7845). It holds services on Friday night and Sedarim in Passover. Its director, Henry Shaw, is not only a diverting individual to know, but is a mine of information on the who, what, where and when of Anglo-Jewry.

There is an inner-cohesiveness in Jewish life which has little to do with religious feeling or belief. Jews like being together, and as prayer is no longer an adequate excuse for being so, a whole host of quasi-religious activities have been developed. These largely take the form of fund-raising. If the typical East European Jew was a *chevrah-man*, an active participant in synagogue life, the typical London Jew is a committee-man. Some collect committees as schoolboys collect postage stamps. The causes are legion and are by no means exclusively Jewish. It used to be said that it's hard to be a Jew. This is no longer true, but it is certainly expensive to be one, for one is surrounded by charity extractors.

If it was only a matter of parting with three guineas here and five guineas there, it would be a comparatively painless matter but one must not only give, but be seen to be giving. Every charity has its annual dinner and it is these dinners which make charity the penance which it is perhaps meant to be. During the high season, from October to March, there are some individuals who are more in their tuxedos than out, and who rarely get home for an evening meal. The charities do not do badly, but the main beneficiary is, perhaps, the West End catering trade.

There is a penchant among Jews—and it is not uncommon among others—to see and be seen, to live and be seen to be living which is of great help to the fund-raiser. The convivial disposition is there, the charities provide the excuse, and the excuse is important. Conviviality in its own right is frowned upon, for although Jewish puritanism is abating, one can find some residual element of it even among the hedonists.

This qualified hedonism arises out of a deep feeling of insecurity. Auschwitz is too recent for any Jew to feel completely at ease in a gentile world. He is too unsure of the future to forego any important part of the present. This is true also of the whole of western society, but if western society is insecure, the Jew is doubly so.

All this may explain a new phenomenon, a Jewish glossy called *Society Illustrated* which combines all that is laughable in William Hickey with all that was fatuous in the old point-to-point *Tatler*, and adds to them a vulgarity which is peculiarly its own. It contains the odd article on fashion, motoring, wine, but its *raison d'être* is pictures of weddings, engagements, and similar social occasions, of wealthy nobodies, of people who are devoid even of the minimal distinction of being photogenic.

To see oneself in a glossy magazine, even as execrable as *Society Illustrated* is perhaps, to the small mind at least, evidence that one has arrived. They can see themselves as they would like to be seen. It is a sort of reassurance. As Anglo-Jewry becomes more established and more self-confident, as memories of persecution recede, as it comes to take prosperity for granted, the deficiencies on which a publication like *Society Illustrated* can thrive should become extinct. They may be too few to sustain it even now.

There is, of course, snobbery to reckon with, but the magazine can hardly batten on that, for the essential thing about Jewish snobbery is to be where Jews are not, or at least not in large numbers. 'Ah yes,' the with-it young man will tell you, 'I used to be at——, the only Jewish boy in the school.' Or, 'I'm a member of —— golf-club, the only Jewish member of the club.'

It is a little ironic that just as some Jewish families were beginning to make the pages of the *Tatler* with fair regularity, it should have undergone its recent metamorphosis.

Eating is the premier Jewish activity. One celebrates a birth with drinks, a male birth with abundant drinks, a *Barmitzvah* with a sumptuous meal, a wedding with a banquet, and the outside caterer—though this is against established Jewish custom—is even creeping in upon the Jewish funeral and stone-setting.

The table, to an extent, was the altar of Jewish life, and a meal is meant to open and close with grace, and be accompanied by some airing of homilies or pious thoughts. The grace, the homilies, the pious thoughts have all but vanished; the chopped liver remains, and it isn't always kosher liver.

In short, if Judaism has waned a lot, Jewishness has waned only a little, and therefore the synagogue-building boom, though extensive, has been out-boomed by a spate of halls. Some communities, indeed, build halls before they build synagogues. (One can adapt a hall to a sacred purpose, but not a synagogue for a profane one.) It is all part of the secularisation of Jewish life. The synagogues have abandoned the holy war, or virtually abandoned it, and are fighting largely on the secular front. They are entering into competition with dance-halls, bingo-parlours and coffee-bars. Some synagogue halls, as a result, come to embrace the menace they are meant to combat. They become dance-halls in themselves.

The young man who is prepared to invest 9d. in almost any issue of the weekly *Jewish Chronicle* will find a ready guide to the abundant social life of London Jewry, and if he is so disposed, can dance his way from synagogue to synagogue, with intermittent pauses for bingo.

Here's an example at random from a typical issue:

Sunday March 28th:

'*Arrange to meet your friends at the Over-27s' dance at the West Central Club, 23 Hand Court, High Holborn.*

'*At the East Finchley Beat Room—the fabulous, handsome Druids. Mems. 4s. 6d. Their guests 6s. 6d.*

'*Hey! Hey! Hey! Tonight at the Highbury & Dalston J.Y.C. . . . . A great night dancing to the latest discs . . .*

'*The Willesden Senior Set presents a special evening featuring another well-known beat group for ladies over 17 and gentlemen over 18, at Cricklewood Synagogue Hall.*'

The purpose of these functions is to bring Jews together, and if they come together for a profane purpose, they may stay together for a sacred one.

This hope may not be as forlorn as it seems. London Jewry has had to strive hard to establish itself in life, often at the expense of life's refinements. The generation now growing to maturity is taking security, and even prosperity for granted. A good part of it has been through university, and if it is not arriving upon a new age of faith, is questioning some of the old materialistic values. Some are turning to a reappraisal of their Jewish past.

Such appraisals are not an orthodox Jewish activity, for Judaism is essentially authoritarian, and the devout must accept all the details of the creed and observance, as defined in the sacred codes, without question. And it is not only the black-garbed *Chassidim* who do so. There are congregations in Golders Green and Hendon which number university professors, physicists, mathematicians, doctors, lawyers and chairmen of important companies, successful men of this world, who will accept without question that every word in the Bible is true, that every jot and tittle in it has some sacred purpose, that the earth is flat, and 5,726 years old, and one must not travel on the Sabbath because one may not ride a horse because a horse too must rest.

These congregations stand a little apart from the rest of London Jewry, but this right to inquire was the central issue of the celebrated Jacobs Affair.

Rabbi Jacobs has been asking a number of questions which have bothered thoughtful, though devout, Jews, and he has suggested a number of answers which have bothered the Chief Rabbi, and this has resulted in the breakaway of his synagogue, and the formation of a new one in 33 Abbey Road, St. John's Wood. He is worth hearing for he is patently the best preacher in Anglo-Jewry, even though he may intersperse his every sermon with commercials for the right of free inquiry.

He has been hailed by some elements in the Jewish community as the new Moses who will lead the thoughtful inquiring young into a promised land where Judaism need no longer conflict with reason, and where the impositions of custom do not conflict with the responsibilities of everyday life; however until now Rabbi Jacobs' disciples have been largely merchant bankers, barristers, solicitors and manufacturers. Such men are not the stuff of revolution.

The affair, though it hit the international headlines (partly because little was happening in the world at the time) caused barely more than a ripple on the placid surface of Anglo-Jewish life.

Theology may have been invented by Jews, but they have been content to resign it to the gentiles. Or to use a peculiarly Jewish form of logic: If God is in His heaven, why worry? And if he isn't, what's the use of worrying?

Polish London

Is the most tightly knit, most Foreign of all Foreign Londons.

Take any activity, and the Poles will probably have it better organised than any other emigrés. Publishing, for example. Since 1939, over 12,000 books in Polish have been published, over 40 Polish periodicals regularly appear and there is even a daily newspaper in Polish which sells 22,000 copies—more than many English local newspapers.

No wonder some Poles say Polish London is more Polish than Poland· Of all the Foreign Londons, Polish London is not only one of the biggest, it is probably the most homogeneous in its hierarchy and traditions.

The Polish 'emigracja' in Britain as a whole, and in London in particular, is an astonishing phenomenon of British social history. In a unique fashion some 150,000 Poles have become integrated into British society, yet at the same time have preserved a strong national individuality.

A middle-aged Pole may have lived in England for the past twenty years, acquired British nationality, learnt to speak English fluently, built up a successful business or practice, and sent his children to the best of British boarding schools. But at the end of it all he will still be as Polish as ever he was. He probably belongs to a Polish club, speaks Polish at home and makes sure his children do, too, attends a Polish Catholic church where mass is said by a Polish priest, belongs to a Polish political party, contributes to a Polish national fund, takes in the *Polish Daily* newspaper.

The global statistics of Polish emigration are as startling as the British statistics. In Poland itself there are just over 30 million Poles today. Another 10 million live outside Poland, seven million of them in the United States (concentrated mostly in Chicago and Detroit). About 600,000 Poles live in France, the biggest emigré community outside the United States; but like the Poles in America, those in France are mostly descendants of people who emigrated in the last century or early in this.

Britain today contains the largest Polish emigrant community created by the last war, or for that matter by any other war Britain has ever fought in. Soon after the end of the war, when the Second Polish Corps under the command of General Anders was brought en masse from Italy to England for resettlement, there were for a short time well over 200,000 Poles here. A few thousand decided to go back to Communist-ruled Poland; several thousands more emigrated to the United States, Canada, Argentina, Australia and other far-flung corners of the earth. But a hard core of some 150,000 is still in Britain, the biggest single foreign influx since the Norman invasion of 1066 (at least, it was until the more recent mass incursions from the West Indies).

Of that 150,000, almost 40,000 have settled in London. For some years after the war the area lying roughly between the Albert Hall and King's Road, Chelsea, with Cromwell Road as its east-west axis, was widely known as 'the Polish corridor'. It teemed with Poles. General Anders set up his headquarters in Queen's Gate (since moved to Prince's Gate, and still the focus of political resistance to Communism in Poland). The Polish Combatants' Association, with its world-wide network of branches, set up its headquarters at 20 Queen's Gate Terrace. And a great variety of institutions, clubs, hotels, clinics, libraries, etc., were established in the same area.

Though most of the headquarters and institutions remain, the area has lost much of its pre-eminently Polish flavour. Hundreds who had bought and converted property there began moving out to such areas as Ealing, Clapham and Willesden in search of smaller and more modern properties. A first-class Catholic boys' school at Ealing was a powerful attraction, the purchase by General Anders of a house in Willesden was another, and in any case ten or fifteen years ago there were good property bargains going in those areas. But throughout London there is scarcely a postal district without its biggish quota of Polish families. There are 5,000 Poles in Ealing alone.

Poles are essentially political animals. Something like five per cent of the community take a lively part in Polish emigré politics and are members or officials of the modern counterpart of the pre-war Polish parties. They elect or nominate members to central national political institutions located in the Kensington area. There is always a good deal of lively debate on the central preoccupation of Polish emigré politicians, namely the concept of ultimate freedom for Poland. A big majority of the Poles abroad regard the present Communist government in Warsaw as yet another occupation which is bound to end one day. Nobody quite knows how it will end, and nobody seriously thinks of a military solution to the problem. But it is a subject which preoccupies all Poles.

Polish emigré politics at the summit in London are decidedly bewildering. There is a President-in-exile, an elderly and distinguished politician, whose claim to legitimacy is challenged by the majority of Poles in London. They for their part have elected a rival Presidential triumvirate which has the backing of most politically minded Poles. This conflict has unfortunately done much to weaken and discredit the political effectiveness of the British Poles.

Despite this, a certain political unity has been sustained among Britain's Polish community by the personality of General Anders, who is the senior member of the Presidential triumvirate. Now in his middle seventies but still an active traveller and effective speaker, General Anders had a fine war record as commander of the Polish forces under British command. His presence in London and his close friendship with many members of the British 'Establishment' explains why London is still the world spiritual capital of Polish emigré resistance to Communism in the fatherland.

General Anders is a figurehead. The hard, active work of keeping the 'emigracja' united and Polish-minded is done by the Polish Combatants' Association. From its Queen's Gate Terrace headquarters it runs clubs, Saturday Polish schools for about 3,000 children, 48 youth groups, 25 amateur drama groups, 20 choirs, an employment agency, a printing works and a bookshop. It does an immense amount of welfare work, giving financial assistance and legal advice. It cares for the interests of a residue of some 1,200 elderly, infirm and pensionless Poles who live in poverty. In addition it keeps a benevolent eye on the 2,000 Polish scouts and girl guides who have their own headquarters in Rutland Gate, and who in the summer holidays go streaming off in coaches to scout camps in the English countryside.

In the main, the Poles in Britain have done well for themselves in material matters. In the first days of re-settlement, in the late 1940s, thousands of Poles took jobs in factories and mines. The bulk of these have bettered themselves by thrift, industry and determination.

Again, the bare statistics are impressive. Since 1945 over 5,000 Poles have obtained degrees in British universities. Fifty Poles are lecturers and professors in British universities. Out of the many hundreds of Polish architects qualified in this country, 200 are currently employed by the Greater London Council alone. Six hundred Polish doctors practise in Britain, a high proportion of them in London. Two excellent medical clinics (with a considerable non-Polish clientele) have been set up in Weymouth Street, W.1, and Rutland Gate, S.W.7.

Several Poles have grown very rich indeed, some reputedly millionaires. They are strong in the property business. Rachman, the property racketeer, was a Pole, but of course they don't like to talk about him now.

At rather more modest but nonetheless successful levels, London is peppered with Polish-owned and run businesses and professional men and women. There are chemists (28 concerns in London alone), antique dealers, bookshops (Orbis in Knightsbridge is best-known to non-Polish Londoners), and interior decorators.

Then there are the doctors, solicitors, architects, artists, sculptors, musicians and composers. Anyone wanting names and addresses will find comprehensive details at the Polish Combatants' Association offices.

(This Association, incidentally, has become so much of an institution that the London police automatically direct to its offices any defecting Polish seaman or other Polish national to whom the Home Office gives a residential visa as a genuine refugee.)

Apart from the Combatants' Association, there are almost two hundred other Polish organisations, such as Cultural, Social, Religious, Scientific, Professional and Sport Clubs. Nearly all of them belong to the 'Federation of Poles in Great Britain'.

Polish cuisine is traditionally good. Some restaurants in the Kensington area worth special mention are: Chez Kristof (owned by Prince Woroniecki) in St. Alban's Grove, W.8 (advance booking essential); Chez Luba, in Draycott Avenue, S.W.3; La Vodka, in Cromwell Road; The Cossack, in Beauchamp Place, S.W.3; Silver Spur, in Earl's Court Road, S.W.5; and Marynka, in Brompton Road, S.W.3. Probably the best Polish patisserie and coffee shop in London is Daquise, near South Kensington Underground station.

The best-known, best-run and smartest Polish club in London is the Ognisko Polski (Polish Hearth) at 55 Exhibition Road, which started as a war-time officers' club. Here good Polish food is served at modest prices in pleasant décor. It is full of former generals, colonels, senior diplomats, actors, writers, political figures; members include many of the old Polish families, Sapieha, Zamoyski, Potocki, Radziwill, Lubomirski, who in this ambience still command a special respect. An invitation to lunch or dine at this club is well worth getting. It is the social headquarters for London's Poles, a clearing-house for all the best Polish gossip.

Poles are terrific readers, and the community supports a huge printing and publishing industry in London and the provinces. It is the only foreign community which still supports its own daily newspaper, the *Dziennik Polski*, with a circulation of some 22,000.

In addition there are some 40 periodicals printed in a dozen or so printing establishments. Most astonishing of all, since the first big Polish war-time influx in late 1939, between 12,000 and 13,000 books in the Polish language have been printed and published in this country, ranging from light novels to serious scientific works. London contains the biggest concentration of Polish intellectuals in the world, outside Poland itself.

It is a characteristic of emigré groups to disintegrate and disperse after a generation or two, as has happened with the White Russians in Paris. But in London the homogeneity and unity of the Poles, if anything, has been steadily consolidating.

The Catholic Church is, together with the intense feeling of nationhood which has enabled Poland to survive so many partitions, an explanation of the persisting solidarity of Poles in London, and in Britain as a whole. In London there are three Polish churches: Our Lady of Czestochowa, in Devonia Road, near the Angel (this was a Polish church even before the war); a modern church, St. Andrew Bobola, in Leysfield Road, near Shepherds Bush; and a Jesuit chapel in Walm Lane, Willesden.

On Sundays London Poles travel enormous distances to attend Mass in these two churches. A Polish service has a special atmosphere of its own, fervent but without exaggeration, happily free of the over-devout tension one often finds in an English catholic congregation; more reminiscent, in fact, of the family occasion feeling of an Irish, Italian or Spanish congregation. In recent years Polish communities in various parts of England have bought ten churches for their exclusive use.

What of the future of London's Poles? Will the next generation continue the tradition of 'Polishness' established by their parents? The signs are that they will. The first reaction of teenage boys and girls born here (who are thus automatically British subjects) has been to try and make themselves every bit as English as their

English schoolfriends. But as they have matured, a curious reaction has occurred. It has been almost as though they suddenly sensed where their real roots were. They have gone back to the Polishness of their own family circle with a kind of pride in this special aspect of their lives, their common heritage.

No doubt this reaction has been helped by regular attendance over the years at one of the 120 or so Saturday Polish schools where they studied the language, history, literature, music and dancing of Poland.

When English-born Poles have visited Poland and returned with a Polish wife it is surprising how the wife, although brought up in Communist Poland, finds little difficulty in adapting herself to London's Polish circles.

Since the 'bloodless revolution' of 1956 in Poland, two-way visiting between England and Poland has grown much easier, bureaucratically speaking. Instead of weakening the cohesion of the Poles in Britain, this appears to have strengthened it.

No doubt time will bring a gradual English dilution of London's community of emigré Poles. A large number of mixed marriages is bound to have some effect. But the sense of being Polish is so powerful, the community is so closely integrated, so well organised and so strongly united by religious faith and national heritage, that it may well retain its separate identity for many generations to come.

West Indian London

The New Irish or the Lonely Londoners?

They certainly work all day and dream most of the night.

Here are some of their dreams and their fears. And some of their own words.

There are approximately 220,000 West Indians living in London. They have come mainly from the capital cities of Jamaica, Trinidad and Tobago, British Guiana, British Honduras, Barbados, and from a bric-a-brac of islets with *recherché* Saint names: Kitts, Lucia, Vincent, Christopher, Eustatius.

Emigration is a very necessary and historical part of the West Indian way of life and Britain is their economic Mecca.

In London they tend to settle in clusters in Brixton, Hammersmith, Shepherd's Bush, Ladbroke Grove, Maida Vale, Willesden, Finsbury Park, Stoke Newington, Islington and in other less dense immigrant areas in Hampstead, Wimbledon and Richmond.

Affectionately called the 'lonely Londoners' and sometimes the 'new Irish', the majority of the West Indians in London are employed in semi-skilled and unskilled jobs. They work as drivers and conductors on the buses and as station attendants and guards on the railways. They are found in substantial numbers on the nursing and domestic staffs of nearly all the London hospitals, nursing homes and clinics. Some teach in the secondary and grammar schools. A few are on the staffs of universities. There are fewer still in the popular professions.

There are, of course, the West Indian businessmen, who, with one or two exceptions only, have all been living in London for many years. They are modest shopkeepers, self-employed artisans, importers and retailers of West Indian bottled and tinned food and other light commodities. There are barbers, real estate agents, calypso records stockists, night club proprietors, and landlords. And there are, too, the cabaret entertainers, actors, and a small intellectual élite of writers, freelance journalists, broadcasters, and political group organizers.

The persistent definitive image of the easy-going West Indian isn't true of the shrewd hustling immigrant. And yet he is also a man who has a keen sense of leisure at home and abroad.

A certain portion of the leisure hours of West Indians is spent in recreating a variety of 'back home entertainments' in the spacious rooms of local town halls and church buildings. There are the usual rounds of 'Irish talk' and domino and darts tournaments.

The men are possibly the finest egocentric talkers in the country. They are capable of holding an audience in a bed-sitter in winter on a number of topics ranging from the vagaries of British party politics and trades-unionism to the economic importance of the Beatles, from the insistence of free speech for the Duke of Edinburgh to the unmasking of the mastermind behind the Great Train Robbery, from the colonising effect, *in reverse*, of West Indian cricket on the British *Weltanschauung* to the Stalin way of death.

They are all gifted self-regarding monologists and exceptionally bad conversationalists. The inevitably militant students are active in and out of the debating societies of their universities, and the workers, anti-Imperialists and political aspirants make frequent pilgrimages on Sundays to Speakers' Corner where they listen and heckle and later on appear on their own platforms with banners bearing the following messages: *Any Difference Between The Tories And The Socialists Is Purely Accidental, Nkrumah Is A Genius.*

The other leisure pursuits take place during the two days of the weekend break. Saturdays and Sundays are set aside for 'open house visiting', cinema-going, reflections on their self-imposed exile, and church-going.

The women take the brisk matriarchal lead in the last two activities and the men and children go along with them passively. The visits to the houses and flats and rooms of relations and friends are the occasions for self-conscious progress-reports, ecstatic exchanges of news from home, community complaints, work gossip, and endless intimations of returning before ' . . . a nex' bad winter ketch we in dis London.'

Many West Indians are devout church-goers. They surrender a great deal of their leisure to help out with the affairs of their local church and to attend regularly on Sundays throughout their stay in England. They are variously Adventists, Roman Catholics, Anglicans, Presbyterians, Methodists, Baptists and Revivalists.

Naturally, the men find time to go to their local pub and to watch and play in a series of office- and factory-planned Sunday cricket matches. The older 'family' men organize poker games with deceptively modest stakes, usually on Friday and Saturday nights, and the younger men go hopefully to Hyde Park and Piccadilly Circus for fruitful encounters with drifting Continental 'craft'.

The successful Byronic seekers move on to jazz clubs in Soho or to the accommodating members' clubs in Brixton or to the basement shebeens in Ladbroke Grove to dance to the latest pop records or to *ad hoc* steel band music.

The London immigrant night club scene has become hopelessly Anglicized since the halcyon nights of The Caribbean Club in Denman Street off Piccadilly Circus, and The Sugar Hill Club in Mason's Yard off Duke Street, Saint James's, and The Caribe in Whitcomb Street near Leicester Square. They are now closed, and the current establishments, which remain to carry on the memory of the doubtful multi-racial delights of the 'big three', are the scattered 'three-to-eleven' imitations in Brixton and Ladbroke Grove with their exorbitant prices, vague promises of the high life, and bad ventilation.

Two West Indian night club regulars were once asked, 'Don't you chaps ever take out your own women?' and the quick reply was, 'Not enough of them to go round, man. Besides, when you're in Rome you gotta integrate with the Romans the most.'

Needless to say, most of the unattended West Indian women are a stoical lot. They play an excellent waiting game. They are proud and appropriately arrogant, and they know their true strength. They are, particularly the older women, nearly all inspired cooks of both English and West Indian dishes.

Most West Indians have extremely finely 'integrated' palates. The housewives can fuse the two culinary cultures effortlessly. At breakfast, the average Brixton family from Jamaica may well sit down to *ackee* (the national vegetable-fruit) and salt fish, fried bread, ginger marmalade, and Blue Mountain coffee. On Sundays, lunch is roast beef, Yorkshire pudding, rice and peas, mixed salad, and baked bananas with coconut milk. For tea, sardine and cucumber sandwiches, banana fritters, and hot country chocolate. Certainly no need for Kit-E-Kat.

Within recent years, shopping for West Indian food has been made easier because of the special market stalls and grocery stores in Stoke Newington, Brixton and Shepherd's Bush which stock an extraordinary assortment of fresh fruits, vegetables and ground provisions flown over from Jamaica and Trinidad to London. The adaptable unsuspecting English butchers provide, quite innocently, certain meat portions which are converted into delicacies: pigs'-trotters and pigs'-tails, tripe, calves'-heels, and sweetbreads. Pickled mackerel, red peas, hot pepper sauces, logwood honey and preserves are sold in the exotic food shops in Soho and in the Berwick Street market on Saturdays. Even a choice selection of Jamaican confectionery is available in Brixton and Shepherd's Bush.

'Life sweet in London, yes, but is a sort o' bitter sweet!' a man from Jamaica may tell his workmate on their way home to a crowded room in the Harrow Road. And the workmate might well remark, 'We not here to count cow but to drink milk, master.'

Most of London's West Indians are here for a very definite purpose. The students in Earl's Court, Swiss Cottage, Queensway and in the other overseas students areas' come and go back according to plan. The working West Indians come to better themselves and to grab at the nearest worthwhile prospect and to return to the West Indies as soon as they have saved enough to start a new life at home.

The phrase used above, 'not to count cow', suggests that the West Indian is not altogether anxious to wage war against inter-racial harmony or indeed to make his peace with it. He can leave the problems of assimilation circumspectly alone, or he can go out of his way to foster integration with the zeal of a crusading multi-racialist.

A distinguished West Indian novelist has described the West Indian as 'a man with a destiny for world multi-racialism, if only he can find the kind of world in which to work to achieve it'.

But if the awkward truth be known, his pride won't allow him to complain or criticise or become assimilated for assimilation's sake. He wants to realise his personal economic plan and get away soon afterwards.

'Is the same thing the British did do in the West Indies with sugar!' a Jamaican Hyde Park orator will say, intending no offence. 'So, what to stop we from doing the same thing back to them in them own country? Besides, the British need we labour for the time being. So, bad to bad, we giving them that at least. When we break even with a little 'pon top, then we cut out back to the Rock.'

But while he is here in London, he lives with fears, his own inherent prejudices, and his great West Indian dream.

His fears are basic: 'I mightn't make it at all. I might dead in this man town before I get set up.'

His prejudices are idiosyncratic: 'I would never want no Cockney attitude to my child education. Them give up too easy where them children concern. Bound to be class killing them!'

Or it might be as simple as: 'People who love animal and don't love themselves is not for me at all!'

His West Indian dream: 'I going go back home and set them backward people o' mine straight 'bout nationalism. Nobody not more nationalistic than English people. I going go spread the word 'mongst we and we going live good.'

Or it might be: 'Is education first and high finance nex'. The culture thing can come later, natural like.'

Or this: 'Is one thing I learn in this town and is this: the national interest always come first, and everything to do with the power of the nation, no matter how many people get brutalized along the way. That's what we got to learn in the West Indies. When I go back I going wise them up 'bout that early o'clock.'

But there are the 'integrated' West Indians, the 'lifers', who remain on and who seldom ever return. They are the tiny clump of practising barristers, doctors, university lecturers, and some of the writers and artists. Many of them are middle class 'exiles'. Some are newly 'liberated' individuals who prefer London's seemingly classless warrens in Hampstead, Fulham and Chelsea to the vestigial Victorian stuffiness and humbug in places like Barbados and Jamaica.

Their kind of typical London sitting-room duologue could easily be spoken in these lines:

'I'm not saying that the winter doesn't get me down year after year, and that there isn't colour prejudice all about, but the great thing is that one's accepted on one's own merit. The English respect quality.'

'In the West Indies, we still wonder about a black man making it to the top in our society. Over here, brains, good manners and sophistication matter.'

But there are levels of humiliation and frustration. The West Indians who come from a rural background seem to be less exposed to abuse. Those with an urban background are less sheltered and more sensitive to the social ups and downs within their immigrant experiences.

This is the sort of commentary that could be recorded in the privacy of an over-heated bed-sitter in West Hampstead any winter evening:

'The Englishman just won't give us certain breaks. Have you ever seen one of us on the staff of a London bank?'

'The B.B.C. has given a lead, though. There's a Jamaican chap who got an announcer's job recently.

'But that's on radio where you can't *see* him. So the boy's got a bloody good voice. Who's to tell he's a Jamaican if the voice matches up with the other announcers.'

'True. If he was on television then that would be a lead all right. Anyway there might be one of us there one day soon.'

'Bound to be one that's so light-skinned that it won't count.'

'The Englishman is a genius in this race relations business.'

'A past master.'

Where have all the leading West Indians gone? Gone back to the West Indies is as good an answer as any. Into politics. Into the Civil Service. Into the top jobs in industry. And some, into obscurity.

Those who remain in London are not so much 'leading' as they are 'holding on'. They hold on in leading positions in political, social and cultural organizations: in CARD (Campaign Against Racial Discrimination), SCWIO (The Standing Conference of West Indian Organizations), A-A-CA (The Afro-Asian-Caribbean Association), NTW (The Negro Theatre Workshop), and in other organizations. There is also RAAS (The Racial Action Adjustment Society), a militant group, and there is one Jamaican prospective Conservative candidate for Bethnal Green and Hackney South.

There is a Trinidadian Greater London Councillor. There are some eight West Indian novelists, and at least two distinguished British Guianese painters whose flexible regional work is being threatened with the flattering description 'British Abstract Art'. And there are one or two quiet academics in London University colleges.

But isn't the West Indian dream really a variant of the British dream with a few colonial nightmare elements thrown in for good Commonwealth measure?

Both the London West Indian working man and intellectual will say that this is so. They will agree that without the colonial nightmare elements, the dream wouldn't be worth dreaming. (Most have come to their 'dream' because of emigrating to London.)

It is rather as a certain British Guianese speaker at Hyde Park once said. 'The West Indies exists and has reality in London but not in the West Indies. God bless the salt in the wound.'

English London

If there is an Indian London and an Australian London, a West Indian London, an Irish London and a Jewish London, is there also, tucked away somewhere, an English London?

There are lots of English around the place. And very funny some of them are. This is what one foreigner thinks about the natives, having studied them in their natural habitat. From a safe distance of course.

Behind all the façades of foreign London, the question naturally arises: is there such a thing as an English London too?

Yes, there is. London has so many faces; if there is an old London and a new London; a rich London and a poor London; an antiquated and an up-to-the-minute London; a London of tiny villages and a metropolitan London; the London of the young and the London of the old; if there is an Indian and an Australian London, a West Indian and a Jewish London, it is almost inevitable that there should be an English London, too. That is, *if there is a London at all.*

Perhaps there is no such place as London? London has been studied and written about so much, sung and abused, investigated and explored by so many for so long, that there is but one single aspect of it that has escaped the attention of students: the fact that no such place as London really exists.

You cannot call such a vast place, consisting of so many square miles and so many millions of people a 'town', any more than you can call the library of the British Museum 'a book'. The library is the conglomeration of many books and London is the conglomeration of many towns.

The people of Bermondsey may never see Wandsworth and the people of Deptford may be farther away from Stoke Newington than they are from Majorca. Because of this vastness there are current as many millions of images of London as there are people who set eyes on London. London is an utterly different place for a Lambeth prowler, for a City magnate, or a Lewisham dentist—and not only because of the differences in their social status and affluence. An image which is so manifold is meaningless and ceases to be an image.

So, it is perhaps best to say that London does *not* exist. It ceased to exist soon after Dr. Johnson's time. But as it can be reborn only if it were to be drastically reduced in size, then let us hope that it will never exist again. As a group of towns, its fascination is endless.

The foreigner coming to London will see basically two different towns. One of these will be almost exclusively foreign and the other staggeringly and stupefyingly English. It depends whether the alien is coming as a future resident or as a short-term visitor, perhaps a tourist.

The overwhelming majority of resident aliens live in a foreign London. Native Londoners have no inkling that London, in addition to being a vast English town, is also a medium-sized Italian, Hungarian or German community, and a small Ukranian or Lithuanian village—to mention a few examples only.

A Hungarian, for example—unless he is a rather exceptional person—will lead a Hungarian life on the periphery of which there will appear the faint silhouette of some English people: employers, employees, customers, colleagues, shopkeepers, cinema usherettes and bus conductors (very faint). But no one who really matters in his personal life will not be Hungarian. His friends will be Hungarian. His doctor and dentist and solicitor will be Hungarian. He will go to one of the Hungarian restaurants when he really wants to *eat*—as opposed simply to taking nourishment in order to keep body and soul together. He will go to a Hungarian tailor, he will know where to buy *debrenci* and other Hungarian sausages.

It is true, he will read the English newspapers and watch local television programmes, but when he is in mellow or sentimental mood, he will turn to his old Hungarian poets and, when happy, he will not hum the Beatles' latest hit but something he once knew in Budapest. With a little bit of luck, he will manage to live in London for years without even seeing an Englishman in close-up.

The visitor, however, will see an utterly different picture. He will be stunned by the Englishness of London. He will feel all the time that he has come to an island and will find himself in a strange land. He was told that Calais is only 22 miles away from Dover. He finds that he has been misled: the two places are 10,000 miles apart. London is much farther away from the Continent than New York or Buenos Aires or even Australia.

Wherein consists then that staggering Englishness of London that hits the foreigner in the eye, which cheers him and upsets him, puzzles and pleases him, fascinates and bewilders him? In what exactly does London differ from all other towns?

London does reflect the English character to a great extent. It comes out in everything the English do; the way they walk, talk, dress, work and joke. And obviously also in the way they build their towns.

The foreigner, if he is sensitive and slightly neurotic, will be left first of all with the impression that London is not simply a town built for the English to live in, but a vast conspiracy to mislead the alien and convince him that he is not really wanted here. Or is it perhaps one of those dead-pan jokes for which the English are famous?

The foreigner, as usual, would be quite wrong. The simple truth is that—as has been said only too often—the Latin races are logical and the English empirical. The result is that Latin influenced towns are planned, thought out, systematically conceived, while London grew like the lilies of the field. In New York, for example, you have the long avenues and the shorter streets, all parallel so that they form neat parallelograms, with a few irrepressible, crazy, zig-zagging monsters, like Broadway, thrown in (one feels, by the British) for good measure.

But in this, the second half of the twentieth century, the British have not yet got round to inventing parallel streets. Their streets begin seemingly quite normally and then suddenly, and without the slightest provocation, they turn left and right and then left again. They zig-zag like a crazy snake and lead nowhere.

Apparent thoroughfares prove to be cul-de-sacs. At least one street, Walm Lane in Cricklewood, becomes its own side-street. It turns suddenly off at a rectangle while that part of it which continues in a straight line—and which in every normal country would be the rest of Walm Lane—acquires another name. Trying to take a short cut in London—relying on your sense of direction, however infallible in other cities—is sheer folly. It is easier to cross the Gobi Desert without a compass than to take a short cut in Soho.

As London grew the way daffodils or stinging nettles grow in the field, and as it is really a conglomeration of villages, one finds innumerable London streets of the same name. The poor unsuspecting foreigner feels that this, too, is a somewhat dirty and completely un-English trick to confuse him. There are 6 Warwick Roads, 9 Cambridge Roads, 10 Avenue Gardens, 12 The Avenues and 42 Church Lanes, Church Gardens, Church Roads, Rises, Paths, Mounts, Hills, Avenues and Drives between Colindale and Wimbledon.

You may object that these Church Roads—just because they are so widely dispersed—cannot possibly cause any difficulties or be confused with one another. Not even the dimmest foreigner, it is asserted, would start looking for a place at Walthamstow when, in fact, he wants Tooting. But you know what foreigners are. They may not know the difference between Walthamstow and Tooting, which, of course, is entirely their loss.

But even the vast distance between similar sounding places will not save him in many cases. He will find in the *same* area Bedford Gardens, Bedford Place, Bedford Road, Bedford Row, Bedford Square and Bedford Terrace; or Belsize Avenue, Belsize Crescent, Belsize Grove, Belsize Lane, Belsize Park, Belsize Road, Belsize Square and Belsize Park Gardens, all neatly piled up on top of one another. Even natives walk round with street maps in those districts.

But let us suppose that the foreigner in question is the indomitable type. He is not deterred by the fact that the names of streets (and groves, rows, mews, gardens, crescents etc.) are one of the most closely guarded secrets in Britain and that at some parts he cannot find a street-nameplate for miles.

Let us suppose that he will not be deterred by drawing 41 blanks and that in the end he does find the forty-second Church Row (or Rise or End) he really wants and then heaves a sigh of relief. How foolish and optimistic these foreigners are! They know nothing of British ingenuity and of the staunch British spirit which just refuses to admit defeat. The foreigner will have to find the *house* too and that is far more difficult than finding the street.

First of all, house-numbers are fewer and farther between than street nameplates. If you do not want to display the number of your house, you just don't: this is a free country. Besides, many houses *have* no numbers. They have instead names: such as *Hill-Top* (recommended for use at the bottom of a hill), or *Bellevue*, when you see nothing but rusty dustbins around; or *The Appletree* when the nearest apple-tree is seven miles away (although, to be fair, in Mary Tudor's reign there *was* an apple-tree in a nearby garden). The street may be two miles long and you cannot possibly have any idea where *The Glasshouse* may be situated.

But even if the house has a number and even if you manage to find house-numbers properly displayed, you are not much better off. In one street they run in the normal way, odd numbers on one side, even numbers on the other. Another street may be a 'good address', so five or six houses in an adjacent street may take the numbers of the 'good' street. Then again, the English have hit upon the happy design of having numbers grow on one side and diminish on the other with the result that you may walk up and down the street two or three times without finding the number you are looking for. In one district houses are numbered in chronological order as in Tokio. The first house built is No. 1, the second (built at the other end of the street) No. 2, and so on.

Another phenomenon that hits the visiting foreigner in the eye is those rows and rows of the same houses which disfigure the suburbs. They are victorian monstrosities and they are depressing. But people are more surprised to find them here than they would be to find them anywhere else. The English are renowned for their individuality, their hatred for uniformity, their contempt for the goose-step. But surely, the visitor feels, to be put in a uniform house is much worse than to be put in a uniform garb. The ordinary uniform deprives you—and only you—of your individuality. But the house deprives your whole family of it.

But if it is true, nevertheless, that the style of a city reflects the character of its builders, then this phenomenon, too—however strange and incongruent it appears at first sight—must reflect something of the English character. And it does. The main reason for building these monotonous and depressing rows of houses was simply to save money. Englishmen were born free and they never, never, never would be slaves: Englishmen—this was understood— should live in specially built houses, planned to suit their individual tastes. But the workers, the people belonging to the 'lower orders', these suburbanites were not really regarded as Englishmen. The inner parts of London are charming and dignified and full of parks and fine, impressive buildings. But the outskirts are dull and dreary. The outskirts, of course, were inhabited not by Englishmen, but simply by workers and servants, in other words uninteresting and insignificant auxiliaries of English life.

Perhaps the uniformity of these suburbs reflects something even more characteristic. Englishmen are indeed great individualists and have a tremendous respect and liking for the eccentric. But apart from the few genuine eccentrics among their ranks, they are great conformers. Not cowardly conformers—not dullards cowed into conformity—but freeborn and proud citizens who choose to conform. Who choose to live lives like others, not to be conspicuous, not to be different, not to draw attention to themselves.

The English—and the visitor will not fail to notice this—wear more uniforms than the Germans did in the silliest seasons of their history. There is the uniform of the City-man, the bowler and the rolled umbrella. The uniform of the students with their coloured, knitted scarves and tousled hair. The uniform of the judges and university teachers. The uniform of the average male with his dark grey suit, cut to the same pattern and recognisable from miles away everywhere in the world. The uniform of flannel and tweed at week-ends, of morning coats at weddings. And even the uniform of rebels, the beatniks and the mods, of the desperate individualists, with their long unruly hair.

It is not only their dress and appearance that is uniform, but their houses. Not only their houses, but also their villages. London is not only the biggest metropolis of the world, it is also its biggest village, or conglomeration of villages.

In a way, village life is better preserved in the diverse high streets of London than in the spoilt countryside of Britain. Experts of London will write interesting and finely observed books on the folklore of Peckham or Brixton, of Beckenham or Hendon.

But the visitor will know nothing of the difference between these places. He will see the uniform suburbs, with the same banks, the shop portals, the big names and very similar small shopkeepers, the same tins arranged in the same way in grocers' windows. The same people going into these shops and greeting one another with exactly the same smiles and with the same 'lovely morning isn't it?'. Every London suburb is a replica of the others.

People do not go from Bermondsey to Camberwell or from

Deptford to Stoke Newington. *There is no need for it.* And there is certainly no need for the visitor to do so. If he has seen one London suburb, he has seen them all. And all this is nothing more than a splendid manifestation of the Englishman's desire to remain a true individual. In other words—as he sees it—his right *not* to be different.

And the visitor is in for yet another surprise—this time a pleasant one. He has heard a great deal about the taciturnity of the British, how cool and how reserved they are. He will be surprised to find how kind and how helpful they really prove to be. They will not be so overwhelming as to offer to accompany him to his destination like the Germans or the Austrians. Nor will they enquire which part of the world he has come from, what his business in London may be and how much his weekly wages are in Stockholm or Yokohama.

But the Londoner will listen to the foreigner's query patiently, will speak to him slowly—and also loudly, as though a language of which you don't know one single word became intelligible if spoken loudly enough. When at last the visitor understands him, the Londoner, before the visitor has had the time to thank him, will walk on with a shy, kindly smile.

People won't push the foreigner around. They may ignore him until he asks for their help but they will not be rude to him. In a shop no one will jump ahead of him to grab his turn. If he hesitates about what to do—in car or on foot—no one will shout at him.

But there is no need to multiply these examples. The long and the short of it is that they will always treat him as an individual. A dull, completely uninteresting, insignificant human being, perhaps. But still a human being. And that is more than enough.

The foreigner will realise in no time that in spite of all the exasperating, annoying, puzzling, infuriating, stupefying little things, he has arrived at the heart of the most civilised human community in the world.

Index

British/American English Glossary

bag (handbag)—purse
bandy-legged—bow-legged
bird—a girl
biscuit—cookie
bob—one shilling
boot—trunk (automobile)
bonnet—hood (automobile)
boozer—drinker, and his drinking place
braces—suspenders
break up—close (of school)
bum—schoolboy for bottom

chambers—lawyers' offices
chips—French fried potatoes
chemist—drugstore
cigarette-end—cigarette-butt
chop (meat)—cutlet
cotton wool—absorbent cotton
cricket—figuratively, good sportsmanship

drawers—pants
dropped a clanger—goofed
dual carriageway—divided highway
dustbin—garbage can

estate agent—real estate agent

flat—an apartment
footpath—sidewalk
foyer—entrance hall
fridge—a refrigerator

ground floor—first floor
guinea—one pound and one shilling
gym shoes—sneakers

haberdashery—notion counter
holiday—vacation

just not on—won't work

knickers—pants

lavatory, loo, toilet—john
ladder—a run in a stocking
ladybird—ladybug
left luggage—check room
lift—elevator
lorry—truck

made to measure—custom-made
mackintosh—raincoat
mansions—apartment building
motorcar—automobile
motorway—freeway

nappy—diaper
nosh—food

odds and ends—junk

patience—solitaire
pavement—sidewalk
petrol—gasoline
pram (perambulator)—baby-carriage, baby buggy.
pillar-box—mail-box
potato crisps—potato chips
pub, public house—a saloon
public school—private school
punch-up—fist fight
prep (preparatory) school—private boarding school, boys 8–13

quid—a pound (sterling)

railway—railroad
ring reverse charge—call collect

slacks—pants
solicitors—writing lawyers
   Barristers are talking lawyers
spring onions—scallions
stone—fourteen pounds in weight
sweet—dessert
sweets—candy
swiss roll—jelly roll

tap—faucet
tart—pie, prostitute
trilby—fedora
treacle—molasses
tube or underground—subway
telly—TV

undertaker—mortician

van—truck
vest—undershirt

waistcoat—vest

Zed—Zee